THE ALFORD BROTHERS:
"WE ALL MUST DYE SOONER OR LATER"

THE ALFORD BROTHERS:
"WE ALL MUST DYE SOONER OR LATER"

Edited by

Richard S. Skidmore

The Nugget Publishers
Hanover, Indiana
1995

Front cover: Dr. Anson Hurd, Surgeon for the 14th Indiana Infantry Regiment, caring for the wounded after the Battle of Antietam. The site is the Dr. Otho J. Smith farm near the Upper Bridge. This Union Army field hospital was set up to accommodate the wounded from French's Division, however, 1,396 wounded from both sides were treated. (Library of Congress photograph.)

Maps and Design
Ligget Graphics
Terre Haute, Indiana

Printing
Greencastle Offset Printing
Greencastle, Indiana

Binding
Franklin's Bindery, Inc.
Spencer, Indiana

ISBN: 0-9623292-6-6

for all children
PEACE and LOVE

CONTENTS

MAPS

Note: The 120 illustrations used in this book are accompanied with an acknowledgement of their origin. Abbreviated credits are used for the better-known sources: (LC), Library of Congress, (NA) National Archives, (USAMHI) United States Army Military Historical Institute, (Miller's) *Photographic History of the Civil War*, (Leslie's) *Frank Leslie's Illustrated History of the Civil War*, (HPHCW) *Harper's Pictorial History of the Civil War*, (B&L) *Battles and Leaders*, (ISL) Indiana State Library and (IHS) Indiana Historical Society.

INTRODUCTION

"We spend our years as a tale that is told." [1]

SIMPLY, THIS IS THE STORY OF three brothers who volunteer to fight in the American Civil War. In seventeen months the story ends, all three are dead.

The tragedy is told, in part, with the letters the brothers sent home. *The Alford Brothers*, however, is much more. A larger drama emerges when the letters the brothers wrote are woven with the letters they received. In total, there are 196 pieces of correspondence which document a family's wartime conversation.[2]

The letters offer far more than chit-chat about a small southern Indiana town or weather conditions in a Civil War camp. An overriding concern is the farm economy as a family stuggles to survive with overdue liens and three less "hands." Likewise, the paths of bullets on battlefields are a major worry. The story also touches on a rural Indiana educational system, newspaper reporting, rumor mongering, postal service, army politics, medical care, battles and the burial of Civil War soldiers. Above it all, *The Alford Brothers* is "a tale that is told" about a family living on the emotional extremities for seventeen months.

The Alfords shared many interests and beliefs although they were individuals with independent feelings – some to be admired, some to be questioned. First, the parents:

	Franklin Alford	Mary Gilley
Name:	Franklin Alford	Mary Gilley
Born:	July 15, 1815	March 19, 1819

Franklin and Mary were married February 21, 1836. The Alford family grew quickly and (almost) at regular intervals. The children and their birthdates were:

Minerva	January 14, 1837
James Warren	December 22, 1838
Wayne	December 15, 1840
Lafayette	December 6, 1842
George	September 28, 1846
Hellen	January 21, 1849
Thomas Greene	March 26, 1852.

misfortune yet we are glad that it is no worse
give my love to all the friends and Brethren and
reserve the same to your self and be careful to
adorn that good confession that you have made
before many witnesses by your Christian
deportment in this time of trial which I
feel confident you will do and if you fall
dureing the campaign I may have no cause
to sorrow as those who have no hope but I
must close by subscribeing my self your affecti
=onate feather
                    Franklin Alford
Say to Brother Houghton that we received
his verry kind and interesting letter and we
fully appreciate his affection manifested throu
the same and will answer in due forea soon but I
must close for the wunt of time and space F Alford

The Handwriting of Franklin Alford, or Father.

unio men ware put down i long to see the soldirs come
home i think sutch camps will have to leave
leave hear i have thaut that i could not stand to
see on my boddy hied but i will tell you what i hav
is whid it can pu i get so ired sometims i feel like
i could do it my self i guess i hav some of the blood
of my grand parens they had to fight toris

Mary Gilley Alford, or Mother.

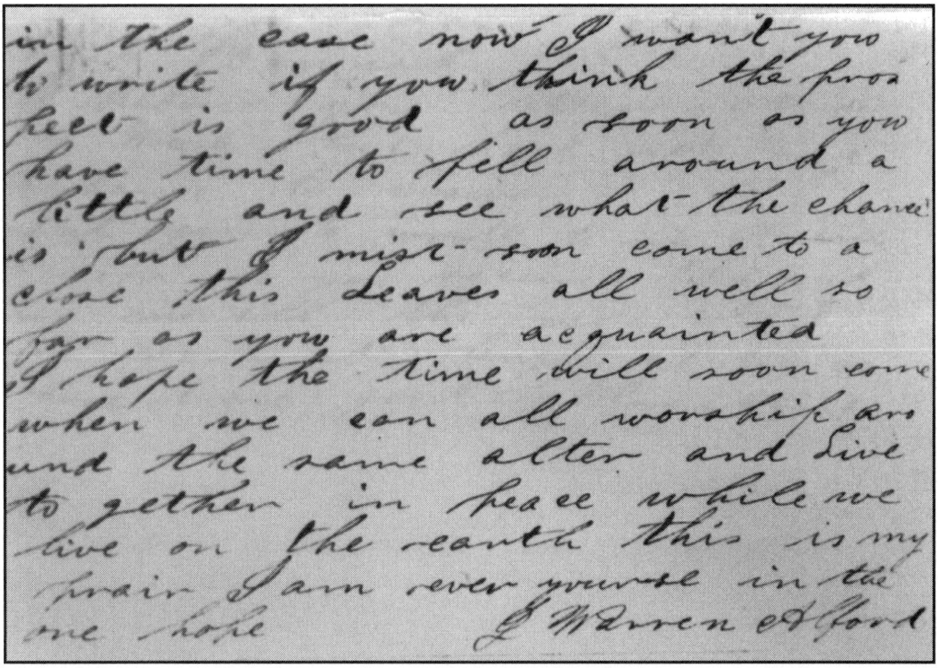
in the case now I want you
to write if you think the pros
pect is good as soon as you
have time to feel around a
little and see what the chance
is but I must soon come to a
close this Leaves all well so
far as you are acquainted
I hope the time will soon come
when we can all worship aro
und the same alter and Live
to gether in peace while we
live on the earth this is my
prair I am ever yourse in the
one hope J Warren Alford

James Warren Alford.

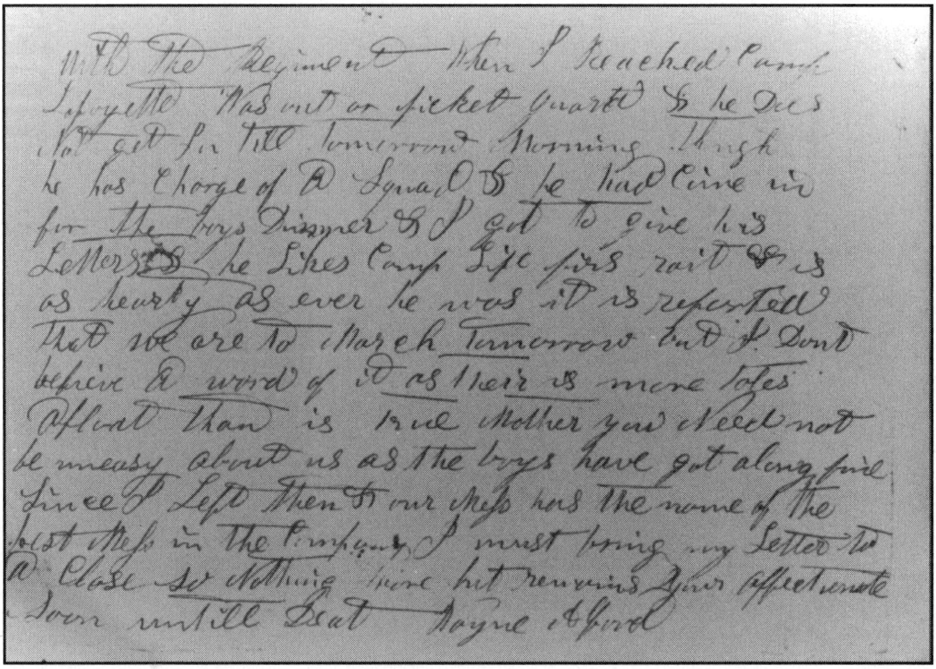
with the Regiment when I reached Camp
Lafayette was out on picket guard & he Does
Not get in till tomorrow Morning though
he has Charge of A Squad & he had Come in
for the boys Dinner & I got to give his
Letters & he Likes Camp Life first rait & is
as hearty as ever he was it is reported
that we are to March Tomorrow but I Dont
believe A word of it as their is more tales
Afloat than is true Mother you Need not
be uneasy about us as the boys have got along fine
Since I Left them & our Mess has the name of the
best Mess in the Company I must bring my Letter to
A Close so Nothing More but remaining your affectionate
Son untill Death Wayne Alford

Wayne Alford.

Lafayette Alford.

George Washington Alford.

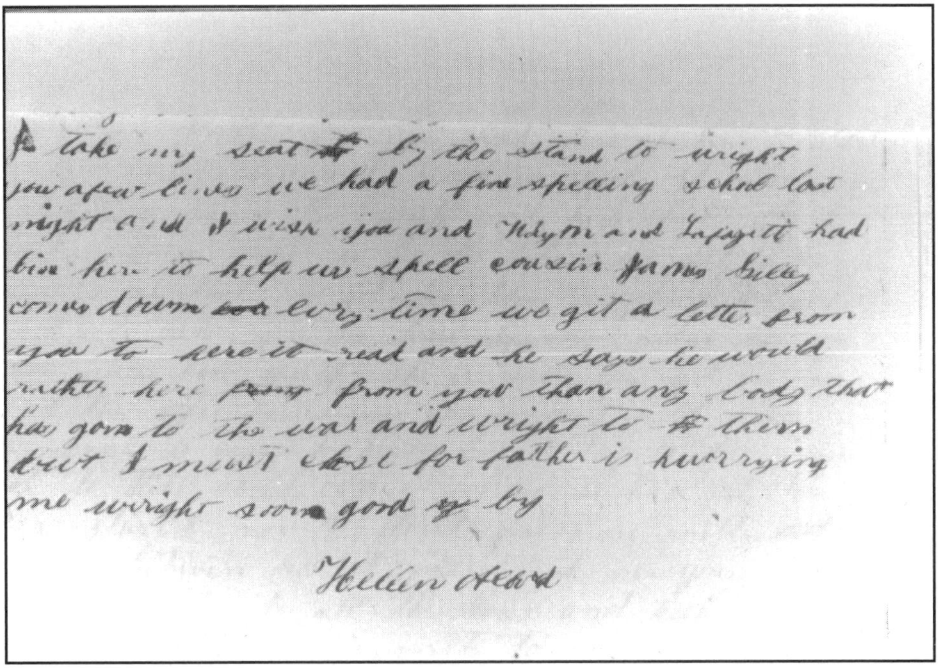

I take my seat by the stand to wright
you a few lines we had a fine speling schol last
night and I wish you and Wylon and Lafayett had
bin here to help us spell cousin James Gilley
comes down every time we git a letter from
you to here it read and he says he would
rather here from you than any body that
has gone to the war and wright to them
but I must close for father is hurrying
me wright soon good by

Hellen Alford

Hellen Alford.

Mr J W Alford
Dear sir we recived yor kind letter of the
and was glad to hear that you was well i havent
time to writ george is going out to feed the fatnin
hogs they are geting tolerable fat Minerva says
that you might wright a letter to her I will
have to close for the want of time wright soon

Thomas Green Alford

Thomas Greene Alford.

last, Monday evening, their was a company
from Camp Patterson ordered to La Lourche
and as the bairs was crossing Beaver creek
the Bridge broke down, and killed some
20 men, beside wounded, Their is no
doubt in my mind but the Tafs was
taken off the end of the Stay road, by some
feind of Hell, Such is life, But I must
stop, writing, as I have to write a note to John
McCrady before the mail comes in You
must excuse this short and hurried note
as I am in a hurry and I will do better
next time Farewell My Friend Warren
may god bless you is the prayer of your
Friend
Dr. J. L. Laverty

Dr. James L. Laverty.

Minerva married Charles Donaldson on January 4, 1855 and a son, Enoch, was born in 1857.

Franklin Alford was the head of the household – absolutely. His position as husband and father in a 19th-century farm family assured him of the leadership role. Furthermore, Franklin's religious fervor provided him with a platform of respect and authority in the home. Outside the home, he operated a sizable farm and was an elder in the family's church. Not surprisingly, in Franklin's letters to his sons he sermonized beyond fatherly advice. At times his letters reflected a missionary's zeal and a bombastic quality. An excerpt from his letter to James Warren on January 12, 1862 exemplifies the point:

> Dear Sir, Yours of the 2nd Came duely to hand by Saturdays
> mail ... and we hope this may Come duly to hand and find you
> enjoying the same incomprehensible blessing. I hardly know how
> to express to you my gratitude to him who giveth life and health
> and all things, for his kind care over us, in sickness & health in
> peace & in War. We are asshured that as is the tender Grace
> before [the throne] so is the feeble Man without the protection of
> him who Numbereth the Hairs of our Heads and without whose
> notice Even a Sparrow doth not fall to the Ground. I hope I shall
> not have intruded upon your patience in Expressing our depen-
> dence on God and our strict adherence to his Council. ...

This was not an unusual opening burst from Father; however, when writing to Warren, he may have been "preaching to the choir." Warren already was immersed with religious thoughts and was striving each day to live a Christian life (in an un-Christian environment).

While apparently functioning within fundamental religious doctrine, forty-six-year-old Franklin Alford was a practical man. For example, in the 1860s, few southern Indiana farmers threshed wheat with a machine. Franklin owned one. In fact, he owned the only one in Daviess County. This modern farm implement was referred to in various letters as "the Masheen."

Father was a financial wizard in a small way. He dealt in promissory notes, both as a lender and a borrower. Indebtedness and dealing with debtors was a frequent concern in his letters. More commonly, Franklin was involved in the barter system. In the time span of these letters, several horses and mules were bought, sold and traded.

James Warren was the heir-apparent and lived in his father's shadow (sons Wayne and Lafayette did not). As time passes, there is a sense of "like father, like son" in James Warren's and Franklin's letters. Warren, as he was called, had been groomed to "take over" and at the age of twenty-two already was a landowner. Therefore, much of the correspondence between Father and the oldest son was of a serious, business-like nature. His letters are less interesting to read than the hearsay and more dramatic material provided by other members of the family. Warren wrote "Dear Parents" on January 2, 1862:

> I am going to send you some Money when I draw again. . . . I
> think I can send you 50.00 and I will send it as we are paid. . . . I
> got a letter from Chester Camp stateing that he had a letter from
> Cooks wife. [He] had saw her [and] she wanted to sell her dowery
> in that land I got from Prater and that it could be got for one
> Hundred Dollars and per haps less. . . .

Warren conforms to the popularly defined role of oldest son. He was his father's confidant, first in the family to go off to war and a steadfast source of advice for his siblings. Warren's acceptance of responsibility and his strong religious beliefs, however, resulted in a personal struggle when thrust into the carefree army life, a dilemma his younger brothers did not experience. On the positive side, the mature-thinking Warren, having entered the army as a private, was promoted to corporal. More importantly to himself and to the family, he persevered in his Christian attitudes to the end. It is Warren Alford's Civil War service which provides the time line for this book, May 1861 through September 1862. Warren saw considerable combat duty in a famous Indiana fighting unit and was a reliable chronicler of what he saw.

Warren served in the east whereas Wayne, the twenty-year-old, and Lafayette, eighteen, served together in the west. Wayne does not write as many letters as Warren, and Lafayette wrote fewer than either. Possibly this has something to do with placement in the family hierarchy, and a sense of obligation. More likely it has to do with differing personalities.

Wayne was the stereotypical young man going off to the Civil War: impatient, self-confident, adventuresome and undaunted by war or death. In a letter to his big brother, who already was in the army when he was not, Wayne wrote on August 26, 1861:

> Most of the boys that I Care for have gone and I am Left almost alone and have a strong Desire to be with you if I could. I want you to Wright to me again on the subject and let me know exactly why you think it Best not to come. It seams to me that the [president's] call [for more troops] is to me as much as to any one else. . . . If you will just recollect the time the excitement was so high here, you can better appreciate my condition. . . .

Seven weeks later, Wayne mustered in the 6th Indiana Infantry regiment and participated in the soldiers' life with gusto. Unfortunately, his enthusiasm for the army did not spill over into enthusiasm for writing home. When he did write, he was far more graphic than Warren.

Lafayette also enrolled in the 6th Indiana and served side-by-side with Wayne, sleeping in the same tent. So, Wayne's letters also reflect Lafayette's experiences. There is a sense that Lafayette was not interested in writing letters, anyway. There was a hint that Lafayette was thought (by Mother at least) to be more rambunctious than his older brothers. Concern was expressed as to Lafayette's behavior once he left home, but assurance came from camp not to worry, he was well-behaved. Little is learned of Lafayette's personality other than he remained a high-spirited boy until his death.

Warren appears the most responsible of the three older brothers, Wayne, next, and then Lafayette; however, the three boys were equally responsive to the needs of their family. All three, realizing the financial hardships at home, faithfully sent their pay to Father.

Just as Lafayette does not write much, so it is with Mother, or Mary. Three letters (two in her hand) are all that is extant; but it is unmistakable, she was tough-minded. Writing (almost illegibly) about the local Confederate sympathizers, she tells Warren, "I have thaut I cold not stand to see anny boddy kild but wil tell you what, I hav wished it. . . . I get so [mad] sometimes I feel like I coud do it my self. . . ." Not always the warrior, she signed off, "your affectionate mother. . . . We do miss thee at home."

There is only one letter written by Minerva, the twenty-four-year-old, married Alford daughter. Like her mother she was barely literate. Nevertheless, we know she dearly cared about her brothers. Minerva and her husband, Charles Donaldson, bought farm acreage from Franklin and are the parents of four-year-old Enoch. Curiously, Enoch is mentioned only twice in the letters. In September 1862, Minerva's husband joined her brother Warren in the 14th Indiana Infantry — just in time to fight together at Sharpsburg, Maryland.

The younger children wrote the most endearing letters. George is every bit a fifteen-year-old farm boy with three older brothers in the War. George provided amusing news from the farm such as when he wrote Warren in October 1861 that "your mule is as fat as a bare and I ride him every where I go." In the same letter he communicates the news of relatives who have enlisted, "that only makes 11 Alfords in the Federal army" and with pride and enthusiasm, "I believe I had better go and make out the 12." George had his own views, too. Referring to what was a (complete) Confederate victory at Ball's Bluff, Virginia, he assured Warren, "they thought they had gained a parshiel victory . . . and they get sorter saucy again. . . . They had better watch out."

Nine-year-old Thomas Greene did not write often but when he did he was preoccupied with the farm news: fattening hogs, the corn harvest, the mare and so on. We know from other members of the family that Thomas Greene's performance at school was outstanding. After he participated in a geography singing contest at the school, Mother wrote Warren that "Green is the best in geography for enny in the school."

Hellen, a twelve-year-old, was fascinated with the idea of her big brothers being in the army. On December 15, 1861 she wrote with great curiosity, "Wrigh to me how you git your washing don and how often you wash. Do you ever shave any? And I would like to know what you look like." Hellen was full of loving thoughts, too, "Warren I wish you was here to eat some Walnuts . . . your letter stated that you still thought that you was comeing home. I hope that you will succeed in getting off for I want to see you very bad, worse than ever I did before." In an earlier letter she wrote, "Oh Warren how I long to see and be with you once more. . . . It just seems as if I could not stand it no longer but I will just have to stor it till you come home, if you ever do come home."

There are letters in the collection from the local doctor who served in the same unit with Wayne and Lafayette. Also, helping fill out the story are letters from Captain William Houghton, Company C, 14th Indiana Infantry, Warren's unit. Houghton and the Alfords were members of the same church before the War. Adding to the overall fabric are letters from aunts, uncles, cousins, nephews and friends.

Consistent with the times, nearly all the letters reflect a Victorian posture. "Dear Sir" is the standard salutation between male family members. The closings are equally starchy, "Your affectionate son, J. Warren Alford." The opening lines, whether Father's long religious discourses or the more friendly greetings, usually ran on and on and on. It all meant, "We are well" and "How are you."(3)

In an attempt to make the Alford correspondence more readable, the letters have been "dressed up" with a minimum of capitalization and punctuation.

Incorrectly spelled words and grammatical errors have been left to reflect the personna of the writer. A majority of the original Alford letters are continuous word streams — no periods, commas or capital letters.

Based on the handwriting and the content of the letters, Franklin was the most literate of his family, Mother the least. He started his sentences with capitals and usually ended them (eventually) with a period. She did neither, and referred to herself as "i." It is revealing that Warren Alford, who had taught school the previous year, showed little inclination for proper punctuation, spelling, capitalization or grammar.

Franklin Alford's education, remarkable for the time, was said to have been acquired in a formal school. Using Pike's arithmetic textbook as a child, he progressed to the "double rule of three," (a method of solving algebraic equations). When Franklin died in 1893, he was remembered as someone with a good memory, a mathematical mind, a persistent reader and "one of the best informed men in the community."(4)

In 1818, Franklin Alford came to Indiana as the three-year-old son of James and Hannah Alford. The small family moved from Wythe County, Virginia, to the southern banks of the White River in Dubois County. James Alford then moved his family across the river to Daviess County where he built a two-story log house. There were no other buildings within five miles, but this was the genesis of present-day Alfordsville. Franklin and his nine brothers and sisters were reared in typical dirt-poor frontier fashion.

When Franklin was twenty, he married seventeen-year-old Mary Gilley and moved into a nearby one-room cabin with one skillet and a makeshift bed. Mary was the daughter of James and Nancy Gilley, founders of the first Disciples Church in southwestern Daviess County. Young Franklin was not a religious person at the time of his marriage, but due to the influence of Mary and her mother, this changed. Before long, he became a stalwart member of the Disciples Church and a "leading Christian."

After the births of Minerva in 1837 and James Warren, two years later, Franklin and Mary Alford moved to a two-room house. The income was derived (at least in part) from the yield of an eighty-acre farm Franklin had obtained as a government grant. Four children were born in the two-room house: Wayne, Lafayette, George and Hellen. In 1850, Franklin built a larger house in, or near, Alfordsville where Thomas Greene was born. As the family grew, so did Franklin's land holdings, reaching 302 acres and a value of $10,000 on the eve of the Civil War.

It is unfortunate we do not have a collection of photographs of the Alford family. More distressing, the three brothers, when serving as Civil War soldiers, never had their images photographed. There had been requests. Father wrote Warren on January 5, 1862, "the Children has written to Wayne & Lafayette for the Likeness and they request the same of you and I Could enjoy It very well my self." An answer came back from Wayne and Lafayette, "their is a man in the regiment who takes pictures but he takes such poor ones that I Don't know yet whether we will or not. If he get to taking them right, we will." Regrettably, it never happened. Warren was more curt in his response: "and as to geting my likeness I [have not had a chance] to get it and do not now when we will have a chance . . . ."

The few bits of information that are available suggest the Alfords were above average in height and perhaps overweight, particularly by 1860s standards. Warren's mustering records indicate that he was 6'1," blue-eyed and fair complexioned. On March 9, 1862 Warren wrote that he weighed 193 pounds "and as good looking as ever." A government record, dated April 1862, denotes Lafayette's physical characteristics as 5'9" tall, blue eyes and a light complexion. Three months earlier, Hellen wrote that she heard "Lafayette is as fleshy in the face as Minerva." Wayne wrote the same month that "Lafe & I are fat and hearty." In March, young George passed along the news that Lafayette "is so fat that he can hardly sea." Beyond this scant information, imagination will have to give form to the Alfords' appearance.

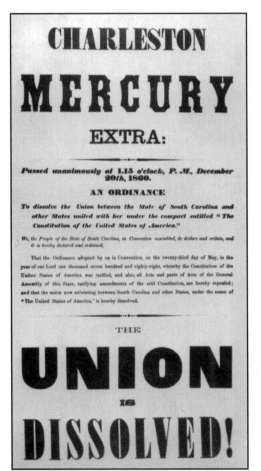

A Bold Announcement in a South Carolina Newspaper. (New York Public Library)

"There can be no neutrals."(5)

Our flag! God! These are words used to stir emotions when wars begin. When *civil* wars begin, flags and God are mingled with more personal words. Our homes! Traitors! Judas! Such were the passions of Americans in April 1861. The words "blood" and "death" were given little regard.

Earlier, the Charleston (South Carolina) *Mercury* had announced to its readers that the "Union is Dissolved." On April 21, 1861, seven days after the surrender of gov-

New York City, Broadway and Fulton Streets. (Harper's Weekly)

The 6th Massachusetts Fighting its Way through Baltimore. (HPHCW)

ernment-held Fort Sumter in Charleston Harbor, the *New York Times* set forth a different attitude with a headline, "The Union Forever."(6) This was the basic question. Did the states have a right to secede, and dissolve a Union? Intelligent, compassionate, God-fearing men could not agree. The question had to be decided with warfare.

Choices were made quickly. Former Democratic presidential candidate Stephen Douglas made it simple: "Every man must be for the United States or against it."(7) In the South, the Stars and Stripes were lowered in defiance of the federal authority. In New York City, patriotism overflowed as Union Square was decorated to resemble a "red, white and blue wonder."(8) President Lincoln immediately called for 75,000 volunteers. The South acted just as urgently as it mobilized for the impending war. Massachusetts volunteers on their way to Washington, D.C., were attacked in Baltimore. In Virginia, the federal navy yard at Norfolk and the arsenal at Harper's Ferry were abandoned and burned. Kansas soldiers bivouacked in the East Room of the White House.(9)

God was invoked by both sides. One southerner wrote, "Thank God the day has come — thank God the war is opened."(10) Confederate President Jefferson Davis declared "our cause is just and holy."(11) President Abraham Lincoln, to the contrary, had warned the South, "You have no oath registered in Heaven to destroy the government, while I have the most solemn one to preserve, protect and defend it."(12)

Abraham Lincoln. (Miller's)   *Jefferson Finis Davis.* (LC)

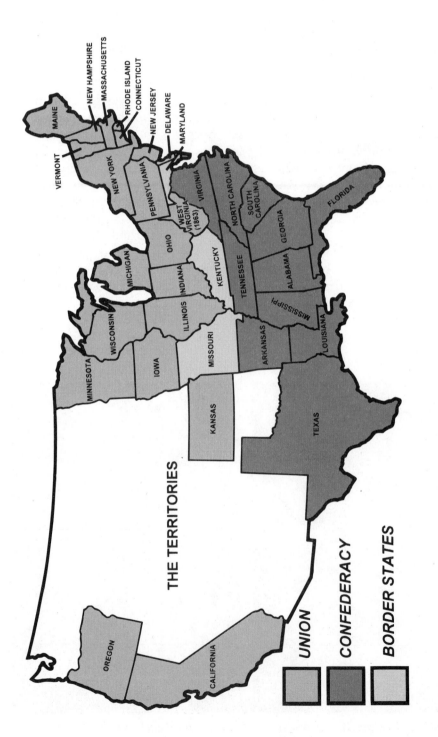

The United States in 1861.

It was not clear whether God was for the United States or against it. Politicians and magistrates continued to search the Constitution and the Bill of Rights for answers — and could not agree on what they found. To make the question more difficult, slavery — long the most inflammatory and divisive issue in the country — was at the core of the argument. Americans differed in other ways, too: economics, religion, nativity, education, and politics.

With all these differences and diverse opinions, how did the fighting-age American sort out which position was "worth dying for"? Decisions, usually made with conviction, were seldom grounded in formal theory or doctrine. Instead, the determination may be as simple as one's address. Only Southern states attempted to secede. It was a situational decision, decided by age and place of residence. In general terms, those living above the Mason-Dixon Line fought for Union and those living below the line fought for the Confederacy. Many times the American Civil War was (is) referred to by geographical reference, The War Between the States, The War of *Northern* Aggression or The War of *Southern* Rebellion.

There were exceptions to this simple rule of residence, most noteworthy being the border state citizens (in Maryland, Kentucky and Missouri) who had great difficulty choosing North or South.(13) For Hoosiers, the decision to risk life and limb may have been agonizing but choosing sides was easy.

The 7th New York Infantry Marching on Broadway. (HPHCW)

"With courage screwed to the sticking point."[(14)]

It could be assumed that the majority of people living in Indiana in 1861 were in favor of sustaining the Union. When Fort Sumter was fired upon, the citizens of Indiana acted with indignation and anger. They gathered by the thousands in cities and towns to demonstrate their allegiance to the federal government. On April 16, 1861, the Indianapolis *Journal* reported the first outburst in the capital city: "There is but one feeling in Indiana. . . . Our streets are blazing with national flags. . . . The drum and fife are sounding all day long. . . . Huge banners wave from the tops of houses and hundreds of flags flutter in windows and along the walks. . . ." The feeling was not unanimous as it was duly reported that there were "sympathizers of Southern institutions . . . but they are few, as pitiful in strength as in spirit."(15)

Indianapolis was not alone in enthusiasm. "Like the sunlight, the 'war fever' permeated every locality," wrote one Indiana historian.(16) At Fort Wayne, the mayor roamed the crowded streets day and night to control the crowds.(17) At Greensburg, the mayor was the first to enlist.(18) In sparsely populated Newton County (2,360 in 1860) it was reported, "*everyone* was wrought up in excitement. No other subject was talked about or thought about. . . ."(19) In the town of Franklin one young man wrote in his journal that "many seemed wild with excitement." He circled nervously about the town, hung around the telegraph office waiting for the latest news, and later tried unsuccessfully to sleep.(20) When the news of Fort Sumter reached Worthington in Greene County, the townspeople immediately erected a flag pole, raised the Stars and Stripes, built fires and closed all the businesses.(21) In neighboring Sullivan County, where Lincoln had been defeated three to one, there was little doubt about where they stood on the dissolution issue. The rural areas were "depopulated" and crowds gathered at the courthouse to hear "loyal mottoes and several martial bands . . . playing stirring national airs." (22)

At Noblesville, when the telegraph failed, two men commandeered a railroad handcar and pumped their way twenty miles to Indianapolis to gather the latest news. Once informed, they headed back on the handcar to the courthouse square in Noblesville. Upon their return, they found a horde of people anxiously awaiting the latest intelligence, in the thick of many bonfires.(23) In Terre Haute, with a reputation for pro-slavery and anti-abolitionism sentiments, the largest crowd in the town's history assembled at the courthouse. The enthusiastic throng adopted a resolution to "maintain the government of the United States with their lives, their fortune, and their sacred honor."(24) All over the state, once profoundly partisan Republicans and Democrats came together as one.(25) At Richmond, it was reported that "even the Quakers are turning out."(26)

The firestorm of excitement was played out with more than flag-waving and cheering. Men, in fact, came forward offering their lives. On April 15, Lincoln called for 75,000, of which six regiments were to come from Indiana. This was the equivalent of sixty companies or 4,683 men. With Indianapolis designated the rendezvous point, an estimated 12,000 showed up and the capital city of 19,000 was choked with rowdy volunteers. On April 26, Adjutant General Lew Wallace reported to Governor Oliver P. Morton that there were 130 companies in camp, seventy more than requisitioned.(27)

In his book, *Civil War Times*, Daniel Howe wrote that he was "living at home with my mother and stepfather. . . . It was felt that either my stepfather or I should enlist; my mother would not decide between us, so we both enlisted."(28) The enthusiasm for war continued into the summer. In Waterloo, Indiana, a cannon was to be fired in recognition of the volunteers who were leaving by express train for the front. When a young man proudly applied the match, the cannon exploded and the man was killed instantly by fragments of flying iron — the first casualty of the war from DeKalb County.(29)

There were many who were deliberative in their decision. John Foster, when relating his feelings in *War Stories for My Grandchildren*, told how his first impulse was to join up, but when the first quota was filled, he decided to "await

Major John W. Foster, A Reluctant Volunteer, Left His Bride, a Small Son and a Budding Career. Foster Would Rise to the Rank of General.
(War Stories For My Grandchildren)

the progress of events. I cherished no desire for military glory, and distrusted my special fitness for the life of a soldier. In my college days I had contracted a horror of war and regarded it as the most terrible and futile of human follies."(30)

Francis Brown had to overcome several persuasive arguments before he enrolled in the 14th Indiana Infantry. An aunt and uncle were southern sympathizers and another uncle felt the South had the right to form a new government. Another uncle thought young Brown would be cannon fodder and end up buried by the Confederates in a far off field.(31) Billy Davis, from Hopewell in Johnson County, agonized before he made his decision, finally writing, "I feel that if I do not go that I will be disgraced, and by staying at home [I] will bring reproach upon the family name." Also, all his friends were signing up.(32)

Not everyone came forth in body. Individuals, families, cities and banks were quick to pledge monetary donations: $25,000 from J.F.D. Lanier, a former Hoosier living in New York; $6,000 from the city of Madison; and $1,000 from T.J. Brooks of Loogootee to Captain Nathan Kimball and the 14th Indiana Volunteer Infantry.(33)

Indiana was not totally of one mind. Some preferred to let the South go in peace. Others were pacifist in principle, or because of religious convictions. Many could not go because of family responsibilities or physical disabilities. A few Democrats and others opposed any action which might subjugate the South. A newspaper editor in Vincennes persisted in characterizing the war as a "wicked, damnable, crusade."(34)

Alfordsville was typical; most of the boys went forward in lock step, but there were a few so-called dissenters. The whipped-up enthusiasm certainly propelled men forward, and without much deliberation. And there were other forces at work. In the case of the Alford boys, their church sanctioned the war, as did most churches. The community, in essence, sponsored their young men when they volunteered. Later, the volunteers were rewarded with bounties. And of course, the most powerful reason of all, "everyone was doing it."

In four years of Civil War, Indiana sent seventy-five percent of her men between the ages of eighteen and forty-five. The deaths would total 26,672. The wounds and misery were incalculable.(35)

"Men whose wildest dissipation had been a horse race or a circus."(36)

President Lincoln issued a second call for men on May 3. Many of the men who answered this call were the overflow from the April 15 call. However, these men had tempered their excitement and had thought longer about going to war. Warren Alford was part of this group.

Warren's company was organized at Loogootee in Martin County (the Alfords lived only nine miles away, but in Daviess County). Loogootee responded to the war news in the same way as every city in Indiana. Folks came from miles around to hear the news and speculate on the next development. Presumably, at least some of the Alfords were there. Wayne, in an August 1861 letter, reminded Warren of the initial excitement and the irresistible pressure that had abounded in April.

A thirty-nine-year-old local physician, Nathan Kimball, stirred the Loogootee gathering with talk of patriotism and treason. Kimball was born in

Brevet Major General Nathan Kimball, First Colonel and Commander of the 14th Indiana Infantry. (USAMHI)

Fredericksburg, Indiana, educated at Asbury College (now DePauw) in Greencastle, studied medicine under his brother-in-law and had fought in the Mexican War as a captain.(37) Kimball's words worked magic and 100 men became the "Martin County Guards," ready for war. Kimball would lead them.(38)

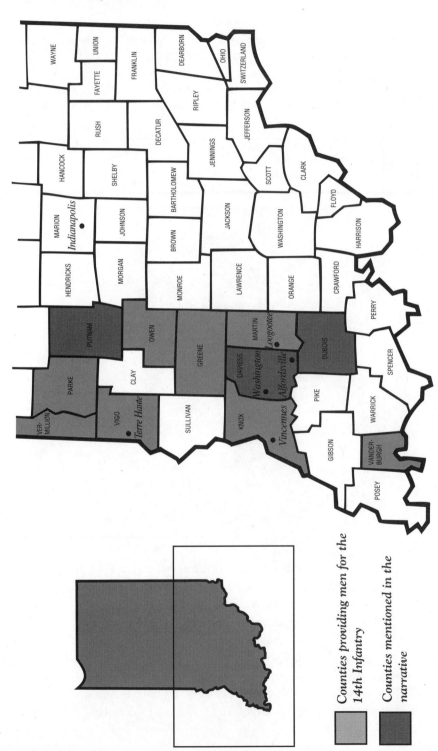

The Indiana Counties Significant to the Alfords and the 14th Indiana Infantry.

Warren Alford and Amory K. Allen were in the band of recruits who left Loogotee for training camp on Friday morning, May 10, 1861. One week later, Allen wrote home from Terre Haute to tell his wife of the recent adventure:

> . . . We got to Vincenes, Friday morning, after leaving home . . . we received a treat . . . and quieted down in the eating house til day-light ---- got up washed our selfs, com[b]ed our heads, and got our breakfast. . . . We then, after promananding some over town, paraded and formed company and marched through town to the Depot on the Evansville and Terrehaute road to Start to Terrehaute. We then marched back in town to go with the Vincennes company [the "Knox County Invincibles"] to receive their flag. We then marched to A tavern and got a free lunch. We then marched back to the Depo led by the Brass Band, heard a speech from Niblec [probably local politician, William E. Niblack] who said we was the finest company of men he had seen and give us bread and cheese enough for supper. And, all in all, we were very highly favered by the people of Vincenes. We then left on the evening train, both companys. We got to Terrehaute Friday evening. We were marched to the fire company hall where we staid til Monday [May 13]. We then march out to Camp Vigo where we are now in regular camp about 2 miles from town where we will be for some weeks. We are sworn and mustered in to service and drill every day. I want you to write to me soon for I have not heard from you since I left home I want to know how you are geting along. We are bound up here tolerable close. We do our own cooking. We have got nothing yet but our provisions and cooking vessels so no more, at present. I will write every opportunity. Take good care of the children and I will not forget you.

> Yours truly,
> Amory K. Allen
> to Mary D Allen(39)

Camp Vigo had a four-month history. It was configured on fifty-one acres of the County Fairgrounds, north of Terre Haute.(40) William Houghton described the camp to his parents as "high ground in the middle and [a] grove to the west, with our quarters running along each end of the ground north and south. They consisted of houses and stalls used in the fair grounds."(41)

Warren, in his letters to Alfordsville, was always optimistic and stated he enjoyed life in Camp Vigo "tolerable Well." It is known, however, that bedding was inadequate and Mother sent blankets from home. Warren mentioned the measles and a hospital. Also, he only had the clothes that he brought from home and was considering buying some more in Terre Haute. In reality things could not have been comfortable, but Warren always tried to relieve the fears of his mother and father. He wrote the officers were not going to let the "boys swair or drink any." To the contrary, a first sergeant and former attorney from Owen County wrote to his girl friend that about half the men got drunk.(42)

No doubt, there was plenty of excitement and new experiences. Both Warren and Amory Allen wrote home about the soldier who had been chained

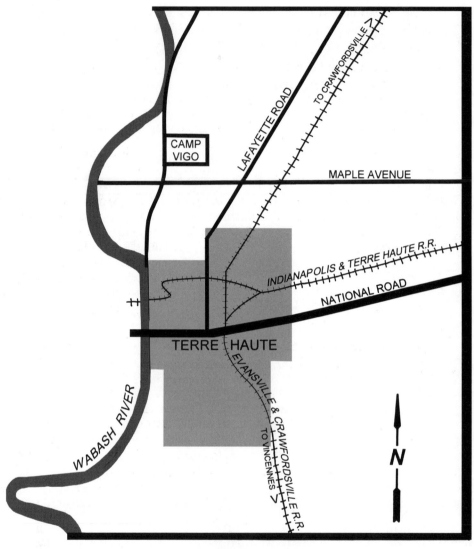

Terre Haute, Indiana, and Camp Vigo.

and drummed out of the service. Allen explained to his wife that the reason was "mis behavior — getting drunk, fighting and abusing the officers." His punishment consisted of dragging a big chunk of wood chained to his feet for two or three days. The scoundrel was displayed in front of the Sunday night dress parade and eventually left camp to the tune of the rogue's march.(43)

A big hullabaloo occurred on May 23 when it was learned that the men would be sworn in for three years of service. Some had left home thinking they were going to serve three months, like the April volunteers. Others believed it to be a one-year commitment. Upon the news of the longer terms, many left camp, including a whole company from Putnam County. A young man in that contingent explained:

On the tenth of [May] we went into camp near Terre Haute. We
were received in the 14th Regt. Ind. Vol. under Col. Kimball, we
were in camp about one month when the three year question
came up. Our company refused to go in for that long a period, so
we transferred to Richmond, Ind. Before this, though, our former
Capt Malin [John R. Mahan] had been promoted to Lieut. Col. of
the 14th Regt. He left nothing untried to get us into the three
year service in the United State Army but with out effect. So we
left Terre Haute . . . [and enlisted in a one-year regiment]. . . .(44)

Others were transferred agreeably to three-month units, some left individu-
ally for home. Warren wrote all the boys from Alfordsville stayed on.

The collection of raw soldiers, 1,134 men strong, was mustered into the service of the United States on June 7, 1861 as the 14th Indiana Volunteer Infantry
Regiment. Nathan Kimball, the firebrand orator from Logootee, was officially
appointed commanding officer with the rank of colonel. John Mahan from
Greencastle was named lieutenant colonel, William Harrow, Vincennes, the
major. There were ten companies of approximately 100 men each, representing
nine counties: Parke, Martin, Greene, Vanderburgh, Vigo, Owen, Vermillion,
Monroe and Knox (two companies). Company C, Private Warren Alford's unit,
would be led by Captain Lewis Brooks, First Lieutenant William Houghton and
Second Lieutenant Harvey Taylor.(45)

Mid-June, the men were issued uniforms (gray satinette) and weapons of war.
Francis Brown recorded: "guns were old flint-lock muskets, some with bayonets.
These guns carried an ounce ball but had not been shot since the war with
England."(46) Properly equipped or not, on June 23, the 14th began to pack up
what they had been issued. Visitors came to Camp Vigo for a "practical sermon,"
a dress parade and the presentation of a regimental flag. The next morning the
regiment marched to the trains as well-wishers crowded into open fields along
the route. At 7:30 a.m. the 14th headed eastward to another converted fairgrounds, this one in Indianapolis.(47) Camp Morton was laid out on thirty-six
acres and the facilities were comparable to Camp Vigo — animal sheds and stalls
with one side exposed to the elements. The interior was adapted for tiers or
shelves.(48) Each shelf accommodated eight or ten sleeping men.(49)

Warren had no complaints.

The Gates of Camp Morton. (Miller's)

The Terrain and Sheds of Camp Morton. (USAMHI)

Endnotes

(1)   Psalms, 90:9.

(2)   The genealogical data and all the letters were provided by the Dorothy Lobban family, descendants of Thomas Greene Alford. The Lobban family graciously donated the letters and other family documents to the Indiana Historical Society in Indianapolis.

  For a scholarly analysis of families in the Civil War era, refer to: Reid Mitchell, *The Vacant Chair, The Northern Soldier Leaves Home* (New York and Oxford, 1993).

(3)   For a more detailed examination of letter writing during the Civil War, refer to: James I. Robertson, Jr., *Soldiers Blue and Gray* (Columbia, South Carolina, 1988).

  Also, the classic two-volume publication by Bell I. Wiley, *The Life of Johnny Reb* (Indianapolis, 1943), and *The Life of Billy Yank* (Indianapolis, 1951).

(4)   The information concerning Franklin Alford's early life was contained in a "Memoriam" printed in *The Martin County Tribune*, Loogootee, Indiana; March 3, 1893.

(5)   James McPherson, *Battle Cry of Freedom: The Civil War Era* (New York, 1988). This is a Stephen Douglas quotation found on p. 274, cited on p. 275.

(6)   Eugene P. Moehring and Arleen Keylin, Editors, *The Civil War Extra: From the Pages of The Charleston Mercury & The New York Times* (New York, 1975) pp. 20, 23.

(7)   McPherson, *ibid.*, p. 274, cited p. 275. From the same Douglas speech as cited above.

(8)   *Ibid.*, p. 278 and *Civil War Extra*, p. 23.

(9)   E.B. Long, *The Civil War Day by Day: An Almanac, 1861-1865* (New York, 1971) p. 61, (April 18). *Day by Day* is an excellent source for concise summations of the significant daily events in the nation, for the entire war period.

(10) *Ibid.*, page 58.

(11) *Ibid.*, page 67.

(12) Don E. Fehrenbacher, Editor, *Abraham Lincoln: Speeches and Writings 1859-1865* (New York, 1989) v. 2, p. 224.

(13) For a study of some men who did not serve in their state of residence, see

Richard Nelson Current, *Lincoln's Loyalists, Union Soldiers from the Confederacy* (Boston, 1992).

(14) Lew Wallace, *Lew Wallace An Autobiography* (New York, 1906) v. I, p. 269. A phrase coined by Wallace.

(15) John Hampden Holliday, *Indianapolis and the Civil War* (Indianapolis, 1972) p. 26.

(16) W.H.H. Terrell, *Report of the Adjutant General of the State of Indiana* (Indianapolis, 1869) v. I, p. 6. Hereafter cited as *IAG*.

(17) Joseph A. Parsons, Jr., "Indiana and the Call for Volunteers, April 1861," *Indiana Magazine of History* (Indianapolis, 1958) v. LIV, n. 1, p 11.

(18) *Ibid.*, p. 10.

(19) John Ade, *Newton County* (Indianapolis, 1911) p. 207.

(20) Richard S. Skidmore, Editor, *The Civil War Journal of Billy Davis* (Greencastle, 1989) p. 8.

(21) *History of Greene and Sullivan Counties, State of Indiana* (Reprinted Evansville, 1975) p. 119.

(22) *Ibid.*, pp. 571, 572.

(23) Joe H. Burgess, *Hamilton County in the Civil War*, np., nd., p. 8.

(24) Charles Roll, *Colonel Dick Thompson: The Persistent Whig* (Indianapolis, 1948) p. 170.

(25) James H. Madison, *The Indiana Way* (Indianapolis, 1986) p. 197.

(26) Parsons, *ibid.*, Phrase quoted on p. 8. For an excellent analysis of the subject, refer to Jacquelyn S. Nelson, *Indiana Quakers Confront the Civil War* (Indianapolis, 1991). Interesting data and conclusions.

(27) Wallace, *ibid.*, v. 1, p 267. The numbers vary and an accurate estimate was difficult because of the traffic in and out of Indianapolis over a twelve-day period. Nevertheless, Wallace stated the numbers as fact.

(28) Daniel Wait Howe, *Civil War Times* (Indianapolis, 1902) p. 9. Howe was from Franklin, Indiana and both he and his step-father, Samuel Oyler, served in the three-month 7th Indiana Infantry.

(29) John Martin Smith, *History of DeKalb County, Indiana* (Auburn, 1992) v. II, p. 1055.

(30) John W. Foster, *War Stories for My Grandchildren* (Washington, 1918) pp. 1, 2. John Foster changed his mind after the first major battle, enlisted, and rose to the rank of colonel of the 65th Indiana Infantry. One of Foster's grandchildren was John Foster Dulles, President Eisenhower's Secretary of State. Another was Elanore Lansing Dulles, an author of fourteen books

on economics and international affairs.

(31) Francis M. Brown, *The Brown Family History*, privately printed, 1976; p. 27. Provided to the editor by Robert Breese, Greencastle, Indiana.

(32) Skidmore, *ibid.*, p. 3.

(33) Merrill and Company, Editors, *The Soldier of Indiana* (Indianapolis, 1866) p. 12.

(34) G.R. Tredway, *Democratic Opposition to the Lincoln Administration* (Indianapolis, 1973) p. 7. Quoted from the *Western Sun*, April 20, May 11, July 27 and August 17, 1861.

(35) David I. McCormick, *Indiana Battle Flag Commission: Battle Flags and Organizations* (Indianapolis, 1929) pp. 657, 658. There are two widely used methods to determine each Northern state's contribution to the Civil War – Indiana ranks number two by either method. The difference in the calculation concerns whether total enrollments are used or if all enrollments are adjusted for a three-year equivalency.

(36) William E. McLean, *The Forty-Third Regiment of Indiana Volunteers: An Historic Sketch of its Career and Services* (Terre Haute, 1903) p. 7. A fascinating phrase. The 43rd was mustered at Camp Vigo, also.

(37) Ezra Warner, *Generals in Blue* (Baton Rouge, 1977 printing) p. 267. As stated, Kimball was born at Fredericksburg, Indiana. In December 1862, he was wounded at Fredericksburg, Virginia.

(38) Nancy Niblack Baxter, *Gallant Fourteenth: The Story of an Indiana Civil War Regiment* (Traverse City, 1980) p. 3. This is the only full-length account of the 14th.

(39) "The Civil War Letters of Amory K. Allen," Editors, *Indiana Magazine of History* (Indianapolis, December 1935) v. XXXI, n. 4., p. 339.

(40) "Civil War Camp Marker Unveiled in Ceremony Here." *Terre Haute Tribune*, November 27, 1962. Camp Vigo lay in a rectangle bordered today by 3rd and 7th Streets, and Florida and Collett Avenues. This is an area just northwest of present-day Collett Park, and U.S. highway 41 cuts a diagonal through the old camp.

(41) Baxter, *ibid.*, p. 36. Quoted from a Houghton letter to his parents, May 12, 1861.

(42) *Ibid.*, p. 36. Quoted from a letter written by David Beem, May 15, 1861.

(43) ". . . Letters of Amory K. Allen," *ibid.*, p. 340.

(44) William A. Alley unpublished journal. John and Emma Walton Collection; Greencastle, Indiana.

(45) Terrill, *IAG*, v. II, pp. 112-122.

(46) Brown, *The Brown Family History*, p. 27.

(47) "A Series of Articles on Vigo County in the War," *Terre Haute Express*, August 9, 1885.

(48) Hattie Lou Winslow and Joseph R.H. Moore, *Camp Morton 1861-1865: Indianapolis Prison Camp* (Indianapolis, 1940) pp. 237, 242. This book contains the definitive account of Camp Morton, both as a training facility and a prison camp. Today the site is bordered by the streets of 19th and 22nd, Central and Talbott.

(49) Skidmore, *ibid.*, p. 6. The 14th Indiana occupied a small area of Camp Morton, which they named Camp Kimball.

CHAPTER

1

Camp Vigo
May the 9th 1861

Dear Parents   It is with pleasure I embrace the opertunity of
Coresponding with you by letter as it is out of my power to see and
talk with you. I am well at this time and have been ever since I left
home and I hope this will find you well. I received your package. . . .
I have watched the office with the hope that I would get some nuse
from some of the friend at home but was much disapointed. I think
that the Folk are a fraid that we will hear [too much] from home as
there are so many of you to write and only one of us [to read].
Enough of this so I will cange the subject. The fourteenth regiment is
now full and we will get our uniform on Monday or Tuesday next.
That Man that they had under guarde was Chained for five dayes
and then drumed out of the Camp. The first sentence Was to shoot
him. We was mustered in to the U S service on the 6th of this month.
. . . Their was not one of the boys [who] backed [out] in our Company.
Their is several of the boys got the measles but they are gettin along
as well as Can be expected. The camp is crowded with visitors from
morning till night. The Mt Pleasant [Martin County] folks was here
this weak and we was glad to see them. Wayne I want you and
Lafayette to write and keep me posted in all of the special matter.
You do not know how much I mis your society. Home society is a
vary desireable thing With me. It is true we have many kind friends
here. I beleive that their is some of the finest Wimen her that I ever
saw any place. They come to the hospital every day to Waite on the
sick. If their aney Cristian people in Indiania they must be here.
Give my best love to all of the Children and all so to all of the friends
and tell them to Write. Remember [me] at a throne of grace. Tell
Charley and Minervy [brother-in-law and sister] to Write to me as
soon as they Can and tell them that this is to them. No more at present but Remaines your son.

J Warren Alford

Wayne give me the best letter you can get up. That is all except I
have a vary sore mouth. Boliver [Gold] gives you his best Respect and
sayes for you two take care of the girles. He sayes for you to write to
him.

[Warren to his father, Franklin:]

May the 12. 61

Dear Father I now take the opertinity to in form you that I am Well
at presen and hope these few lines will find you injoying good health.
We landed safe in this place on the eavening of the 10th. It has been
raining for the last two day. We have bin housed up sleeping on the
soft Side of a plank and bording at the Bunton house. We expect to
go in to camp to morrow. Their are about ten companies in Camp to
day. Ours boys are all in fine spirits. When you Write Direct to
Tarrehute Vigo Co. ind. So no more at present. But we reamin you
affectionate son. J Warren Alford

[Warren to the family:]

May the 16 = 1861

Dear parents brothers an Sisters and friends in General. I now
embrace this opertunity to drop you a few lines to inform you of my
good health. We came in to Camp on monday last and have had fine
Weather since. Our encampment is in regular order. We have a regular Mounted guard of eighty men. It is a beautiful place about two
miles from town. Terryhute is a fine town of about Eighteen thousand inhabitantce and they are fine looking Hosiers. No scandles to
the hosier state. Their are about eleven Companies in Camp of fine
looking Hosiers. We have some fine fun. Some of the boys that [are]
a frade of gunn powder have bin drummed out of Camp. The boys
are all Well and in fine Spirits. The laws and regulations of the Camp
have not bin fully explaned yet. They [are] not going to let the boys
swair or drink any. I think Indiania is looking up. I think it is
thought that We will get our uniform in abought ten days and per-
hapse our aremes [weapons] at the same time but we cannot tell positive. I would like to have some more Close [clothes] but I supose I Can

by them here Cheeper . . . than you Could send them to me. If not I
will Write to you. . . . I have time to Read about a dozen letters each
day. I was on gard last knight. Give my best to all friends. Wright
often. Let me know how you get along With disunion at home. I
have no heared a word of disunion since I left home. As it is now
time for dinner I Will give you a bill of our fare . . . on 1st bacon 2
beef . . . 3 potatoes 4 hommony 5 three kinds of vegetables 6th Coffee.
Direct you letters to Camp Vigo Tarryhute Ind in Care of Captin
Cimble [Kimball]. No more at present but remains your Deutiful son.
JWA

★

[Wayne to Warren:]

Home Monday
May, 20 - 61

Mr Warren Alford. Dear Brother   I am Seated again to Wright You
A few Lines. We are All Well at present. We received your Letter
Saturday Eavening. I Have Nothing of importance to Wright. Only
that Trimble Was at our Meating And preached three Noble Sermons.
You Wanted to Hear [about] Disunion. Our Guard Numbers over 100.
Dr Key of Haysville [Dubois County] Has been Coming over for the
Last two Weeks to Make a Cecession Speach but He takes care Not to
come [lately]. We are gowing to Slicers to Muster Next Saturday and
our Capt says if they Cheap [cheep] Well [we'll] thresh them out.
Charles Allen [talked to me about] that Money for that threshing. He
is under the impression He payed it. . . . He says He paid it to you in
town one Day their by Kyles smokehouse & remarked that part of it
belonged to Lafayette and it Ought to Have been payed Long ago. He
said inquire of you and He thought you would recollect it. If Not He
supposed He Was Mistakened. I expect to Come up to Terry Haut in A
Week or to if We get Along With or Work. Well I rote to you Last
Monday but Did not know Whether it Come to Hand or not. We sent
a blanket to Vergil [Virgil Alford, a cousin]. Wright if it came to Hand.
His Mother is gowing to Send Him a Comfort this Morning. Mother
Has started you a Can of peaches Last Eaviening by Bob Bally. The
people are generally Wel so far as I know. Father says that as soon as
We get through the push of our Work He Will Wright to you as he is
Slow A Hand to Wright. Now Wright Who is in your Mess and if
you Want any thing. Wright to us Nothing more but Remains Your
Brother untill Death.

Wayne Alford

Lafayette is gowing to Wright

[Separate sheet from Lafayette:]

Special

Genette Was Here With Trimble and the Bethena Girls were up to.
Our Girls Were out to [Church] Meating And are All right. Say to the
Boys I Would Like to See them. Tell them We are All Right Down
Here.

Yours Respectfully
Lafayette Alford

Did you Get your Revolver and What Did it Cost?

[Warren to Father and Mother:]

May the 23rd 1861
Camp Vigo Ind

Dear Father and Mother

I am seated agane to drop you a few lines to inform you that I
received your letter of the 20th and was glad to hear from home and
to hear that you was all well and to inform you that I am well and
that I am enjoying my self as well as I expected when I started. I
find that if a Man Conducts him self right he will find friends
where ever he goes. We received your favor with thankfulness Lewis
brook [Lewis Brooks, soon to be named Captain of Company C] sayed
them was the finest he had eaten for sume time. From your letter of
the 20th I supose you did not get my first letter. Captain Kimble
[Kimball] has bin promoted to the Colonels office over the fourteenth
regiment of Indiania volunteers and we are with out a Captain but
we have a man that will fill his place . . . I Cannot say positive now
If he payed [for] it. . . . We enjoy Camp lif tolerable Well. We do not
expect to stay here more [than] fifteen Dayes longer. I Will Write to
you as sone as I asertain where We are going two. I got my revolver
and it Cost fifteen Dollars. I Deposited twenty Dollars With Lewis
brooks for safe keeping unitil I need it. I stood picket gard last night
and am some What nervous and in a bad fix for Writing A flourish-
ing letter. I supose you can cook over arough letter. I want you to
Write to me as soone and Often as you Can. I would like to her from
home for I do not expect to be their for some time. Tell Hannah that
I would [like] for her to Write to me. It is though[t] We Will get in the
united States Service. So no more at present but remains you
Affectionate Sone and Brothers.

J Warren Alford

Wayne Beleive this in answer to your letter and look for another.

★

[To Warren from Robert Gilley, an uncle or a cousin:]

May the 23 1861
J W Alford
Dear sir   I take this oppertunity of wrighting to you to let you no
that we ar all Well and hopping that this letter may find you enjoying the same.   But I would like to heare from you as is convinent
with you.   I suppose you hav plenty of time to read all the letters
that is sent to you from many of your friends so this ends my letter
Robert Gilley

[Warren to all the family:]

June the 11th 1861
Camp Vigo
Brother Wayne and all the family   It is again I seat my self to drop
you a few lines to post you in regard to some matters that their
seams to be great excitement in regard to and allso to let you know
that I am well at the present time. All of the boyes are well so far as
I know. John McCord [Warren's cousin and a fellow member of the
Alfordsville Christain Church] is not able to drill yet but is gettin a
long as well as Can be expected for he was vary low. Wayne we are
expecting to leave heare every day. The Col [Kimball] thinks that we
will go to Cumberland Maryland. We are getting tolerable well
drilled and if we get a chance at the Ceesesions we will show them.
As the Col sayes that it [will] take ten secessionist to whip one union
man and that the hoosiers is not such a coward as Jeff Davis
[Confederate president] would have you think and if we meat them
by the help of god we will whip them. For I can [not] in my own
strength but go forth in the strength of the God. . . . Mother I would
like to come home but I think it not prudent at the present time taking every thing in Consideration. Wayne we have our uniform and
are going to get our Rifles. The governor [Oliver P. Morton] is not
going to let us go With out being prepaired fully to meat the enemy.
Wayne I will write to you as soon as I Can find out when and where
we [are] going to. Wayne tell Dr. Laverty that I received his vary
Welcom letter. Sam Cragen [Samuel E. Crego from Martin County,
soon to be in Company C] is in Camp this week. [He] sayes he is going

Indiana Governor Oliver P. Morton. (ISL)

with us. Tell Charley and Minerva that I will answer the letter as soon as I can and for thegm to rite as soon as they please. Tell the boyes of your Sunday school I would like to be with them. So as this sheet is full I will Close. Good by. J Warren Alford

[Same envelope, a note to Father:]

Father I Want you to get of W J Brown pay for servin on the board last Spring. He toled me that he Would give me one Dollar for it. Give him a Receite for me if he wants one. We are going to send our Close home and you Will be expecting to get them and distribut them for we thaight that you would do it for us as we are going to pack them in Step trunk. Write soone. J W Alford

to
F[ranklin] Alford   H[ellen] Alford
Mary Alford   Gr[eene] Alford
W[ayne] Alford   C[harley] Donaldson
L[afayette] Alford   M[inerva] Donaldson
G[eorge] Alford

★

[Wayne to Warren:]

Home June 13th 1861
Mr James Warren Alford   Dear Brother As you are Now gone from
Home and placed in Circumstances Which require Decission of Mind
and Character I though it Not amiss to Put you in Mind that the
responsibility of your position Requires that you Should Lay aside
childish things and stand to your post as [a] true Lover of your
Country. Though your Company is Sweet We Had rather Bid a final
farewell in this World With the Bright Prospects of Meating you in
the World of Happiness than to see you Come Home Disgraced as some
Have Done. No Rather than this We Would see you Had Death and
When the grim Monster Had Laid His . . . fingers around your Dear
Boddy We Can Remember that you Have Stood up Shoulder to
Shoulder With those of your friends in Defence of the Liberty
Bequeathed to us by our Fore fathers and in Defence of the
Constitution of our once Glorious union and for the flag of our
Country So Nobly Defended on Concords Hill on Bunkers Crest. These
are my feeling if I were in your Situation and I am Confident those
are yours. That Letter Which Some of the Boys Sent to F Bartl made
Him Just Rair on his hind Legs. The shoe fits so Well it Pinches I
think. I Say the one that rote it Was the Best guesser I ever saw for
a Strainger. I Want you to Wright Me Who Rote it. He is gowing to
try to find out who Wrote it But if I New He Would Be None the
Wiser of it. He Has With Drawed from the Home guard and We are
glad of it. Mr Bingham Has also Withdrawn and We are glad of that.
We expect to Organize in the Militia Line in a few Days or as soon as
We Can obtain a copy of it. We Drill Regularly every Saturday and
Some eavenings through the Week. Their is a . . . Comotion about
McCords store being Robed an their are several Out on the Lookout to
Night. We are all Well except father and george. Father Had a Shake
with the ague Sunday Last and george Has been poorly for several
Days but they are able to Plow to Day. Charles & Minirvia are here to
Night. The Girls are all Well So far as I know and are in for the
Union. . . . I Was in hopes you Could Have Come Home Before gowing
into the U S Service. If you Have any Chance Come for it May be the
Last Chance for Some time. But I mist Bring My Letter to a close. Oh
that God of Battles Would Preserve you from Harm is My Prair. Your
Kind Brother.

Wayne Alford Jr

★

[Lafayette to Warren:]

Home June 17 /61

Dear Brother   I take pen to inform you that I am well [and] hoping
when you receive this . . . [you] will be enjoying the same. I went
into the molitia company last saturday. We expect to Commence cutting Wheat next week. Excuse me for not writeing you [a longer let-
ter]. You must write. Nothing more only remains your brother.
Lafayette Alford

[Same letter, Wayne to Warren:]

Warren   Wright to Me if you Nead any More Money on your trip
and if so We Will send it to you. Wright soon and tell Me if you
received My Letter of friday. Your Brother   Wayne Alford

[Warren to Father and Mother:]

Terrehaute
Camp Vigo June 23/61

Dear Father and mother
        I embrace the present opportunity to write you a few lines for
the last time I will write from Camp Vigo. We have orders to march
at 5 oclock in the morning. We go from here to Camp Morton [in
Indianapolis] where we expect to remain but a short time, probably
eight or ten days and when we leave there we expect to go the scene
of action but we cannot exactly [tell] where yet. But the general sup-
position is that we will go to Virgina. The regiment all appear anxious to get off with the exception of a few who would like to desert
Though they are few. The boys are all in good health. John Stafard
[Stafford] and Lemuel Kelley was in Camp thursday and Friday last
and from what they sayed their was great excitment around
Alfordsville about that letter. Those that wrote it understands them
selves. Some of the boyes sayes that they wuld like to see them in
Camp Vigo. If they were to show them selves in the Camp they would
be used a little rougher than they are accustomded to. All the boys
would like to be there longe enough to tell the boys of Alfordsville
what they think of them. . . . If it become necessary they could do
more than tell them the straight thing. They have got so embittered
against the least sign of toryism that they could do anything. [Such as]
hang seven heads or anything else. We expect to gratify our selves

soon by getting at the rebels. When you write again write to
Indianpolis. If you can make it canvenient mail your letter at
Loogootee so that I will be sure of getting it before we leave
Indianapolis.

Yours Truly,

J. Warren Alford

Direct your letters in care of Capt Brooks Co C 14 Reg Ind Volunters

[Wayne to Warren:]

Home June 23 /61

Mr James Warren Alford. Dear Brother   I am Happy to embrace
the opportunity this Sunday Eavening of Wrighting to you and to
inform you that We are all Well at present and Hope you are enjoying the Same blessing. I was at Loogootee Last Eavening and When I
reached Home your Letter and William Houghtons was at Hand
Which Were thankfully received. . . . As you Have heard of Dr
Jackmans Hostilities to the Union Cause Here I will Just state that he
received a Letter from Loogootee Signed Many Loyal Citizens of
Martin and the Adjoining Counties [stating] that he could Not Stay
Here and utter His Cecession Slang and Make His Brags as he has
done. That He Could Make a Cession speach if He chosed to Do so in
spight of us . . . [but] if He Didnot Leave Alfordsville against [before]
the twentieth of July they Would Hang Him Higher than Haman
was Hung.   He caired around for a While and Said if He New Who
Rote the Letter he Would Blow their Brains out or something to that
account. He then mounted the old [?] and Rode Down to Capt Slicers
to Show it to Him. He red it and expressed great Surprise at it.
Jackman then told Him to Hand it to Wm Jackson Who Was standing by and [he] refused to do it. Jackman then told Him to read it
aloud Which He Did and then Handed it to Jackson Saying that I
Believe they Will Hang You but Dont fear for I can furnish 500 men
in one Day Who Will stand to your Back. This report I suppose
Creditable But the Hour is growing Late and I Must Close for the
Night. Promising if the Lord [willing, I will] Wright more in the
Morning. All well this Morning and I am seated again to Wright and
it is raining this Morning. James Briant [Bryant] Commenced Friday
eavening Last to rais A Company for U S Service. He Was Down to
our Drill Saturday eavening to Solicit volunteers and I think James
Lyons is going or he says so at Least. Our Malitia Company is Nearly

full and We are gowing to organise in a few Days. We Cannot for a
few Days as harvest is uppon us and it Must be attended to immediately. Some of the boys says they Wish Me to [stand] for first [the
word "second" was crossed out] lieutenant. I told them that Was just
as they Pleased. If they Desire it I will run. Mr Bingham has Cleared
up the charges brought against him and is Now in the Company
again. I Have . . . A great deal more to Wright But as I Want to
Wright Houtin [William Houghton] You can just refer to His Letter
for the rest Which is important I assure you. I must Bring My Letter
to a Close so No More only remains your Affectionate Brother until
Death. Wayne Alford

PS A Word to Boliver [Gold]   Dear friend. Your folks are Well so far
as I know and in fine Spirits.   Henry & Bill Says With regard to that
Letter that Wm Houtin [Houghton] sent to [Jackman ?] We Will Stand
to any thing you Boys Have Said. And if they Want to Say any
thing about you boys just Come to us we are Responsible for it all. I
hear it Whispered that [?] Says if you get Back He will shoot you. I
Dont hardly Now Whether He Said it or Not. If He Did He can just
shoot Some of us and that Will Do just as Well as to shoot you. Wright
to me Whenever you Can. No More But With Respect remains your
friend.

Wayne Alford

[A companion letter to William Houghton, a fellow church member and Second Lieutenant in the 14th Indiana:]

Home June 24h /61

Much esteamed friend Wm Houghton. Dear Sir. I am Seated this
Morning to answer your kind Letter Which came to Hand Last
Saturday and found the friends so far as I know enjoying good
health. I will just say that I have Wrighten Warren Some of the par-
ticulars and Nead not repeat them as you can just refer to his Letter.
With regard to Bartl and his Letter I will just say that the company
Was Drilling Saturday eavening and they all Desired that I Should
read aloud that Letter you Sent Me. I Did so and then some of them
publicly declared that any Man who Would Wright Such a Letter as
Florian Did Was a tory. As Bartl [and his] Son Had Made such a Blow
about the other Letter they Said He should read this or hear it Read.
So We went Down and Had him to read it. He Said it was verry easy
to Lose the Letter and then Say He Said so and so. We told Him Not

to Say that for We had sooner Believe you as him and his Son. His Wife then come in and begain rairing on Her hind feat and as Might be expected fifty Men Could Not stand the fire so We Just retredded and Left it. So When florian Came Home He said He Would Like to see that Letter if I Had No objections. I told him I had None. Of course He Said it Was a Ly about His [implying] that their horse Company [was] gowing to Help the cessionests. I told Him Not to Say that if he pleased for When He Said Wm Maddin Was expected to Be their Captain that Was enough for He Was a Known Cecessionest and further more that I Was Willing to stand up to any thing You Boys Said and When He said you Would Ly it all Just came to me [that] I would stand good for [anything you said]. We concluded then that He Would cecede and So We just Left at once. The Home guard here has been verry slow to anger but believe Me thay are completely aroused Now. . . . I Have Nothing More to Wright only give My Respects to all the Company. Wright as soon as convenient and Let Me know . . . Where I Will find you. But if I can I Wish to keep up regular Correspondence. If you Wright tell Me Where to Direct my [mail]. Nomore But remains your Brother in the One hope. Wayne Alford

[Father to Warren:]

Home June 26th 1861
J Warren Alford

Dear Sir. Through the Mercy of God we are all still enjoyng Common health and we hope this address may find you and all our friends enjoying the same Blessing. We received your verry kind and affec‐ tionate letter of the 23rd and we were all glad to hear that you were well. Your Aunt has moved on your place and wants to know where you want her to Clear. . . . I lifted the Note Prater held against you yesterday with $75. Your friends are well and appear to be verry much interested for your wellfare. We had some excitement over the Letters Wayne received on Saturday from the Camp. And I said I would help tar and feather some of them. And as I was passing through the street Monday morning Bartell and Jackman gave me more abuse than you could think. Calling me all the bad names they could think of. I went on about my business and when I came back in the evening I learned that the town had been in an uproar all day and did not disperse till about midnight after a Council of about 30 men of the citizens and a number of them armed to the teeth. They was [called] upon the next morning by a Committy. But enough of this. We went out to work Thursday morning and Lafayette fell on his Sythe and cut his wrist badly.

Friday morning and raining. We [are] driveing on with four Cradles and the promise of two or three more tomorrow. We expect to keep Goldsmyth till our grass is cut. We hope to be remembered to or by all our friends. Wayne says he will wright again soon. Wright again as soon as convenient and keep us posted in all your movements. Nothing more but honor your calling that you may have hope of eternal life.

ever yours   F Alford

[Warren to his brothers:]

Camp Cimble [Kimball]
Indianapolis June 61/30

Dear brothers. It is again I take this opertuity of fulfiling my promice to you. I am well at presant and hope these lines may come to hand in due time and find you enjoying that Heaven favored blesin. I received fathers letter Friday last and was glad to hear from you but was sorry to hear that Lafayette had cut his hand but hope he will soon get well. You sayed in your letter that my ant had moved on my land and you wanted to know where she should Clean. I want her to Clean on the south half of the west eighty and on the North east quarter of the forty. I am glad to hear that you lifted that note prater held against me and allso to learn that you are geting along so well with your work. Wayne I went to Town to hear preaching to day and who should I heare but Jimmy Mathley. It was quite a feast for me after hearing nothing but Methodism for nine weeks. Then it appeared like I was at home. He delivered quite an able discorse on the subject of rightly dividing the word of truth. He was followed by an able speake. I did not learn his name. The meeting was closed with praying by Elden goodwin. We had quite a pleasant meeting. Brothe goodwin promised to visit us if we remain hear a few days. This is a fine Citty. It is pleasan weather here. You sayed something in regard to our Masheen [threshing machine]. All I have to say is do the best you Can. And all is right in regards to that letter. I want you to wrigh the particulars and all so about what they say about you and me in particular. L Brooks has gon home.... Wayne ... in regard to our opposers [I want you] to alwayes be prepared for them never let them find you [off] your gard. I want you to [always] be on your gard. Do not let your tongue go before your knowledge but remember your deuty to god and your Cuntrey. So I must bring my letter to a close. Hoping to hear from you soon. Tell hillery [Hileary Houghton] and [my brother] green that I received them notes. Tell them that I see many strange thing to look at here and would like to help Green harvest. So no more. Good buy. Warren Alford

★

1
BACKGROUND

"their works do follow them"[1]

When James Alford built his two-story log house in an isolated area of Daviess County, little did he know he had founded a community. On June 3, 1845, the town of Alfordsville was laid out into sixty-four lots.[2] The community is in Reeves Township, in the southeast corner of Daviess County. Reeves Township comprises approximately forty-five square miles, and in 1850 there were 1,000 inhabitants living in 171 dwellings.[3] Alfordsville is sixteen miles southeast of Washington, Indiana, the county seat. More relevant is the town of Loogootee in neighboring Martin County, nine miles to the northeast.

James Gilley, Mary Gilley Alford's father, was an early settler and was the first Alfordsville postmaster, appointed on April 1, 1856. Isaac Jackman (probably the same Jackman mentioned in the Alford letters) was the second postmas-

Alfordsville at the Turn of the Century. (*Howard Gabhart*)

Alfordsville, Indiana, and the Alford Farms, 1862.

ter and he was followed by Joseph A. McCord on June 26, 1861.(4) McCord had married Franklin Alford's sister, Emily.

It was recorded that the first settlers were intently concerned with providing an education for their children.(5) The success of this objective is reflected in the literacy of Franklin Alford. As a boy in the 1820s and 30s, Franklin obtained a formal education in Daviess County.

The first school in the Alfordsville area was thought to have been a log structure built on land donated by James Alford. It is known that a second log school was built one mile south of town in 1853.(6) The Alford children probably attended this school.

The establishment of churches also was important to the early settlers, particularly for the Gilleys who organized the first Disciples Church in Daviess County. The Gilleys formerly were Baptists. The Disciples Church denomina-

tion originated in southern Indiana and the first church service is believed to
have been conducted in Washington County in 1819. The church gained popu-
larity in the 1820s and 30s by reaching out to disenchanted Dunkards and
Baptists.(7) In 1846, the Alfordsville Christian Church was founded.

The files of the present-day Alfordsville Christian Church contain the following historical document:

CHURCH RECORD

In the year of our Lord and Savior Jesus Christ one thousand
eight hundred and forty six (1846), we the undersigned being
moved by the love of God and our Lord Jesus Christ, after con-
sulting together on the subject of the glory of God, do unani-
mously agree to unite ourselves in a body as members of the
body of Christ's church at Alfordville and we do agree to live
together in the bonds of the gospel. We acknowledge no other
authority but that expressed in the inspired word of God,
embodied in the book called the Old and New Testament.

We do therefore give ourselves to God, to each other in the love
of our Lord Jesus Christ. "Amen"

Franklin Alford	Wayne Alford
Joseph P. Gilley	Elmer Gilley
Benjamin Gilley	William Harmon
Henry Edwards	Alfred Wilson
Wayne Wilson	Joseph Wilson(8)

Franklin Alford and his brother Wayne are believed to be the founders of
the Alfordsville church, with Wayne serving as the first preacher. (This would
be uncle Wayne Alford who wrote a letter to Warren dated September 9, 1861.)
One of the early members remembered the strict church policy, "If they heard of
any member going to a dance, playing cards or getting drunk, they sure went
after them." Offenders were required to acknowledge "they did wrong or else [it]
was written in the church record `Withdrawn from for misconduct'."(9)

In 1860, a new Christian Church building was erected approximately one-
fourth mile north of Alfordsville.(10) It is likely the land for the new church
was donated by Franklin Alford. The Alfords' home, in 1860, was one-half mile
west of Alfordsville and they probably walked to the church. Other church
members came by wagon, some from the area near Loogootee. It is the 1860
church that Warren saw in his mind when writing home in 1861.

"The enemy in the rear"[(11)]

There can be no doubt the Alfords were agitated about the secession and disloyal element in Alfordsville. One such resident was given until July 20 to get out of town or he would be hanged. A man who reportedly uttered "Cecession slang" was threatening to blow out the brains of his accuser. And Father was ready to "help tar and feather them."

This was not just an Alfordsville phenomenon. It was believed by many that there were "secesh" all over Indiana. Any study of this situation must start with the knowledge that, in general terms, Indiana overwhelmingly supported Lincoln and the pro-Union sentiment. There were exceptions and these exceptions created the uproar.

Franklin and Wayne Alford's letters reflect the hysteria in Alfordsville. Father wrote, "the town had been in an uproar all day and did not disperse till about midnight" and there were people "armed to the teeth." Wayne related to Warren a story of a confused indictment. A Mr. Bingham, already a member of the local militia company, was thought to be a secessionist and was run out of the company. Later, the charges were cleared up and Bingham was re-admitted to the same company.

The "facts," then and now, are shadowy. In the summer of 1861, there were people living in Indiana who were staunchly pro-Confederate. The emotions of the time, however, prohibit any reliable estimate of the number. One thing is clear; there are few facts to buttress any examination of the so-called disloyalty issue.(12)

One reason a Hoosier might have been firmly pro-Confederate was the racial issue. If the Confederacy lost and slavery was abolished, freed Negroes would flood the state, take away jobs, mix the races, etc., etc. A group in Dubois County was on record in February 1861 as to their attitude toward the African-American population: "We hold to no equality with the Negro, and we will have no social intercourse with them, for we look upon them as an inferior race and believe that the Almighty never intended the races to amalgamate."(13) This feeling also might have subsisted in neighboring Daviess County, but there is never a hint of this attitude in any of the Alford letters.

For some Hoosiers who were not supporters of the Confederacy there were well-founded reasons to be against the war, any war. Pacifists opposed killing for intellectual and moral reasons. This faction may have been vocal in their convictions and their intentions may have been misunderstood. For those caught up in the "Union Forever" fever, these anti-war advocates were no better than "secesh."(14)

There were those who opposed the war because they thought there were better alternatives for solving the slavery and state's rights problems. Before the firing on Fort Sumter, Democrats in particular advocated negotiating.(15) After the firing, some continued to cling to that hope. These "negotiators" were accused of being disloyal by those with a different view.

There were Hoosiers who had been born in the South and still had relatives living in the South. They may have chosen to avoid the "brother-fighting-brother" possibility. Nine percent of Indiana residents in 1860 had been born in slave-holding states.(16) The lower third of Indiana, in particular, had been settled by Southerners and there would have been an understandable reluctance to go to war and shoot at family members.(17) Although not "secesh," these Hoosiers easily fell into the category of Southern sympathizers.

Personal sentiment and politics aside, economic concerns had an influence on opinions. The southern counties of Indiana certainly were vulnerable to economic disaster if cut off from the south. At a meeting in Washington County it was declared, ". . . the State of Indiana['s] . . . commercial, agriculture, mechanical and manufacturing interest . . . [are] interwoven with the south . . . and a separation therefrom would be fatal."(18)

Another factor for controversy in small rural communities (and harder to validate) may have been based on life-long animosities. Not everyone got along. The differences may have been based on political party preferences, religious beliefs, economic status, etc. These past disagreements may have carried over into disloyalty accusations during the Civil War.

Later in the War, the charges of disloyalty in Indiana became more harsh, and the consequences more severe. Today, historians tend to discount the threat of the Copperhead "movement," or secret and disloyal enclaves. If there was such formal activity, it was poorly organized and certainly of inconsequential effect on the Union military effort.(19)

There is "documented" evidence of incidents of Copperhead activity in Daviess County. A 1915 county history reports the story of a secessionist by the name of Rice who cut the rope on a flag pole. This was considered an "act of desecration" and Rice was arrested and fined.(20)

Another, more celebrated, Daviess County case involved Captain Eli McCarty, Company G, 42nd Indiana Infantry. As recorded in the Indiana Adjutant General's Report: "On the 3d of October, 1864, Captain Eli McCarty, while serving notices on drafted men in that [Daviess] county, was murdered by Sons of Liberty concealed in the woods through which he had to pass. His body was thrown into the [White] river and not discovered for several days."(21) Carved in McCarty's grave-stone is the explanation that he was "killed by eight peace Democrats." Strangely, no one was ever convicted of McCarty's death and an examination of the military records indicates McCarty had resigned from the Union army eighteen months earlier with a fifty percent disability, "unfit for duty."(22)

In next-door Martin County another, unresolved, incident was attributed to the Copperheads by the local newspaper. A young soldier home on leave, Jackson Ballard, was assigned the task of locating an army deserter. On March 18, 1864, Ballard left his home on his assignment only to be shot down by seventeen bullets. Supposedly six of the shots were from his own revolver. The body was buried in an unmarked grave. The same newspaper provided its readers with an accounting of the quantity of weapons in the possession of the Martin County Copperheads: three hundred pistols, seven kegs of powder, four hundred pounds of lead, and several thousand musket caps.(23)

Whether a real or an imaginary threat, great quantities of energy were expended at the time: arguing, worrying, writing, threatening, stewing, etc.

"immunity . . . from invasion, plunder and murders"(24)

Governor Oliver P. Morton enacted a militia law on May 11, 1861 to provide protection for the State from internal and external enemies. Wayne's descriptions of the local militia company in June 1861 are apt characterizations of the actual situation. Although Wayne was eager, there was not much formal structure or potency to various local units. In fact, they held off training and issuing weapons until the crops were harvested. While waiting, some units disbanded and impatient men enlisted in the regular service.(25) It was September 10, 1861 when a serious, systematic effort was undertaken to organize the Indiana Legion. Competent individuals were appointed to leadership positions, military regulations distributed and formal instructions provided to subordinate officers. The Daviess County unit was assigned to the First Brigade, Second Division. The brigade was made up of units from twelve southwestern Indiana counties. Within the Daviess County Legion, (eventually) there were companies called the Alfordsville Legion, the Clark's Prairie Guards, the Morton Cavalry and seven others from around the county.(26)

The volunteer Legion units were intended to suppress internal disorders and resist Confederate invasions. These objectives were of great significance to the residents of southern Indiana.(27) The Legion generally lacked a sense of serious purpose until there were outside threats, such as Confederate General John Hunt Morgan's Indiana Raid in July 1863.(28)

The Legion units practiced military marching drills and, later in the War, performed the manual of arms with authentic weapons. The volunteers did obtain an appreciation for military life and the Legion served the purpose of training men who would later enlist in regular units.(29) And no doubt, the absolute numbers were useful in times of emergencies. An estimate of the Legion's total enrollment would be unsupportable although it is known that 18,000 small arms were issued to the organized units.(30)

As to the level of competency, it can be noted that in 1863, Virgil Alford, a former regular army private with one year of service, mustered in the Alfordsville Legion as the First Lieutenant.(31)

"I take pen in hand"(32)

The Alford letters are unique in many ways and the subject matter certainly was of a personal nature. The opening and closing phrases, however, are typical of most letter writers in the 1860s. According to Bell I. Wiley, a renowned Civil War historian and reader of thousands of Civil War letters, the "average Yank" opened his letters with "I seat myself . . ." or "I will take the present opertunity. . . ." The Alfords were typical in this regard. Many of their closing lines included "no more at present" and references to "death." These, too, were characteristic of the time in which they lived.(33)

A common element in soldiers' letters was the plea for more letters. Warren's first letter, written May 9, 1861, relates that he "watched the office with hope." When Wayne and Lafayette left home they also pleaded, "write often and tell the friends to write." Of course, the folks at home were equally anxious to get mail from their soldier-sons. "Wright and give us a description of your new home," requested Mother and Father.

"Due 3" Envelope.

"Due 3" Envelope.

There were never enough letters. Incorrect style or illegibility was never a deterrent. When Minerva wrote Warren in September 1861, she apologized with: "I am tired of riting . . . not being in the habbit of ritin . . . read what you can and gues at the rest."

The Alford letters usually were written with pen and ink on 8" X 10" paper, prefolded (by the manufacturer) to provide four pages, 8" X 5" each. Occasionally the boys used stationery with small patriotic figures and verses in the upper left corner of page one. Envelopes also were available with icons preprinted on the front, upper left-hand corner. Three-cent postage stamps had been in use since 1847 but there were no post cards. Military personnel were permitted to forward their mail franked, "Due 3," to be paid by the recipient. Most of the Alford boys' mail arrived at the Alfordsville post office "Due 3."

In 1861, the United States Post Office Department in Washington, D.C., reported revenues of $8,349,296.40. This was an increase of $50,000 over 1860, in spite of eleven states seceding in 1861. Operational expenses dropped sharply but the department was still in the red by $2,481,000 for 1861.(34)

The Post Office Department in the North remained intact during the Civil War. Judging by the dates referenced in the Alford letters, postal operations were remarkably efficient. The railroad network was used extensively throughout the War. The Railway Mail Car system, by which mail was sorted en route, was implemented in 1864. When the draft act was enacted in August 1862, those

The Mail Wagon. (USAMHI)

exempted included, "post officers and stage drivers who are employed in the care and conveyance of the mail."(35) It was intended the system was to work uninterrupted.

Government officials quickly realized the importance of the mail service. Special Agents from the Post Office Department were appointed the rank of colonel and assigned to an Army Commander's staff. Extant documents indicate excellent cooperation between the military and the postal authorities.(36)

General Grant, in an 1864 letter to Postmaster General William Dennison, used exuberant compliments to describe the efficiency of the Post Office Department personnel. Grant also boasted that he had worked closely and agreeably with his postal agent since February 1862. Grant described that he was able to eliminate the need for civilian postal clerks to work within the lines of the Army. Instead "intelligent, reliable enlisted men" were detailed to handle the military mails.(37)

The volume of mail during the Civil War was staggering. It was documented in 1861 that some regiments of 1,000 men were forwarding an average of 600 letters a day.(38) The quantity of military mail reached 90,000 pieces a day through Washington D.C. and double that amount through Louisville.

From beginning to end, letters were exchanged between citizens of the United States and the Confederate States. Letters sent from the North to the Confederacy were required to have only the U.S. postage. Letters coming north from the Confederacy also were required to have U.S. postage. Private express companies were allowed to operate between the two adversaries. In addition to packages, the commercial entrepreneurs brought letter mail from the South and entered it into the U.S. postal system, but only with postage purchased in the North.(39)

There were enormous collection and delivery problems to be solved as the Northern armies moved South. These were the areas where the old United States postal routes had been disrupted. As soon as Union forces moved into the once-seceded territory, former postmasters and contractors were contacted, given the oath of allegiance, and rehired at their old rate of pay.(40)

The system worked. Grant wrote, "Our soldiers receive their mail matter with as much regularity and promptness as possible for armies in the field . . . and as [quickly as] the most favored portions of the country."(41)

William Dennison, Postmaster General of the United States in 1864. (Louis A. Warren Lincoln Library and Museum)

Endnotes

(1) Walter R. Houghton, words to eulegize Franklin Alford, February 26, 1893, *The Martin County Tribune*, March 3, 1893.

(2) A.O. Fulkerson, *History of Daviess County Indiana* (Indianapolis, 1915), pp. 281, 282.

(3) Bureau of the Census; records for 1850. The numbers reflect 3.8 dwellings per square mile and 5.8 residents per dwelling. Alfordsville was (is) the only community in Reeves Township. In 1886 it was stated there were 171 residents of Alfordsville, two churches and one school; refer to Goodspeed's *History of Knox and Daviess County* (Evansville 1886) p. 741. Today, there are approximately 125 residents and two churches.

(4) Editors, *Atlas of Daviess County, Indiana* (Philadelphia, 1888) p. 296. Joseph McCord is the father of John McCord, Warren's tent mate (and cousin).

(5) Fulkerson, *ibid.*, p. 282.

(6) L. Rex Myers, *Daviess County Indiana History* (Paducah, 1988) p. 165, 166.

(7) Logan Esarey, *A History of Indiana from its Exploration to 1850* (Fort Wayne, 1924) 3rd edition, v. 1, p. 323. Also, James H. Madison, *The Indiana Way* (Indianapolis, 1986) p. 100. The Dunkards were well known for their anti-slavery beliefs, but there is never any sentiment about slavery in any of the Alford letters.

For a recent analysis and interpretation of the churches' importance in Indiana during the mid-1850s, see Barbara J. Steinson, "Rural Life in Indiana, 1800-1950," *Indiana Magazine of History* (Indianapolis, 1994) v. XC, no. 3, September 1994, pp. 224-226. This article provides an excellent summary of the Indiana farm culture, and particularly the evolution occurring during the Alfords' lifetime.

(8) From the Alfordsville Christian Church Record Book, p. 206. Access to these records graciously provided by Steve Remmel, the current minister.

(9) From a letter found in the Alfordsville Christian Church historical records. The letter was signed by Lou and Wayne Gilley (Mrs. and Mr.) each having been child-members of the church in the 1860s. The Gilleys had moved to Kansas and the letter, or brief memoir, was written as the church neared its centennial celebration in 1946. Mrs. Gilley remembered the time "someone gave mother what was left of the loaf after The Lord's Supper and us children ate it." Mrs. Gilley did not relate the end of this story, but it is assumed this was a serious transgression. She concluded her letter with, "wish we were able to be with you." And then, "We have spent many happy times in the church at our old home in Alfordsville."

In Myers, *ibid.*, p. 182 there is a note beneath a 1902 plat map of Alfordsville "as remembered in 1969" which states, "there was never a saloon in Alfordsville."

(10) Again, from the Record Book, p. 206. The 1860 church building no longer exists. Franklin Alford also donated a portion of his land for the church cemetery. This is where Warren and Lafayette were buried in 1862. The cemetery is still "active" and well kept. Curiously, Franklin and Mary Alford were buried at Loogootee in the Goodwill cemetery.

In 1888, another church building was erected (back) in the town of Alfordsville. Church membership at that time was 180.

(11) A popular phrase to characterize disloyal citizens in the Northern states.

(12) The standard sources on the subject are: Emma Lou Thornbrough, *Indiana in the Civil War Era 1850-1880* (Indianapolis, 1965), and for the 1860s Republican Administration viewpoint, see W.H.H. Terrell, *ibid.* v. 1, passim. Also, John D. Barnhart, "The Impact of the Civil War on Indiana, *Indiana Magazine of History* (Indianapolis, September 1961), v. LVII, n. 3.

(13) Tredway, *ibid.*, p. 2. Article XIII of the 1851 Indiana State Constitution prohibited Negroes and mulattoes from entering the state. For more background, see Emma Lou Thornbrough, *Since Emancipation A Short History of Negroes, 1863 – 1963* (Indianapolis, n.d.), pp. 1-4.

(14) Not all pacifists remained neutral. See Jacquelyn S. Nelson, *ibid.*

(15) This attitude did not always follow party lines. Both Democrat Daniel Voorhees and Republican Walter Gresham were on record as being against

United States Senator
Daniel W Voorhees. (ISL)   *Union Brigadier General*
Walter Q. Gresham. (Millers)

coercion of the South. Daniel Voorhees, a Seventh Congressional District Democratic candidate before the War was quoted as saying he never would "vote one dollar, one man or one gun . . . to make war upon the South." (Stampp, *Indiana Politics During the Civil War,* Bloomington, 1979, p. 55) He later changed his mind. In February 1861, Walter Gresham told future Indiana governor Oliver P. Morton that he "would not fight in a servile or domestic war." Refer to Matilda Gresham, *Life of Walter Quintin* (Chicago, 1919), p. 136. When the war started, Gresham enlisted as private and rose to Brigadier General although he was dogged with charges of being disloyal.

(16) Stampp, *ibid.*, p. 12.

(17) Thornbrough, *ibid.*, p. 540.

(18) *Ibid.*, p. 100.

(19) Franklin L. Klement, *The Copperheads in the Middle West* (Chicago, 1960) passim, and Klement, *Dark Lanterns* (Baton Rouge, 1984) passim. Klement is regarded as the authority on the subject.

(20) Fulkerson, *ibid.*, p. 155.

(21) Terrill, *ibid.*, v. I, p. 288.

(22) McCarty was buried in a small cemetery in southern Daviess County. A sign near the highway, State Road 257, reads, "100 feet east of this point is the grave of Capt. Eli McCarty Company `G' 42 Infantry killed Oct. 12th [sic.] 1864 while serving notices to drafted men." McCarty's military records were obtained from the National Archives. He had been wounded in the shoulder at the Battle of Perryville, October 8, 1862.

(23) Harry Q, Holt, *History of Martin County Indiana* (Paoli, 1953) p. 292.

(24) According to Governor Morton, this "immunity" was provided to the citizens of Indiana through the efforts of the Indiana Legion. This phrase was part of a message to the Legislature, date unknown. Quoted in Charles Walker, *Sketch of the Life, Character, and Public Services of Oliver P. Morton* (Indianapolis, 1878), p. 93.

(25) Terrell, *ibid.*, v. I, pp. 106, 107, 136.

(26) *Ibid.*, v. I, pp. 107, 108. Also v. III, pp. 555, 556.

(27) Thornbrough, *ibid*, p. 142.

(28) Arville Funk, *The Morgan Raid in Indiana and Ohio* (1863), (Corydon, 1971) pp. 13-26. The Indiana Legion was utilized to a greater extent during the Morgan Raid than at any other time during the Civil War. They did, however, participate in other military actions; i.e., the Adam Johnson Raid on Newburgh and the Hines Raid. Mostly, they exercised "utmost vigilance."

(29) Stampp, *ibid.*, p. 80.

Confederate General John Hunt Morgan's Raid in Indiana–Burning &
Looting in Salem. (Leslie's)

(30) Terrell, *ibid.*, v. 1, p. 110.

(31) *Ibid.*, v. III, p. 556. Virgil Alford had served with his cousin, Warren Alford, in the 14th Indiana Infantry.

(32) Wiley, *The Life of Billy Yank*, p. 185. An often-used opening phrase in an 1860s letter.

(33) *Ibid.*

(34) *Official Records of the War of the Rebellion*, (Washington, 1880-1901), series III, v. II, p. 888. Hereafter cited as ORs. Assume series I unless stated otherwise.

(35) *Ibid.*, series III, v. II, p. 334.

(36) *Ibid.*, v. XL, part II, p. 271.

(37) *Ibid.*, v. XLII, part III, p. 506.

(38) Wiley, *ibid.*, p. 183.

(39) ORs, series II, v. II, pp. 12, 13.

(40) *Ibid.*, v. X, part II, pp. 3, 4.

(41) *Ibid.*, v. XLII, part III, p. 506.

CHAPTER

2

[Warren to folks at home:]

Cheete [Cheat] Mountain
Summit Camp
July the 20th 1861

Dear Father and mother brothers and sisters and all that this may interest. I am well at this time and have bin since you hared from me. I have not bin sick aday since I left home and I hope this may reach you injoying the same blessing. For it is truly a blessing. The boyes are able to eat their rations and they think it quite a blessing. We are a bout Fifteen miles From any place. Right among the Mountains. We have a fair view of the Allegheny and about Eighty miles from Stanton [Staunton] and about 100 miles from Clarks burg [which is] alittle town Where we left the rail road for Rich Mountain. [After] three dayes march . . . we expected to get in to a fight but they wer fighting when we came in sight and we wer only held in reserve. . . . I suppose you got the detailes of the battle more Correct than I can give them. Their were about six hundred of the rebels that were take prisoners [and they] passed here yesterday going home this morning. The [dust] Cloud were floting right among our tents. A sold[iers'] life agres With me first rate. I have not heared from home for about one Week [or] before I lef Indianapolis. I would be glad to hear from you as the time for thrashing has come. I guess you [are] a abustle with your work. I would like to be With you and if uncle Sams Work goes on as it has I think it will not be long. . . . God has blessed us in the work. Their is no doubt of that and if he be for us [who] can be against us. General McCelon [George B. McClellan] sayes that we will be at home in time to [harvest] our Corn this Fawl. In regard to my spiritual health. It grows stonger Eavery day and I hope by the help of god never to get Weary. . . . He is a preseant help in eavery time of need and I hope that we may all be favored to meat againe on Earth and Enjoy friends and society but if it should be other Wise I hope We may all meet in that blessed land. I shall Wind up by saying We are in the hand of a Just god. . . . Direct your letter to the Fourteent Regiment of Indiania volunteers. For want of space I close.

J Warren Alford

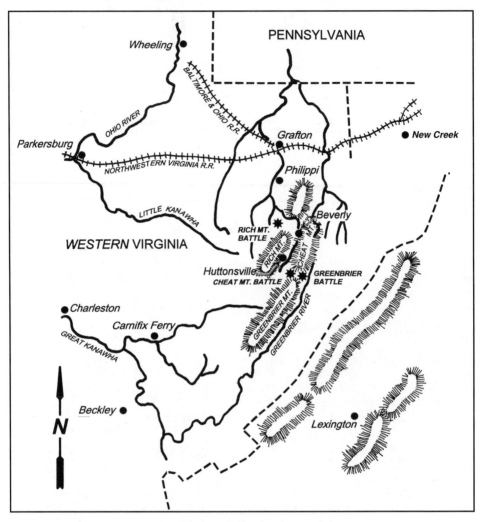

Western Virginia, Warren Alford's Area of Activity, 1861.

[Warren to Wayne:]

> Cheate [Cheat] Mountain
> Summit Pass Camp
> July 21st 1861

Dear Brother. It is with Pleasure I take this opertunity to Drop you a few lines to let you all know that I am yet well and hope these few lines may find you all injoying the same great blesing. I started a letter to Father yesterday not knowing when he would get it. As the Chanse for it to get lost was vary good I thought I would scratch a

Union Major General George Brinton McClellan. (USAMHI)

few lines to you and send it to you by our Commissary Mr Bunton
as he was going right thrue Loogootee starting in the morning. I
knew it would be a good Chanse for you to get it. We are in the
rougfest Country I ever saw. About 200 miles from Bellair [Bellaire,
Ohio, across from Wheeling] on the Ohio River on the Road Leading to
Stanton [Staunton, Virginia] [in] sight of the Alleghanes [Allegheny]
Mountains. [About] fifteen miles from any place you could mention.
We are awaiting orders to march the Western division of the Armey
having done the work assigned for her to Do. We have not bin in
any battle and do not know when we shal be for they seam to think
it is not quite so easy to Defend them selves as to get out of the Way
of the federal armey. It is not [as quiet] for them as they thaight. . . .
The Federal troops hold the strongest position in the State that is
Manasas junction [Manassas Junction] and Scot [General-in-chief of
the Union Army Winfield Scott] sayes [we] will be [in] Richmond in a
few dayes if no bad luck. It is thought that the Rebels will have to
seeke some other place than old Virginia in a few days for it is giting
to hot for them. We were [in] sight of the battle of rich mountain the
boys were vary Eager to go and help do the work for the traitors.
Tell [everyone] you know that I am all right . . . and will Wright as
soon as I can get Leasure. Our Company is in vary good health and
in fine spirits. Some of them did not find our last march as light as
they thought it would be but they are Willing to do any thing for
the good of there Country. I would like to see you vary well but first
my God an then Country and then my friends at home. I would [be]
glad [to] be with you [but] my Country Calls and I must obey. Chere
up and trust him that sayed let their be light for doeth all things
well. Remember your deuty to god and do not forget to pray. I hope
that this may greete you all and find you all well. Give my love to
my inquiring friends

                                        J Warren Alford

[This may have been an enclosure in this letter:]

Bolivar [Gold] sayes for to tell those that wish to Write to hime to
direct as before mentioned and all so that he is well. Virgil [Alford]
Wrote to day. Tell his mother he is well allso. It is now about nine
Oclock and I was on gard last night and to day and I am slepy. Good
by for the present. May god bless you all and save you at last in the
Prair of your unworth brother in the Lord as in the flesh.

[Perhaps another enclosure in the same letter:]

As I hope that you will get my letter that I wrote to Father soon [I
will not include details of my trip in this one.] I want you to Wright

to me soon and Just Direct your letters to the 14th Regt of Indiania
Volunteers Company C in Care of Cap L Brooks and I think I will be
most likely to get them. I do not know how long we will stay in this
place . . . if so Directed the [mail] will follow up the Regment where
ever [it] goes. Wayne give my love to those [who] gladley receive it
and oblige your brother. J Warren Alford

★

[Wayne to Warren:]

Alfordsville Daviess County Ind.
July 25th/61

Mr Warren Alford. Dear Brother   After Waiting in Vain for
Sometime for A Letter from You And Not Knowing the reason of
your Not Wrighting Untill yesterday. We learned that William Houtin
[Houghton] Had Wrighten Home And that Paper Was Verry Scarce in
camp at this time. We are All Well at present and Hope these few
Lines May find you enjoying the Same Blessing. We are getting along
With our Work as Well as Could Be expected. We Have our Wheat
and Oats all Up and Will get 10 acres of our grass cut today if nothing Happens. And Charley [Donaldson] and James Alford are cutting
the upper Meadow. Health is Verry good in this place Now and the
Boys are Nearly all gone and gowing to the Ware. Capt James Briant
[Bryant] Started for Indianapolis With His company Night before Last
[which became Company E of the 18th Indiana Infantry]. Included
were: [Isaac L.] Alford, William Collins, Henry William, and Albert
Cochran. Albert Patric [Patrick], William Canary [possibly Conay], E P
[for Ebenezer P.] Gilley, William Porter, and one of the Patses [probably
Patts], A [for Alexander] C Camp, Michael Burch. And I Learn that
John Gold & William Patric [Patrick] are gowing Monday with him
Also Hillery Seay, Robbert Porter and Milton Jackson and one of the
Patses [Patts] are gone With Capt Boaltin [Nelson F. Bolton who orga-
nized Company D of the 24th Indiana Infantry] from Washington
[Indiana] and James B Kellams has gone With Capt Magoffin [Samuel
F. McGuffin from Loogootee who organized Company I of the 24th
Indiana Infantry]. It Was Hard for Me to stay When they Were
enlisting But if I go you may expect Me to Come to your Company [C
of the 14th] if I Can get in. The Boys [are] All gowing off [and] I am a
feard [it] Will break up our [local militia] Company Here. We Have
Sold the Machine and Swaped Jack for a fine imported Mare and
Sold Tiger for $90 for a Waggon Horse in the Army. Mayby youd See
him if He comes to Virginia. I Have Bought Me a Revolver Just Like
yours. We Learned from the papers that McClellons [General George

McClellan's] Divission is ordered to Washington. If you go their You
Can Wright oftener I Hope. Father Says He Will Wright Soon. I Wrote
you and Wm Houtin [Houghton] a Letter When you were at
Indianapolis But did not know Whether you Received them or Not.
If not you tell Houtin [Houghton] How it Was and I Will Wright as
soon as I Hear from you. Wright if Whether I can get in your Co or
Not. Our Love to all the Boys. We Send you Paper and evelops and
stamps. Wright soon   Nothing More But remins your Brother untill
Death.

Wayne Alford

★

[Wayne to William Houghton:]

Alfordsville Daviess Co Ind August 2/61
Lieutenant Wm Houghton.

Dear friend and Brother   I am Happy this Morning to inform you
that I am Well at preseant and Hope When this reaches you I May
find you enjoying the Same blessing. I Wrote you a Letter While you
were at Indianapolis But I Suppose you never received it. The excitement in our town Has Gone Down and I think Cesession is Dead
enough. At all events they Have Dried it up. Capt Briants Co [Bryant,
Company E of the 18th Indiana Infantry] Has taken of fifteen or
twenty of our Boys. I Wroat to Warren and gave their Names. I suppose you Have seen them if the letter has come to Hand. It Was
mighty Hard for Me to hold Back When the Boys were enlisting
though I had Writ to Warren to see if their Was a Chance to get into
your Co. So I Had to Wait to Hear from Him. Ill tell you Wm this is
no place for Me. All the Boys (With a few exceptions) that is any
company for Me are gone and I am Left allmost alone. All that I
Have to regret is that I Didnot stay With you When I was at Camp
Vigo. If I Had Known their What I found out When [I] got Home I
Would Have Stayed Sure. I am appointed to go to Washington to see
When the oficer Will . . . swear in our [local militia] Co. I Have
Nothin More to Wright only remember you Have a friend in the
Person of Wayne Alford. Nothing More but With Much respect.
Remains your friend and Brother untill Death.

Wayne Alford Jr

By your Permission I Would Say to Warren that I received His letter
and that We are all Well and Have Done our Harvest. Warren Just
tell the Boys that Mess with you that I am all right yet. I was Hapy
to see John McCords Letter and to Learn that you all got through
your skrimish safe. Tell Conolty [Richard H. Conolly] His People are

all Well so far as I know at present. Vergil [Virgil Alford] and
Stephen [Stephen H. Collins] and Bollivers [Bolivar Gold] folks are Well
But Verry Loansome since the Boys Have gone. Remember Me With
Much respect. I remain yours till Death. Excuse my Scibling for I
am about Worked Down and am verry nervous at present.

Wayne Alford Jr

PS I forgot to tell the boys about Wm Gold & Henery Edwards &
Alexander Robertson & John brown & George W Gilley. They are the
ones that Vounteered [in Company E of the 18th Indiana Infantry]
Since I Wrote to Warren

★

[To Warren from William M. Porter, recently enrolled in Company E of the 18th Indiana Infantry:]

Mr Warren Alford ... Give my best respects to all the Boys. Tell them
to Write soon and Remember their Friends.

Camp Morton Ind
August the 6

Dear Friend. I Now embrace first opportunity that I have had from
many days of sending you a few lines. Never did I feel as happy as
when Engaged in writing to an old friend. I suppose that you have
not heard that we all have enlisted [and are] now preparing to follow
you. We are all well and in good spirits as fighting Cocks. We was
Glad to hear from you. As soon as we got the letter we all engaged in
writing. The 19th Regiment left here yesterday and I never seen as
much Excitement as was. I only wish we was ready to go with them
but we are here enjoying all the pleasures of Camp life of plenty to
eat and lots of Fun. I would give you the names of some of our Boys
but there is so many of them I cant. Alfordsville gets the Brag.
When we get ready to Come look out then we will make the secessions
git. Oh who wouldt be a soldier to fight for their Contry. But alas
dear friend who [would] have thought that one year ago then our
peaceful shores now should be made a military Camp. War ... is horrible but all is for the Better I think. They have been making the
plot or a good while to destroy our american independence but how
they are mistaken. There is thousands of free hearts and Loyal
Citizens who left their homes and every thing wich they loved and
rushed on to rescue their Country from an impending destruction.
We have bid adieu to those thats left behind and gone. [We] have
pledged our lives [and] left our prospects to secure for them peace

[and] domestic tranquility and a peaceful inheritance to future pos-
terity. I dont mean them who aid the Cause but those who Can go
but yet they Remain neutral and say the weakes Class must fight.
But I do say that if ever peace is again restored it will be done by the
Common people of our land and not by those who throw on the aris-
tocratic air and say greasy mechanics and Club fisted farmers is not
fit for office. We will show the small sum of three hundred thousand men who have attempted to over throw our liberties of the
north because they was industrius. . . . Never will we surrender the
flag until the mountains begins to shake and the earth tremble . . .
for I would ask nothing better for a winding sheet when death
appears. But you boys know all these things and are on the same
principal. Remember all of us who are fighting the same battle but
think of home with pleasure and not regret and of the dear girls
who have promised to wait till we get back for us. I would like to be
with you but I could not go when you did. I enlisted with Capt
Bryant the same day we started and left a weeping mother and kind
friends and Come up here Wednesday and went thursday home after
volunteers and never [saw] as much excitement in Alfordsville [as] at
the muster. I got up [and] told them my purpose and made a few
Remarks on the important question and then made a Call and to my
astonishment that evening and the next day. [?] came forward and
went with us to Camp Morton. I Could get an office if I wanted it.
. . . I must Close for the want of paper. But Remember us and write.
Tell Bill houghton not to forget friends if he has an office. You must
[write] soon. Farewell for this time. Wm M Porter

[In the margin:]

Direct to Camp Morton Ind In Care of Capt Bryant 18th Ind Reg

[William Porter was a sergeant at the time of this letter. He was promoted to second lieutenant on June 4, 1862 and first lieutenant on
July 1, 1862. Porter was discharged on February 15, 1865 after being
wounded.]

[Warren to Wayne:]

Camp Cheat Mountain Summit
Virginia August the 3rd 1861

Dear Brother and the rest of the family. I received your letter of the
25th yesterday Which gave me much satisfaciton to learn that you

was all well and doing well. I sent one letter to Father and one to you and one to Charley Donaldson [brother-in-law] since the 15th of July. [These are] the onley letters I rote since I came from Ind to this place. But [I] learned in your letter that you had not yet received them though I hope you will in due time and answer them imediately. I am well at present and in good spirits hoping this will come to hand finding you all injoying that heaven found blesing. In answer to your request to know whether you Could get in this Company I suppose you could get in with this Company as it is not full at present but my advise to you and Lafayette is for you both to stay at home and put in your time well on the Farm for I think farmers will be neded worse than soldiers by far. At preasant time this is the best advise I can give you at the preasant. You can now exercise the Cool Judgment of a sound mind. Those are my sentiments precisely for I think 700,000 men is enough to over come . . . the enemies. The boyes are well. Stephen Collins [a private from Martin County] sayes tell his folks that he wrote two letter home lately and would be glad to hear from them. I have nothing of importance to wright you as we get no nuse onley by letter. We would like to have more of them. If their is any thing in the nuse papers that would interest me cut it out and send it to me in your letters and do not be afraid to wright often to me. Tell father and Mother and Lafayette and Charley and Minervia and hannah and all others that I Can get letters if they would only write and start them as I directed . . . to the 14 Reg Ind. Vol. Co C Western Virginia in Care of Cap Brooks and do not for get to wright your self. I am as fat and black alimost as a bair and in a mile of wher plenty of them [bears] stay. So no more at preasant but remains your affectionat brother ever more. Excuse this letter
J Warren Alford to Wayne Alford

[Father to Warren:]

Home August the 5th 1861
Warren my dear Boy with love and affection that I cannot express. I am now Seated to Wright you a few lines to let you know that we are all well and we hope these lines may find you and your associates in the enjoyment of the same Blessing. We received your Letters of the 20th & 21st of last Month which gave us pleasure undescribeable. And [even more when we read] your Closeing remarks [probably the references to God]. . . . Our constant Prair Both day and night is that God may protect you in all the dangers to which you are exposed and Bless and strengthin you in your efforts to serve

him. We wrote you a few lines about a week ago tonight from
Loogootee and sent it with Paper and invelops by express which we
hope you have got before this time. We have got up all Grain and
Grass. Ten large Stacks of the latter without any Rain for it is getting verry dry here. We have Sold the Machine for 175 bushels of
good White Wheat and the Thrashin of our Crop. Wheat is verry low
but I hope I shall be able to realize 75 cents for it. I intend to Sell
such things as we can spare and pay our Debts as fast as I can. I
want you to imbrace every opportunity to keep us posted with regard
to where you are and what you are doing for there is many things
told here about the 14th. Give my love to all the Boys and asshure
them that they with your self have the Prairs of all the Brethren
and friends who pray ... and especaly [those] of your own family.
Lafayette wants to give you a line. I must close till Friday so good by.

Warren   F A   Mary Alford

[Same paper, from Lafayette:]

Dear Brother. It is once more I take my pen to Wright to you but as
you see I Cannot Wright. My arm is Well enough to Mow or Stack
Hay But is is So Nervous that I Cannot Wright. It is verry Warm and
Dry. The thermomiter standing at [90 something] in the Shade but We
think if it Rains in a few Days Corn will be good. We Learned yesterday that thomas sutton has got Home. We Learned How [they] Were
all taken Prisones and this Morning I Hear that Some 14 of your Men
Were Lost. While I am Wrighting Hillery Houghton Came in and Says
tell Wm [his son] that they are all Well and Have got in their Harvest.
Tell [our cousin] Vergil that I Was at His Mothers yesterday and they
are Well and Have received His Letter. The M. E. Camp Meating came
of yesterday. Some of the boys and girls Went Down. I was Not
guilty Myself though they Say it Was perfect.... Bryants Co has left
and I suppose our [local militia] Co will be sworn in Saturday Next.
Remember My respects to all My friends and Wright as Soon as
Convenient and I Will Do the Same. With Much respect your Brother
untill Death.

Lafayette Alford

[Warren to the folks:]

Camp Cheat Mtn Summit
August the 18th/61

Dear Parents and brother and sister. I take this opertunity of writing
you to let you know that I am well at this time and hope this my

reach you in dew time and find you all well and enjoying all the pleasures of home and Chistian society and the luxuries of a plentiful harves. And I hope you will not have as much hard work as Common as you have sold the mashiewn which will take a vary heavy burdon [off of] you and give you more time to prepare and cultivit your farm for it [was not] one of the most payinges business-es that thier is. One acre well Cultivated is worth two half done. . . . As Wayne talkes of comeing to our Company I would be glad to have him with me but I do not think it is . . . prudent at the present time. . . . It is strongly thought by some of the regment that we will be at home in a short time or at least in Indianapolis in less than two months. . . . If we . . . Reorganize their will be a chance. . . . But I think he can do more at home. I talked with Capt Brooks and he gave me that as his advice but if [Wayne does volunteer] after take-ing every thing in Concideration I would be glad to have [him] with us. Those Remarks you Can consider and then act acordingly. We are still on the same Mountain not knowing wher we will move. Theire is a small party of rebbles in about fifteen miles from here but we have no orders to Cross the line of old and new virginia which we are in one mile of. We have done the work assigned us. That is of dri-veing them from Western Virginia and now have nothing to do but guard the pass. . . . Their is two Reg at this place and two more tenn miles in the Reare. I received a letter from Wayne by the hand of Wm Houghton and one from Father and Lafayette on the 15th & 16th and I thought that I would answer it with Hannah['s] letter as [paper] and envelopes are Scarce. You stated in your letter of sending me some by express. I have not yet received them. . . . Right to me how they were directed and I will try to get them. I have nothing of importance . . . only the boys are all well. I would say [as I] close to live close to your deuty so that if we Should never meet on earth that we may all meet Where parting will be [no] more. Your Sone from home J W Alford

[Wayne to Warren:]

Home Alfordsville Daviess Co
August 19th/61 Ind
Mr Warren Alford. Dear Brother I Received your Letter [in] Saturdays Mail Which Came to hand & found us enjoying good Health and was glad to hear from you and to Hear that you Were on the Land & among the Living and enjoyng a reasonable portion of health. I Have Nothing of importance to Wright to you. I Was pre-

pared to come to Virginia When I received your Letter But as you
think it Best for Me Not to Come yet I have Countermanded the order
[to join you] this Morning. As the friends all say under the circumstances that it Would Hardly be prudent in as much as I Had asked
advice and Had got it. It Would Be good sense to act accordingly.
Notwithstanding it was a verry hard thing to give it up though it is
allways my Disposition to please my friends rather than myself. I
have Nothing more of importance to Wright. The times are about as
usual. Our Company Will be mustered into Service next Satuday and
then I Can tell you Who our officers Will be. I Will Bring My letter
to a close. No more but remains as ever you Brother Wayne Alford
until Death. PS I forgot to tell you We have received all the Letters
you Said you had Wrighten and have answered them accordingly.
Mother says if their is anything in that country to eat or Wear [for]
your comforts buy it.

[Same page, a note from Father:]

Dear Son
As we think it unnecessary to [repeat] the things that has been written there is but little left for us to wright but in order for your
Comfort we will inform you that there is nothing that you would
[have] done that would have given us half the comfort that did your
remarks relative to your spiritual health. And our constant Prair is
that our Heavenly Father may give us all grace whereby we may
serve him with reverence and Godly fear. Tell Virgil [Alford] we
received his letter and his folks were all well and glad to hear from
him. Tell Bro Wm Houghton his folks were well yesterday. His Father
Jennet & Aunt Eliza was at Meeting yesterday. Tell John [McCord],
Steve [Collins], Boliver [Gold] & Conolty [Richard Conolly, all Warren's
mess mates] that there friends are all well. Give my love to all [our]
friends and a double portion to you. So fare well. Your affectionate
Father. F Allford

[Wayne added another note:] Their has been a big fight in misourie
[Missouri] Lately in Which Gen Lyon [Union General Nathaniel Lyon]
With 5000 men engaged 23000 of the rebals and drove them back
With Considerable Loss. Our Men however Lost their brave comman-
der Gen Lyon. Rebals Lost their Commander also Gen McCulloch
[Benjamin McCulloch] & General price [Sterling Price]. They captured
McCulloch Horse & Sword. We had more particulars but the paper
Has been misplaced. [This was reference to the Battle of Wilson's
Creek, Missouri, fought on August 10, 1861.]

Wayne Alford

Union Brigadier General
Nathaniel Lyon. (USAMHI)

Confederate Major General
Sterling Price. (USAMHI)

[To Warren from Clem Reily, a friend on leave from the 14th Indiana:]

Loogootee Aug 20th/61

Dear Friend
      I now inted to drop you a few lines to try and tell you the particualrs. I was at yur Fathers yesterday and found the friends all well there is Nothing of importance going on there. . . . It is the dullest time everywhere I ever Saw. I have not done a days work since I got home. My health is about as usual. There is Still Some Simpathy felt for the South in certain localitys in this and Daviess Countys but they are afraid to express themselves. Everywhere there is more lies told than truths. I had quite a fight last week [about] your company. There was a man by the name of Lewis Cissell came into the Post Office and got to telling that Kimball and Brooks was treating their men worse than Negroes and I asked him how he knew and he Said that he heard Lem Kelly read it out of a letter that he got from Billy. I told him that it was a lie he drawed a chair on me and I [took it]

from him [and] knocked him down and whiped hime. There is a
great rush of Soldiers to the west now. There is not a day but what a
train passes here with them. I wish I was out there with you now
for I beleive I could Shoot as hard as any of you but I am here and
you are there and I beleive that I will have as much fighting to do
here as I can attend too. . . . I heard this morning that there is threats
made that the Black Republicans have got too be cleaned out [of] here
and . . . soon. Well all I have got tosay is that they will have a good
time of it before they get through with us. I heard that the Report
had reached you that I was Speaking hard of the officers there. . . .
You may set it down as a base lie. I have written nine letter to the
camp and have never received a line from there as yet. I wrote one
to you three to Barney [probably Sergeant Barney Berry] the balance
to the boys in my [old] mess. I want you to Show this to all the boys
and I want you to let me know whether you have received your pay
yet and if you have ask Capt Brooks if he has drawn mine. . . . There
is Some Misunderstanding in camp in regard to the time you have to
serve and the best information I can get is that you will have to
serve the three years unless peace is declared Sooner than that.
Thomas Sutton is getting well. I wrote to Col Kimball telling him that
if he would Send me a pass I would come back to the company and if
I could not get in the Company I would fight on my own hook. . . . To
tell the truth I am almost spoiling for a fight give my respects toall
the boys. Write as soon as you get this and you will much oblige
your Sincere Friend.

Clem Reily

[Written in the various margins:]

The girls are all well about alfordsville and other points where you
are interested. I joined Capt Bryants Company but was rejected. They
are in Mussouria. George Riggan and & Laura Wood was married
last night. Tell Barney if he dont write to me he had better. I am not
married and dont intend too.

[Wayne to Warren:]

Home Alfordsville Ind Aug 26/61
Warren Dear Brother.

Again I am Seated to Wright to you without waiting to Hear from
you in answer to my last leter. We are Still jogging along about as
usual. Times still remain hard without much prospect of a change
either way. [Concerning] that Noat that we held on Braxton I rote to

Him about it the other Day and he has not answered it. I expect to have to go and see him and if I do I shal talk pretty strong to him. I am getting tired of waiting on him. After I wrote you about comeing out to where you are I Learned that your Capt Had Written home for three more men and I immediately Set about getting ready to go and I had Just about got ready to go When you rote me not to Come. This flustraited my Design altogether and I Had about given it up and I came to Study about it and I Didnt See how I Could. Most of the boys that I Care for have gone and I am Left almost alone and have as strong Desire to be with you if I could. I want you to Wright to me again on the subject and let me know exactly why you think it Best not to come. It seams to me that the call is to me as much as to any one else and if you Will just recollect the time when the excitement was so high here you can better appreciate my condition and then wright to me. Their may be something about Soldiers life that you know that I Donot and if you Will Just Wright it to me in a private letter I Shal be Satisfied and it will greatly relieve my mind at the present. And as for them 700,000 troops you spoke of I think I am a Little better posted in regard to that than you are. I Dont think from the best information I can get from the papers that their is more than 500,000 in the field and a great Many of them is not Drilled fit for service. Consider these things ... and wright me as soon as you receive this. Though the last call from Ind does not extend to us if I go it will make one. The 1st 2nd & 3rd Congessional Districts Have filled there quota and they want to get the rest from the North Part of the Stait if they can. [Alfordsville was in the Second Congressional District.] I want to know also if I [got] into your Co[mpany] if I would be Discharged When the rest of the Co was or if I would have to stay 3 years or till the war was ended. Wright me the particulars about these things if you Please and as soon as possible. I send you Hannah Morens respects By request. I Was at H Houtins [Hillery Houghton's] yesterday and they are all Well. Give my love to all the Boys especially to vergil [Virgil Alford] and H [probably William Houghton] and retain a Double portion for your self. I must close. Good By.

Wayne Alford

[Warren to the folks at home:]

Camp Cheat Mountain Summit
August the 28th 1861

To the Friends at Home.
I am now seated to drop you a few thoughts to let you know that I am well and hearty and am happy to be privaledged to wright to let

you know something of a soldiers life and how they have to live we
do not have as many of the comeforts of life as many people have yet
we live better than a great many do at home. We have enough to eat
and that is more than some people have at home. We draw our
rations from two to four times a week. The articles are beef, bread,
Rice, Pork, Coffee, sugar, Vinegar, and some times beens. This consti-
tute our grub. This Cooked up in such stile as is not ofter gotten up
in a common Cuntry hotele. . . . We can make as good a dish of soop as
any french cook [or] as good a black berry py. The black berrys are
just ripe here. A Soldiers live is a life of adventures. He does not
know one hour what he will have to do the next. Some times word
comes for a company or two to go out on the scout and then we have
to go some times. The guards get frightened and shoot at anoise and
rase an alarm and then they bring us out on double quick time.
Their was three regiments brang out in line of battle night before
last but it proved to be a false alarm and we went back to Camp some
what dispointed for the boyes say they would like to get a chance at a
secessinoist be fore they go home. We are the advance guard and
have had a hard time of guarding this place. We have had [to] do
guard duty about twice a week but their has come to our relief two
regiment of Ohio infantry and one artiley Company and now I think
that we have force enough to hold the place against any force that
the enemy can bring agains us. We are now building a Fort sufi-
ciently strong to hold it by a few men. I think that this is going to
be a military post as it is about half way be tween Clarksburg and
stanton [Staunton] and in a vary important place . . . it command the
pass Cutting off Eastern from Western Virginia. It is sayed that their
will be some more of the Ohio trups here in a few days. Their was a
man shot him self thrue the ankle last night so that it had to ampu-
tated. He belonged to Cap Coons Co [John Coons' Company G from
Knox County]. One of Cap Thompsons Co [Noah Thompson's Company
E from Evansville] shot his hand off the other day. Their has [been]
several of our officers sent in there resignation in the last two Weeks.
I think it is mostly feer casued them to do it. This is my private
opinon of the matter. Some of the boys are on guard to day and it
has be gan to Rain. I was on guard last night. It Rains here when
ever it want to and is vary Cool. Their has frost nearley eavre week
since we came here while you have been scorching wit heat and
parched with the Drouth. I would be glad [if] you had some of the
Rain [as it is] not necessary for our benefit here as Soldiers. . . . We do
not need Rain here every other day. The boys are some of them sleeping while others are about in squads talking some about home . . . others are complaining about the bad weather. The boy that are a
quainted get to gether once an a while and talk over the pleasures
left at home. Yet we feel proud to think that we are counted worthy
to go in defence of a Cuntry the cause of which is so deeply found in

justice. Such are the Clames of a Cuntry that cost so many of our Countrymans lives to establish and not only there lives but there for-tune. And now shal we not maintain it I for one say we will neve give up the ship so long as their is one left to cry out against it. The boys that came from Alfordsville are all well and eaver ready to give there lives for a sacrifice on the alter of there Cuntry if necessary. They send there best respects to all the friends. Give my love [to] those that have a desire to hear from me.

This [that follows] is to all my friend and I shal expect to hear from them shortly. Friends pardon me for not writing to you personaly for stamps cannot be got here. All though I do not address you sevar-aly [separately] my love to you is the same.

From J Warren Alford

[Now, to the family:]

Dear father Mother and brothers and sisters. I will attempt in answer to your request to give you notice that I have Received four letters from home since I have ritten to you. I have received one from Wayne on the 20th and allso one from father on the same day. One from father on the 23rd [and] Wayne riting in the same one from father. [Another] one on the 25th. One from Donalson on the same day. [I] was glad to hear that you was all well and was glad to hear the Wayne was willing to stay at home. This is in answer to all of the letters as I have no stamps to pay pastage wit. You will receive this by hand of Mr L[?] or J[?] Acmeton. And as Water is to the thirsty sole so is good nuse from a far Country. Wright to me often. Write to me vary soon. . . . Good advice from father, Mother, brother or sister will be thankfully received. Pray for me while I pray for my self and you that god fineally may save us all and that he will do [it] if we obey his Commandments.   J Warren Alford

[In the margin:]

Write long letters but do not make it long between my love to all.

[From Father to Warren:]

Loogootee August 29th

J W Alford. Dear Sir. Being at Town and finding an opportunity of dropping you a line I embrace the opportunity hoping that it may afford you some pleasure to hear that we are all well and in the

quiet enjoyment of the old homestead. We hope this may find you
and all our friends in health. We have but little time to wright but
haveing heard a great deal about your Skermishing we have some
fears that you may become to bold and on account of you success
venture in to dangers and hazzard unnecessarily. Now we say act the
Man and discharge your whole duty to your God and your Country.
The friends is all well. If you have any money to spare Council Capt.
Brooks and if you think it best send it home with instructions concerning the same. Times is pretty hard but we hope to live over. We
must now . . . close haveing wrighten twice as much as we expected.
So nomore but ever Praying for your welfare in Time and Eternity
ever yours. Give my love to all my friends. Tell them to wright to
me if they can get time and wright your self as often as once a week
if you can as we look verry anxiously every Mail. Nomore but
remains you affectionate father until Death.

F. Alford

[Cousin Robert Gilley to Warren:]

August the 31 1861
Alfordsville ind

Dear Sir. I take this opportunity of Writing to you to let you know
that We ar All Well at present and hopeing that these few lines may
find you enjoying the same health. . . . Time is verry hard here. We
are not Going to raise verry good cropse. We have had A verry dri
Summer. Our corn is verry lite. We have just finished threshing our
wheat. It is not verry good but [we] out to be satisfied. . . . I must sort-
ley Come to A close. We thought that the men Around here wer all
pretty loyl but thare are some not. But nomore at present. I would
like to see you but as I cannot I [would] like to here from you. Please
write as soon as you can. So remaines your friend as long as life.

Robert Gilley

to J Warren Alford

Excuse this

If you please.

[Father to Warren:]

Home Sept the 1st 1861

Mr J Warren Alford. Dear Sir Yours of the 18th ult came duely to
hand yesterday and met A hearty welcome. . . . Your Mother is not

verry well but improving and much rejoiced to hear from you again.
. . . I have been much delighted to hear you express a determination to
give God the supremacy in your affection . . . for if you put your
trust in God you have a strong Tower like a mighty rock . . . which
you may fly for refuge in a time of danger. I know you are anxious
to know how we are getting along. Religuously we have to confess
that a luke warmness pervades the Congration to some extent but we
are glad to find out there are many good soldiers of the Cross who
will stand firm in defence of the cause of Truth and Righteousness
and importune with the God of our Fathers to guide among us our
armies and especially our Brethern in defence of the Libertys we
enjoy. . . . Joseph Murray is employed at $1.10 per day to teach School
for us till the funds are exhausted which will take him from the middle of present Month till the middle of March and by that time we
hope you can come home and take part in the closeing. . . . Our [local
farm] boys are with holding from the secessionist all the fine fruit
and every thing nice. . . . [The local boys say that] if you should be
so fortunate as to get back again [next] spring [they hope] to share
with you the luxuries which . . . are so common but to you are so
rare. . . . We hope the time is not far distant when we may receive
our friends again to participate with us in the quiet enjoyment of
home. . . . I must let you have a line about the [weather] here. We
have had fine Rains which has greatly increased our prospects for
Corn and we hope to have plenty to Fat all the Hogs. . . . Jackson
Allen thinks we will have 35 or 40 Bushels per Acre. . . . Tell the boys
that their friends are all well. I want all our friend to share with
you in these few lines. Lafayette and George and Hellen and Green
all sends thier love to you hoping to receive the same from [you]. . . .
The want of space admonishes us to close. Ever your dear Father and
Mother. Franklin & Mary Alford

[Warren to Wayne:]

Camp Cheat Mountain
September the 2nd 1861

Mr Wayne Alford
Dear brother. I received you kind letter of the 26th yesterday
Which gave me much pleasure to hear from home. I am quite happy
to be provided the opurtunity of being able to answer yur request.
You wanted me to give you my reasons for not wanting you to come
to the Company. You seam to think that their is something about soldiering that I do not want you to know. But you are much mistak-

en as to that for I do not think that their is any thing that is dis-
graceful or any thing that you would flinch from. It is not that I
would not like to have you with me for their is nothing that would
give me more pleasure than to have you with me. . . . We have the
best Company in the Regment. We have the best Officers in the Reg.
I would not give Brooks for any Captain that I ever saw. He has his
Company to obey all orders and has them under the most strictist [dis-
cipline] of any Company in the reg. If it was not for his being strict
I Would not like him. . . . If a Company is not disspline they are of no
account. Order is the firs thing in any thing. Keep up your [militia]
Comapany at home and put in your time on the farm untill next
spring and then if you are neaded then I shal say come. As it is getting along to wards Winter and you Could not [do much here] . . . and
if you did not get a full pass it would cost you about twenty five dollars out of your pocket. I consulted Brooks and Houghton on the sug-
gestion. They boath thaought that if it [were] them in my place they
would advise you two stay at home for the present. Houghton rote
you on the subject which I hope you have got before this time. . . .
Those are my reason for writing you not to come. But if nothing
Will do you but to come Brooks thinks he will be at home in about
twenty days and then you can make arrangements with him as to
being discharged when the rest of the company gets there discharge. I
have answered all the letter I have got from you and I think I have
got all you have sent to me so I shal close for the present. Remember
your brother at a throne of grace for it is in and through the mercies
of god we live. . . . It is my prair that we may all [be] blessed. Wright
soon soonir soonest. This is from your brother. J Warren Alford

[From married sister Minerva Donaldson to Warren:]

September the 8 1861
God morning Warren. It is with pllasure that I take my seat
to rite a few lines to let you kno that we are well. Father was her
yesterday and mother has bin sick but is well now. They wither is
fine here now. The sun shines hot in they day. The nites are coo.
They corn is ripening fast. They people are broke ing up follow [fal-
low] ground. Charley is going to sow wheat in corn. He expects to
commense next week. He has to work at they mill more than half of
his time. We have fruht A plenty. I never saw as plenty of peaches.
I wish we could send you over A few. Charley was at loogotee last
satur day [or rather it] was a week a go and heard that your lieutenant had resigned his office and had got back thare. We would lik

to know they reason of his doing that way. I saw a pease in they Commershal [*Commercial*] that dind not give them a very good name. We understood that Inman [William R. of the 14th Indiana] rote a let-ter home stating that you would start home next week. We would be glad to see you but are a fraid it is not true. Thare is a rumor a fote that Jeff Davis is dead but weare afraid it is not true. Last [week] was cort. Charley Allen was Juryman. He says they govener sent A Committee of men to Washington [Indiana] to pri in to they secession-est move ment. We under stand that they took they whole secesh gang from about high rock to Washington [local communities] and that Slicer and Barton and other was sworn. Thare is A litle curious movements About it and we do not exacly understand it. We have understood and supose it to be true that Bartle and Jackman [alleged Copperheads] are going to move away from Alfordsville. They people generally will be glad [when] they go. I must bring my letter to A close as i am tired of riting not being in A habbit of ritin. Read what you can and gues at they rest. Rite to us as son as you can. Give Virgil [Alford] our best respects. No more at present but remains your brother and sister until death.

★

[Wayne to Warren:]

Alfordsville Daviess Co Ind September 9, 1861
Mr Warren Alford. Dear Brother   I am Blessed With another oppor-tunity of wrighting you a few lines to let you know that We are all enjoying a reasonable portion of health at this time. You requested to keep you posted up on local matters. For fear you would think the time Long if I waited to receive another Letter from you So I thought I would right to you this Morning. I have verry Little to wright that would interest you though I suppose you would Like to hear from the old farm once more. We have about 25 . . . acres of ground Broke for wheat and intend Breaking about ten acres more Which we expect to get Done this Week if Nothing happens. We expect to sow that feald at Allens that we planted . . . in corn. They says that our corn Looks fine. I have not Seen it Since we laid it by. But enough of this. Our Company has been ready for to be mustered into the service but it Seams that Richard Clemants Wont come out and Do it. I dont know whether he is a ceccesh or not but we have Sent Chester Camp to See him and tell him that if he Dont Come We will wright to the Governor about it [and] see if he cant be made to do something. The Company at Washington [Indiana] have their arms and I think we

could get ours Son if We Could get organized. Ely [Eli] McCarty [from Washington] is progressing with his Comany [presumably Company G of the 42nd Indiana] and Kirk Mc is getting along verry well. I believe McCarty beats up [?] for volunteers [each] Saturday. The Rumors about the 14th Coming home are plenty. If all the Lies that have been told were in receipts a ten Bushel Box wouldent hold them. I give you one which I heard yesterday. Whether it is true or not you can tell better than I can though it is a likely story. They Said that Co C was sent out on a Scout with orders to take everything they Saw So they brought in all the Hogs & Cattle & everyting they could find. So when they got Back the Colonel was mad and Said they were a Set of Damd thieves and at this the Company rushed at Him and it was with great Difficulty that the officers could restrain them from killing him. This is a fair Specimen of the talk that are about in this part of the Country. Wright me the Cause of those officers resigning if you know. I must close for it is about mail time. I send you a letter from minervia & She Clear forgot to sign her name to it. You can do it for her. No more but as ever yours in hope of seeing you on earth again. Your brother until Death. Wayne Alford

PS Lafayette Sends his love to all the Boys But espetially to those that went from here & Wm Haughtin [Houghton]. And retain a double porton for your self. I Send My own also to those and to Capt Brooks. Lafayettes hand is well but it is so nervous that he cannot wright yet. Tell us why an officer has the authority to throw up his commition [resign his commission] and Come home any more than a Soldier Would.

No more Wayne

[From Warren to Wayne:]

[Date unknown]
Well Brother Wayne I read your letter with much interest and now attempt to give you a few lines in answer. I was very glad to hear from you and so were all the boys. But we expect to hear of you getting along witt your company better than you are. I expect you will come and help Co C yet. We have not so much picketing to do since we got off the mountain. There is no enemy here for us to watch for like there was before we cam down from the mountain but we are drilling as regular as we did in Camp Vigo. We have had fine weather Since we have been In the Valle but cant expect it much longer.

As for our destiny this winter I am entirely ignorant. I have no
idea how long we will stay here or where we will go when we leave.
Nothing more
Your Brother
Warren

[From Uncle Wayne Alford to Warren:]

Alfordsville Daviess Co Ind
Sept 9th 1861

Mr Warren Alford my nephew.
Dear sir. I now for the first time since you left home Avail myself
the opportunity of addressing you A few lines to let you know that I
am still amongst the living through A kind Providence: I hope that
this may reach you in due time and find all well. You will feel surprised when I tell you that I have received not A line as yet from
any of our `Boys' & that this is the first that I have written for
myself though I have written Many for others More or less every
week. You are doubtless well posted with regards to our affairs at
home as well as abroad. You may have perhaps learned that
Secessonism is a great secret organization. I mean that its devotees is
Oath bound Sworn to do anything and Everything within their
power [to] Destroy the Governmer: I have taken some paines to hunt
it in some of its hiding places and now think that we are very nearly redy to shell it out. Their is A Man in our state that has fiendish-
ly gone through their Secret lodges in the south and fully Exposed its
inner temple and learned all of their nefarious designes and has now
published in Indianapolis A full Exposition of their hellish trickery.
He tells us that after the Bombardment of Fort Sumpter that they
sent their [despicable] Spies out north of mason and Dixon line to
make sure of their friends in the free states. This Man who betrayed
them says that they now have some two or three hundred Sworn
knight in southern Indiana and Illinois. Their Name is Knights of
the Golden Circle. If you will answer our letters I will keep you
Posted as we proceed to ferret it out. Things are tolerable quiet here
at the present. The Secesion Clan has heretofore made a labored
Effort but appears to have failed to some extent. They have however
Called a mass meeting of the Dimocrat party at Dover Hill on the 14th
of Sept to try to gather from them Some help. Write immediately
upon the reciept of this. Remember my respects to Brother Wm
Houghton, Brother Mathew Stafford, Brother Virgil Alford, Steven

Collins, R Conolty [Conolly], John McCord and in fact all the Boys in Camp of my acquaintance. Tell them to write.

> With respect. Eld[er] Wayne Alford

★

[Warren to the folks at Alfordsville:]

> Cheat Mountain Summit
> September the 12th/61

Dear Father and Mother brothers and sisters. After wating ashort time after receiving your letters one by the hand of Cap L Brooks and one the next day I thought I would drop you afew lines to inform you that I am well and hope this may find you all enjoying good health again. You rote in your letter that mothers health was pore but getting better. I hope by this time she is quite well agane and I hope you are getting along well in a simular point of view. As spiritual health is preferable to halth I hope thet their may be no panes spared in strengthening the spiritual man. May the lord help us to use the meanes put in our hands to strengthen us and keep us in the way that we should go. May we allways be found engaged in the things that we should be and ever shun the pathes of vice and folley and may we be ever like Paul when he sayed I am hense forth ready to be offered. For may we eaver be ready to live with god. You do not know how much good it does me to get a letter from home. Yet I think I get many letters from home. When I get a letter from home the boys get around me to hear what you have to say. I would love to hear from you at least once or twice a week so long as I may stay from home. I think I have got all of the letters you sent to me as yet excep that package you sent to me with stamps in it which I would be vary glad to have. I would be glad if you would in your next letter send me some stamps as I can get paper and envelpoes here. You need not send me any more of them. We have not got our money yet but we have the promise of it in a few days. And I think I will have some money to send home and as to the way I shal send it I cannot say but I think that Cap L Brooks will go home be fore long and I can send by him. And if he does not go he will send his money home and I can send with his. If he does not go I will write and let you know how it is comeing as soon as I find out how I will have to send it. He thinks he can get a check on the bank. We are yet in the same place. We have got our fortification done but when we will make are foreward move I can not tell. The prospects to stay for awhile longer at this place looks as good or better than it did the day we came here. But as the movements of the armey is not known we may go frome here in a short time and we may stay two Months. You sayed in your letter some thing about ther being fine

Raines at home and something about so much fine fruit and that you hope that we would get home this winter. I hope we may get home in the corse of this winter for I think that our southern broth- er will get tired of the fun and as great many of there troops are in onley for one year and by that time they will be tired of soldeiering and there armey will be some what reduced and they will not be in clined to volunteer agane. . . . I received a letter from Clem Riley say- ing that he had heared that their was a bad impression in the camp on regard to something that he had sayed about the officers. Such was the report but we did not know wheter it was so or not. I shal bring my letter to a close for the present. Hoping you will pray for the spedy termination of this national calamity and for your sone and brother that he may ever discharge his duty as a Cristian and a soldier.

[In the margin:]

I ever remain your sone and brother. James Warren Alford

[Now, a note to the brothers at home:]

Dear brothers. I now turn over to the last page and I thought I [would] wright some things to interest you as I had written as much to father as was necessary and all that I had that was necessary or interesting. Boys I have learned a great many things since I left home. Soldiering is some thing like farming on the river and staying in a shanty. Our tent is just about comefortable as our shanty was last summer but the weather is more disagreeable here than it was their and the fare is about the same. We get crackers and they are tolerable hard. We have to do our own cucking but we have more time than we had last summer. When we have to march it is vary hard work but it is a vary small portion of our time we put in marching. And we spend the biger part of our time in our tent or siting about talking with the boys. Children I would glad be wit you and spend the ours as we done Reading our good books and tell you what I have saw since I left home. Children be contended and Wright to me all of you and Remember they creator in the day of thy youth be fore the Evil day comes X X

[In the margin:]

Forget me not but pray fore me that I may live a Christian [life] and be an honor to the family and at last get home to heaven.

From James Warren Alford to his bothers and sisters at home.

[From Father to Warren:]

Home Sept the 15th 1861
Mr J Warren Alford

Dear Sir. We received your verry kind and also verry welcome letter
of the 2nd Inst by yesterdays Mail. It found us in the enjoyment of
Common health and all the luxuries that is Common in this vicinity
of Country. And we hope this . . . communication to you may come
duely to hand and find you in the enjoyment of health and free
from the Iron hand of rebel authority. We see that Rosecrans [Union
Brigadier General William Rosecrans] has defeated Floyd [Confederate
Brigadier General John Floyd] on gauley [Gauley Bridge, Virginia]
near Carrex Ferry [Carnifix Ferry, Virginia]. We . . . hear that you
have been attacked by Lee [Confederate General Robert E. Lee] on one
side and Wise [Confederate Brigadier General Henry Wise] on the
other. But they were repulsed by your galantry. We have no further particulars. We are verry anxious to hear from you again as we
suppose you was in the latter engagement . . . . We hope your life has
been [spared] in the sight of him who is able to shield his Children
from dangor. We feel quite anxious to hear the particulars connected
with the fight but doubtless we will get it in the nuse before you can
wright to us. But we hope you will give us a statement of the facts
as soon as you can. [Frank] Nolan[d] got home on Sunday I have not
saw him yet but will soon. I am glad you are so well pleased with
your officers. We think it would be difficult for you to esteem them
to highly and especialy those of our acquaintance. Our boys is not
sworn in yet but it is on acccount of neglect of Clemments. We have
thrashed our Wheat and Oats. We had 250 bushels of Wheat & 62 of
Oats. You had only about 25 bushels to your share. Aunt Cicily [has]
come to hear . . . every time she hears that we have a letter from you.
She told me the other day to send you her love when I wrote again.
Wayne says he will wright about saturday and if we can get them
we will send you a few stamps. If you have got our last letters you
will find inclosed four or five sheets of paper and seven invelopes
but we must close. . . . Verry respectfully your Father until Death.

Franklin Alford

I send 1/2 sheet Blank. Use it if you kneed it.

[From Father to Warren:]

Loogootee Sept 17

Mr J Warren Alford

Dear Son. We are all well and your Mother and I is at Logootee today
and we send you A bunch of Invelops. I want you to wright as

often as you can and we will be glad to pay all Postage. I wrote you
yesterday and wayne will Wright Saturday. I saw [Frank] Noland
this morning and he thinks he is on the mend. [Noland recently was
discharged from the 14th Indiana.] I was glad to see him and hear
from you. Give all the Boys my love. . . . When these [envelopes] are
gone we will send you more. No more but affectionately your Father
and Mother.

F & M Alford

★

[From Wayne to Warren:]

Home Alfordsville Daviess Co Ind
Sept 20/61

Mr Warren Alford. Dear Brother.
Again I am Seated to Wright to You A few Lines to Let you know
that I am well at present and trust you are enjoying the Same. Your
Letter gave me great Satisfaction though I Did not answer it immediately for father was Wrighting to you and I thought it best to Wait
till the Next mail so that your letters would Come in regularly. I was
highly gratified with your answer to my questions and if it Should
be that the war is not over I Hope to be with you Next Summer
though I have no Say it will Last till then though it may. Their is no
telling. Frank Nolen [Noland, recently discharged,] has got home. . . .
Father & Mother went up to See him and was highly pleased with the
information he brings with regard to your position and your Doings.
We learned from the papers that 300 from the Ind 14th & two Ohio
regiments had a Severe Skirmish the other Day with a body of Cecesh
and drove them back Without loss on our Side. Wright me if you
were in it and all about it if you can.   And wright me if you have
Joined the Masons. We are gowing to School. . . . I was verry hardly
pressed to take a school where you taught Last winter. They Seamed
to think as you taught them Such a good School your Brother Could
Do as well but I Could not Do it and go to School myself. . . . So I
Declined thinking that it would be of more advantage to me to go to
School myself. You Wanted to know how F B got along with the girls.
I will tell you in the first place He was acting post master. . . . J. W.
and Nan Collins Suspected him of not Sending her Letters an So She
went and rummaged every Corner about the office and gave Him to
underStand that She thought he was guilty. . . . [Another] time he was
at Charles allens and the Subject came up and he Said he was a
Cecesh and Nan Said you had better leave here right quick and She
Said he looked like he would rather it was not him. But he takes Care
not to go back. . . . Tody [a girl] has turned Cesesh I believe and Says if

She loves any Body and they was to turn Cesesh it would make no
difference with Her. Lizyan McCord had a notion of him Some time
ago but her and tode fell out and quarreled about a letter that was
Droped by Somebody. I never learned who but they passed Several
times and So H. B [a boy] had to give one or the other up and so he
Droped Elizy and now goes with tode all to gether. He Seldom ever
goes out only when he is gowing Down there and then right Back
again. Their is nothing more of importance to Wright. I spoke to Nan
about your letter and She Said She got your letter and answered it So
long ago that She was getting in the Same fix of yourself. But I must
bring my letter to a close. John E Mathews begins a Meating of Some
Days tomorrow Night (4th Saturday in Sept) and I Should Like to See
you Here if I could in your terms but I Cannot I Suppose. I expect to
See Net then. . . . This is badly wrighten you must excuse me for I am
extremely nervous at this time. Since I am Wrighting I recollect that
I am mistakened about the fight. We had 8 Killed and that of the
enemy 80 Killed and the Loss of most of thier baggage. We Could Not
learn from the paper how many of you were engaged in it. Wright
us the particulars. No more but remains your Brother until Death.

Wayne Alford Jr

[From Dr. J.L. Laverty to Warren:]

Alfordsville Daviess Co Ind Sep 20th 61
Mr Warren Alford

Dear Friend

I received your kind communication of last Week, and I now
sit down to answer it. My health at presant is good altho I have
enjoyed very poor health for some time Back. But I thank god that I
am now able to mount my horse once more. We have . . . a great deal
of Sickness and if it keeps up I do not know what I am to do. It is
more than I am able to attend to But I will go as long as I can before
I give one case into the hands of Old [?, the name of another doctor].
I acually feare that we are going to have a Sickly fall. I was very
much pleased with your letter, as it was the first one I have ever
Received from you. I should like very much to enjoy camp life and
be with you in Va. But owing to the Situation that I now occupy I
deam it best to stay at home for the presant. I have no news that
will interest you. The ladies Warren are all Well in this portion of
the county or at least your acquaintances. Some of them talk about
getting married but I think they are only jesting about it. We still

have companys making up in the neighborhood around us. Mr [Eli] McCarty is now collecting men to go into a company [G of the 42nd Indiana] to rendavouise at Evansville. The young men are nearly all gone out of our county and still more going. I was offered the appointment of assistant surgeon in the Cap Boltins company of Washington [24th Indiana Infantry] if I go. But the people heare would not heare to My going away So I had to sing mum on the sub-ject. Their Was a terible accident happened on the St Louis Rail Road [Ohio & Mississippi RR] above the Shoals last Monday evening. There was a company from Camp Patterson ordered to Va ... and as the Cairs was Crossing Beaver Creek the Brige broke down and killed some 120 men besides wounded. Their is no doubt in my mind but the taps was taken off the end of stay rods by some fiend of Hell. Such is life. But I must Stop writing as I have to write a note to John McCord before the mail comes in. You must excuse this short and hurried [note] as I am in a hurry and I will do better next time. Farewell my Friend Warren. May god bless you is the prayer of your Friend.

Dr. J. L. Laverty

[From Warren to Lafayette:]

Cheat Mountain
September 22/61

Dear Brother

I now take the ... opertuity ... to inform you that I am well and hope this may find you in the ... same. I would inform you that I received Waynes letter of the 9th on the 13th which gave me satisfac-tion to hear that you was well at that time. We was in quite an excitement for on that day. ... We had a brush which terminated in the loss of five of our Reg. Two killed out of Co E. [and] one of Co. D. Two out of Co G. ... The loss of the Rebles [was] from 50 to one hun-dred from the best account we have. Our Co got the first shot. Your brother got to see the Rebles and fired the third or fourth shot. Forty of our Co. fired in to one hole Reg and they fired some five of six shots and fled like fritened Rats from an old barn on fire leaving eavry thing behind. Some two Wagon loads of eqipage, blankets, nap-sacks, even ... gunns and haver sacks with all of their provision. For four days they came in site every day for four days but did not git us a chance at thems. Suppose the first metting did not sute them. ... From the account that the prisoners gave their was some two of them to one of us. This perhape is true I would have ritten sooner but I

run the Ramrod in my hand and I could not Wright for some five or
six days. This accounts for my not Wrighting sooner and on this
account I have got behind wrighting. Tell my friends I will answer
as soon as I can. Thier is some fight in the hoosiers and the Rebles
say they do not like hoosiers and we do not care for it. How does my
letters take at home and is their any get up about them. Tell Hannah
Alford I received her letter and was glad to hear from her. How does
the Mule grow and the Colt. And how does the hogs look. Father if
you can get the Money please pay my arearage to the Bible union. I
would like that payed If I am away from home. . . . The claimes of the
lord are as binding on a Christian in the armey as at home. I [feel]
my need on him as I ever did and am as willing to serve him and
may he enable us all to trust in him is my prare. Wright to me soon.
From Warren to Lafayette Alford.

[Along the margin:]

Send me a number or two of the Review if you please. [The Review
was not a local paper, probably a religious publication.]

★

[From Virgil Alford to Wayne:]

23 Sept 1861
        Der cousen. It is with much plasure i now set my self to rite
you a few lines to let you no that i am will at this time. I hope
these lines may find you injoying good helth. I recieved your leter
of the 2th. I was gald to here from you. I had a brush with the
enemy the twelfth. They attack us both in frunt and reer. Our los
was about 5 killed and sum eight or ten wounded. Thur los can
not be properly ascertained. We buried about sixth of them and
found several graves which they had buried them selves. They will
not com out and fitt us a fair fight. . . . We air as good at bush
whacking as they air. . . . We drove them back and every thing is
quiet to day. I think they air will trained for running. I think
they execute that order beter thun any thing els. I would [hope you
could be with us] but as you cant you must do our part of going to
see the girls and keep them chired up till we get back then i think
they will be a chance for them to al git marryed. I her they air al
going to wait and marrye a soldier you can tell them i think it a
good notion. . . . Tell lafayette i think he mite rite to us. I have not
received a [letter] from him yet. If he wants me to rite he must rite
to me. I no he has more tim to rit than i hav for i hav had to stand

gard nerly every day for aweil. ... I am high privit in the frunt
rank. Warren is apointed corporal. ... So nothing more but remain
your Most affectionate friend until death. Virgil Alford to Wayne
Alford

[From Warren to Father and Mother:]

> Camp Cheat Mountain Summit
> Sept the 25th 1861

Dear Father and Mother
It is agane with pleasure I seat my self to in form yu that I am yet
on the land and among the living. Blessed with health and the proper exercise of our mind. We have reason to believe that our life and
our health is pecious in the sight of our heavenly Father. We do not

**Confederate Colonel John A.
Washington.** *(Courtesy West Virginia
U.D.C., via Tim McKinney)*

**Union Major General Joseph Jones
Reynolds.** *(LC)*

dout for one moment but he will bring us back home safe if it is for the best. And if not let us be resigned to his will and let us live so that if we neaver meat on eart that we may be prepared to live together aroun the throne of God where parting . . . will be nomore but one continual see of Joy and peace for ever and ever. I receive Your vary welcome letter dated the 15th on the 21st which gave me much pleasure to hear of you all being in good health and in the enjoyment of the luxuries common to that part of Cuntry. We do not get many nice thing but we get plenty of the substantals of life and we are conten and a contented mind is worth more than all the gold of California. We come out to be a Soldier and live or Dye for our Cuntry. . . . Their [is] no place [for] Idlers . . . in the armey in Western Virginia. You sayed you wanted me to give you a details of our bat-tle. I guess you will get it in the papers before you can get my letter. I Rote a letter to Lafayette giving you some of the most important facts conected with the figh and will not go over it agane. . . . You sayed you heared that they made the attck frount and Rear and as to Wise [Confederate general and former Virginia governor, Henry Wise] being thair. He was not as I know of and as to them making the attact they did not do it but they was in our frunt and Rear in large numbers but we was to fast for them. We made the attact our selves and we made it count. We must have kiled something over one hundred of them at this place and took prisoners and wounded as many more. It was reported by our officers that there losses was one thousand in the hole action while ours was vary small at this place. We only lost at this place five or six men. Our Co did not lose a man in the hole action not withstanding we made the [fight] with only 40 man and drove back 12 or 1500. We got a large amount of eqipments that they fled and left in the woods. They lost one Colonel by the name of Washington [Lieutenant Colonel John Augustine Washington, an aide to General Robert E. Lee]. They sayed they would Rather lost a hole Reg. He Was the owner of George Washington estat at Mount Vernon. I must bring my letter to a close and will write againe soon. Ever yours Sone in the one hope. J W Alford

[In the margins:]

I started a letter to you on the Morning that we was attacted and the Wagons Was [overturned] and the male [was thrown] out of the Wagon. But we was so clost on to them that did not get off with it nor open it.

Say to Minervia that I receive her letter in Waynes. Wayne I give my love to all inqiring friends.

★

[From Warren to "brother":]

Cheat Mountain
Sept the 26th 1861

Dear brother.
I now embrace this opertunity and it may be the Last time for some
time an it is not imposible that it may be for ever as We are going to
start in the Morning to go for them and a life is uncertain and deat
is aboad [death is about] in our land and we have no [control] of our
lives. [I] thought we would write you a few lines to let you know
that we was Well at this time. I do not know wher we are going two
but we are not going far as we are not takeing our things. Their is a
[Confederate] Camp about 18 Miles [from here]. Their is not More that
21 thousand [or] less than 17 thousands [of us] and we are able for
them if we know ourselves which I think we do. We have not had
any male for four days for some cause or other. I know not what
[happened]. I think we will get a Male this eaevening. . . . We was a
fraid I would not have time if I should wate. I think we will get to
rest in afew days for we have held the advance for the last 75 days.
Our General says we have done more service than any Reg in
Virginia and he sayed he would give us Rest in a short time. Their
has bin several Men . . . Discharged in the las few days on account of
disability. It is thought by some that we will go in Winter quarters
in the [border] Stats. This is only hear say. We heared that their had
bin amove on washington but could hear nothing reliable. I go from
this place trusting in the Lord fore he alone is able to save us both
spiritualy and temperaly and he says he will protect his Children if
they put there trust in him and heaven and Earth can pass away
but his word cannot so we must aclose for the preasent. Remember
us at a throne of grace.   J W Alford

[In the margins:]

I have wrote so much that I could not Wright along letter. I write
two a day. Write to me soon and oblige you brother away from
home.

[From Warren to Wayne:]

Cheat Mountain Summit
October the 6th 61

Dear Brother   It is agane with pleasure I attempt to write you a few
line to let you know that I received your vary kind letter which
came to hand on 1st inst and found me well and [I was] glad to hear

that you was all well. And I had a chance to send you this by one of
our men that was going home in about one hour. After I Received
your letter we was ordered to get Ready to march to fight the enemy
and I shal not have time to give you the detailes in [this letter] as this
has to be ready to go in a short time. We all got back safe except one
man by the name of Boid [Amos Boyd, a private from Martin County
who was killed at the battle of Greenbrier River, October 3, 1861. He
got shot dead at the first fire [of] the cannon [which] was vary heavy.
We fired about fifteen hundred shot and nearly every shot taking
affect. Their loss was vary heavy whilst ours was lite only about 25
kiled and wounded. I shal have to bring my letter to a close for the
present. I am well and in fine spirits and will write againe soon. So
I ever Remain yours in the one. In one of your questions I can not
answer. . . .

J Warren Alford

[From Warren to Father and Mother:]

Camp Cheat Mountain Summit
Oct the 6th 1861

Dear Father and Mother
I now take the pleasure in writing you a few lines to inform you
that I am well at this time and Hope when this come to hand it may
find you all Well and living in hope of eternal life. I received your
kind letter under date of the 17th of Sept and one from Wayne Dated
the 22nd which I answered this Morning and sent it by hand to
Loogootee by a man by the name of Walls [Corporal Columbus Walls]
who was discharged. He lives in Loogootee. We had an engagement
with the enemy on the 3th. We only lost in the hole engagement 8
kiled and 13 wounded. The 14th Reg only lost three men. One of our
Co was kiled by the name of Amos Boid [Boyd] he Lived in Pitsburg.
Co A lost one by the name of Price [Sergeant John Urner Price]. He
was a universalist Preacher and a vary high learned and talented
Man. He lived in or near Rockville Park [Parke] Co Ind. It was said
he was the best learned man in the state. You have no dout heard of
hime. He was second Sargreant in his Co. Our Co and Co A was to
geather at the time those two men fell. [This happened] five minuts
after the firing Commenced. This was about 7 in the morning. Our
company Was detailed to go forward to find out where they was. Our
Reg Was in line of battle when the General [Joseph Reynolds] sayed to
Col Kimble [Kimball] have you a Co that will advance to find out
where they are. When the Col Called our Co to advance which we did
imediately. The Gen and Col both advancing with us. When we

advance about 300 yards . . . they opened fire on us. We held the line till some two other Co advanced to our Relief. Then We advanced immediately on them. Routing them with heavy loss on there part not geting another man hurt. An other Reg [was] advancing at the same time to our Right. They was about all infantry fighting that was done. At about half past seven we opened a heavey cannonading which last for 5 1/2 hours. They returned the fire but did no damage searcely. Our baterey fired about 1500 shot and shell. They nocked a wheel off of one of our gunn Carages while we disabled all but one of there gunn. We was geting Ready to finish the work with musketry when they was strongly Reinforced [while] our forces [withdrew] slowly and sulenly hoping they would leave there intrenchments to follow us but [they] appeared to [want] to quit. Their loss was supposed to be 500 kiled and a great many wounded. There shot fell around us for a while thick and fast but did not take affect. Our boys acted nobley [and did not] dis grace our selve nor the Cause for which we fight to Maintain. I will close on an other sheat [not found].

★

[From Lafayette to Warren:]

Home October 8th [1861]
Dear brother   It wilth pleasure I seat my self to let you no that we are well hoping this will find you enjoying the same.   Warren I can not write much as . . . my hand is nervous but I will do the best I Can. We have got 32 in our company and they have to go to a Catholic Church today out by downeys and from thence to the harts school house to morrow. They say up there we will git 40 out of there militia Company. The sesesh of kentucky say they intend wintering in our state but we will giv them a hot place if they do. My Colt is fin. Your mule is fat and fin. He sides furst rate. We have hade the [hogs] about a month and they are fattenning fine. Our Corn is Very good. We have got 34 Acres of wheat sown and it looks fine. I had like to forgotten. [I] received your letter the first day of this month which gave me mutch satisfaction. Let us know how you are off for cloths. We lern from the papers that the troops there are thinley Clad. Rite immediately concerning it and we will try to relieve you if possible. Prey daily that you may discharge your duty both spritualy and politicaly. Do the same for me when Conviniant. Nothing more only remaining your brother. Write soon. Lafayette Alford

[To Warren from Mother, although written by Father:]

Home Oct the 13th 1861
Mr J. Warren Alford

Dear Sir   I am now seated to wright you a few lines from your Dear
Mother. We received your letter of the sixth Inst which found a
verry affectionate place in our bosom and gave us great comfort to
hear that you had passed through your conflict of the 3rd unhurt.
Though I have sympathised verry cosiderably with you on account of
your deplorable condition in the way of Clothing but [I have been]
greatly relieved by the presentation of an opportunity of sending you
a few old clothes. I say old ones because I had not time to make new
ones. And again I am cheered with the welcome tiding of you haveing received some new ones. I now hope there may be no more mis-
takes when useing the word rugged in connexion with the Indiana
Boys and especialy the Fourteenth Reg. I am in hope it will not be
long before you will get rest and be moved to some pleasant place to
enjoy it and as near home as would be prudent. [And] that we may
be better able to accomodate you with such things as you may need. I
see from the nuse of the Eleventh that general Reynolds [Brigadier
General Joseph Reynolds] has had a second reconnosance in force and
has driven Lee [Confederate General Robert E. Lee] from Big springs.
I would like to know if you had to perform any part in the second
engagement. We are verry sorry to hear that so many of the boys are
on the sick list but I have heard that the Alfordsville Boys were all
well. I want you to use every possible means to preserve your health
and ability to perform your rugged task. I learn from the particulars
connected with your visit to Greenbrier that you took a prisoner by
the name of James Alford which I think is likely to be our Cousin.
If you can find out anything about him wright and let us know it
in your next letter. Now in the close of my letter and in the fond-
ness of an affectionate Mother I beseach you that by the grace of God
that you continue to walk worthy of your high calling and . . . present your body a liveing sacrifice to God which is your reasonable service. So no more but remains your affectionate Mother untill death.

Mary Alford

★

2
BACKGROUND

"Fighting means killing."[1]

THE ALFORD LETTERS PROVIDE AN EXCELLENT sweep of the events in the summer of 1861. There was much excitement at home, more men were being organized into volunteer units, and those who had been organized were being sent to the front. As for the Indiana troops, the "seats of war" were western Virginia and Missouri.

Hoosiers first saw action in the small engagements fought in western Virginia. The first Indiana soldier was killed in June.

Warren wrote in July that the 14th Indiana was about to take part in its first engagement – they were approaching the Confederate encampment at Rich Mountain, western Virginia. This was after a "three dayes march [and] we expected to get in to a fight." The 14th did not get into that fight, as they were

The Battle of Rich Mountain. (HPHCW)

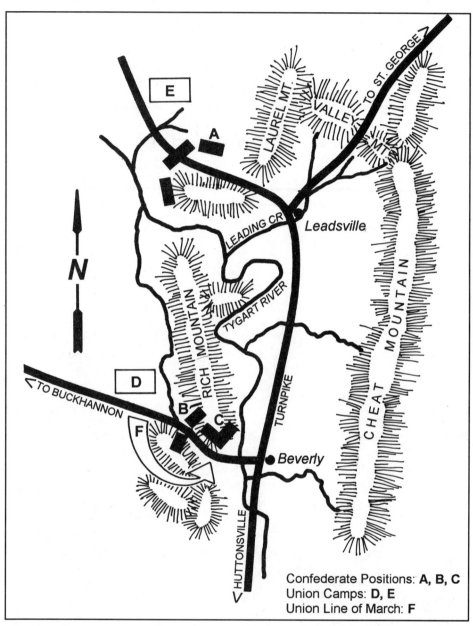

Battle of Rich Mountain, July 11, 1861. *(Redrafted from Similar Map in The Soldier of Indiana.)*

held in reserve during the battle. Of the four Union infantry regiments taking part in the Battle of Rich Mountain, three were from Indiana.

General George Brinton McClellan, the commander of the Union forces, reported "Our success complete and almost bloodless." McClellan thought casualties were "perhaps twenty killed and forty wounded."(2) The official number was given as twelve killed, fifty-nine wounded.(3) After the Union triumph, the 14th Indiana took part in the pursuit of the fleeing Confederates.

The most momentous military event of the summer was the Battle of Bull Run, fought near Manassas, Virginia. There were no Indiana troops in this battle, fought on July 21, but at least one Indiana congressman left Washington, D.C. and traveled to Manassas to watch the festivities. Never again would the Civil War be looked upon so light-heartedly. The casualties totalled approximately 4,700 Americans, North and South.(4)

The Battle of Bull Run was a humiliating defeat for the Union Army. The once-rampant euphoria was being tempered with reality. Three weeks after Bull Run, on August 10, the Union Army suffered another defeat at Wilson's Creek, near Springfield, Missouri. This time, 2,100 Americans were killed and wounded.(5) As at Bull Run, there were no Indiana troops at Wilson's Creek.

So, the War did not end in three months as many had predicted. In the North, the call for troops reached 650,000 and preparations were underway for a lengthy contest.

In late August, there was a Union victory on the Outer Banks of North Carolina followed by another win on September 10 at Carnifix Ferry.(6)

After the battle at Rich Mountain, six companies of the 14th, including Company C, moved their camps to a summit of the Cheat Mountains, near Beverly, western Virginia. Many of the soldiers complained about their new situation. George Lambert, Company F of the 14th, wrote that the name of the mountain could not have been more appropriate: "for we have been cheated in various ways and various times. . . ." He went on to explain that the boys were cheated on food, "half rations." They were cheated on the weather, "cold, colder, coldest and rainy, rainier, rainest." And they were cheated on clothing, "the boys have to wrap their blankets round them . . . to hide their nakedness."(7)

The references to the cold rainy weather and the lack of clothing were not an exaggeration. Captain Elijah Cavins of Company D remembered that "horses chilled to death" in September.(8) Colonel Kimball, in official correspondence with General Joseph Reynolds on September 14, 1861, closed with a pointed reminder, "Though almost naked, my command are [sic] ready to move forward."(9)

One soldier summed it up by saying the region was "the country God forgot."(10) Warren thought otherwise, "we are in the hand of a Just god."

"Captain Brooks, deploy your Company and meet the Confederate skirmishers."(11)

In Civil War history, the Cheat Mountain Campaign is significant because of the presence of Confederate General Robert E. Lee. This campaign was Lee's first as a Civil War field commander. Also, it was significant for the

Elijah H.C. Cavins of the 14th in His Latter Years. (IHS,M42,C6335)   *Confederate Colonel Albert Rust.* (LC)

Confederacy because of its disastrous results. For some members of the 14th Indiana, it was best remembered for the "cold and rain of [a] dreary and uninhabited country, and lack of sufficient rations and clothing."(12)

Lee's goal was to clear northwest Virginia of all Union troops. His first move was to attack the blueclads, in and around the Cheat Mountain summit, with five columns – from five directions – simultaneously. Things did not go well for General Lee: a measles epidemic among his men, an overly complicated plan, terrain features which favored the Union forces, and a downpour of rain. The turning point, however, occurred when a Lee subordinate took council of his fears. One of the Confederate wing commanders, Colonel Albert Rust with 2,000 men, was to lead the assault on the Cheat Mountain summit. Rust also was to fire a signal shot alerting the other commanders that the general offensive was to start. As Rust approached his objective, he became fearful that he was grossly outnumbered and retreated, without firing a shot.(13)

As Rust and his men fell back, they encountered a Union wagon train on a routine assignment. When word of this chance engagement reached the summit camps, Colonel Kimball assembled two Ohio regiments and Companies C and F

The Cheat Mountain Summit. *(West Virginia University Archives)*

from the 14th Indiana. Captain Brooks led Company C into their first fight. Colonel Kimball described the sequence, "My captains immediately opened fire, and informed me the enemy was there in great force. I ordered them to hold their position. They did so, and soon had the pleasure of seeing the whole force of the enemy take to their heels. . . ."(14) Warren described the situation in his September 22 letter to Lafayette as "fritened Rats [running] from an old barn on fire." Warren also told how he had fired the third or fourth shot in the skirmish.

Fighting took place at other nearby points, and with the same outcome. All the Union forces, serving under Brigadier General Joseph Reynolds (from Lafayette, Indiana), successfully held their positions. The casualties were light considering the troops involved and the importance of the battle. The Union lost twenty-one killed and wounded, the Confederate estimate was set at seventy.(15) The Cheat Mountain Campaign ended and Lee rode toward Gauley Bridge and Carnifix Ferry, to join another Confederate campaign that had failed.

Warren Alford and the 14th Indiana remained encamped at the dreaded Cheat Mountain Summit. Finally the regiment, which numbered about 600 men, obtained some protection from the cold. A private in Company G submitted a letter to the Vincennes paper with the explanation: "Overcoats for the Thirty-second Ohio came up on Tuesday and were distributed to the "ragged Fourteenth" — a good joke on the Thirty-second, which marched up the next day and were welcomed by our boys with their coats on."(16)

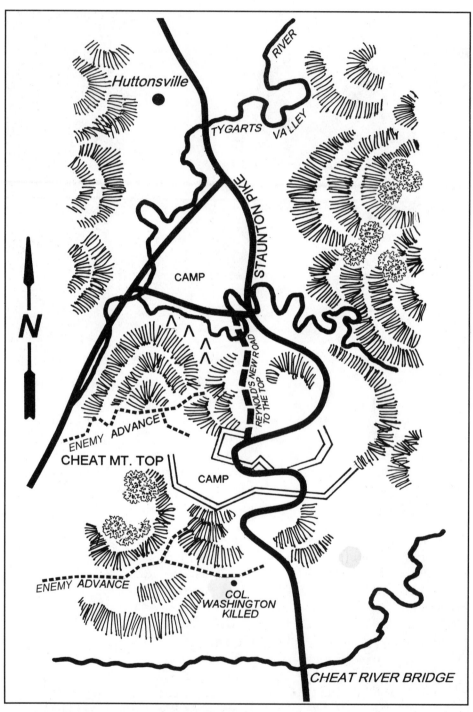

Area of Cheat Mountain Battle, September 11, 1861. *(Redrafted from Similar Map in The Soldier of Indiana.)*

After the retreat from Cheat Mountain, Confederate soldiers, under the command of General Henry Jackson, made a new camp twelve miles to the southeast. The carefully selected site was near the juncture of the Greenbrier River and the Parkersburg-Staunton Turnpike. In addition to favorable terrain, the Confederates heavily fortified their position and took special care to protect their flanks.

On the night of October 2, Union General Reynolds assembled 5,000 men for a march on the Confederates at the Greenbrier River. Colonel Robert Milroy (from Rensselaer, Indiana) and the 9th Indiana Infantry drove in the Confederate pickets; then the 14th

Confederate Brigadier General Henry Jackson. (LC)

Indiana was ordered to make a frontal assault.(17) Company C was sent ahead of the regiment as skirmishers. The battle quickly became a standoff with artillery dueling artillery. The 14th pulled back to protect a Union battery and consequently became the target of enemy fire. The fighting took place in a valley or an area "almost an oval in form, encircled by hills."(18) The enemy shells and the thundering noise were relentless, but Kimball reported his men "did not waver."(19) At about 12:30 p.m., General Reynolds called off the engagement. Nothing had been gained.

Union Major General Robert Huston Milroy. (West Virginia University Archives)

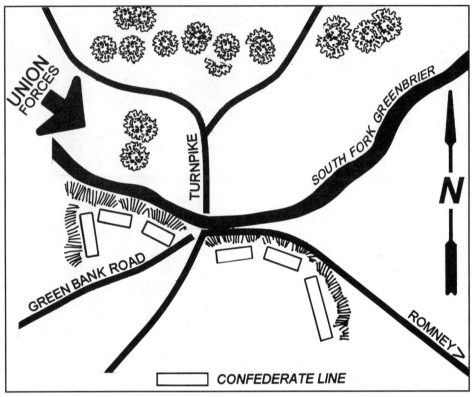

Battle of Greenbrier River, October 3, 1861. (Redrafted from Similar Map in The Civil War in West Virginia.)

The 14th Indiana lost three men, just as Warren reported to the folks at home.(20) All three men were hit with artillery shell or shell fragments. Amos Boyd, Company C, was killed on the field and two others died back in camp. Warren's description of the Battle of Greenbrier River is basically accurate with the exception of the obvious overstatements, particularly the numbers ("500 kiled"). John Kuppenheimer, a German immigrant serving in Company F, wrote home, "I am informed that the Rebel loss is about 400 killed."(21) Officially, the Confederate casualties totalled fifty-two, of which thirteen were captured.(22) Again, it was a small engagement with little military importance, except for those who were there.

Colonel Kimball filed a glowing account of the 14th's behavior in battle and added, "we are ready again."(23) As winter weather set in, there was no more fighting and the region remained in Union control.(24)

"Blueprint for Modern America"(25)

The Civil War has been characterized as "the Second American Revolution," suggesting that the course of the nation was abruptly altered.(26)

Perhaps, but for those living day by day in the Civil War era, the changes were not so far-reaching, nor the coming of better times so predictable.

In 1860, Indiana's economy was based on agriculture and when the eleven southern states seceded, many traditional markets were closed to farmers in southern Indiana.(27) Fortunately, the Alford farm was situated seven miles south of the east-west Ohio and Mississippi Railroad. This line was completed in 1857 and connected Cincinnati, Vincennes, and St. Louis.(28) The Alfords, therefore, had direct access to the expanding eastern and western outlets.

Corn and pig production was the primary output of Indiana farmers and it is known from the Alford letters that their farm operation involved feeding fifty-five hogs with the corn grown on their land. The Alfords sowed wheat in the Fall for which there was a broadening market in the west and northwest.(29) Also, the Alfords may have obtained cash for their timber and possibly even wildlife hides. As related in the letters, some funds were received through cash rent of their land. Franklin also earned income by contracting out his threshing machine or "separator." In various forms, the Alfords' livelihood was tied to the agricultural economy. (There was a coal vein below their land, but probably unknown at the time.)

There were some in Indiana who foresaw the impending changes. One historian has written, "Enterprising Hoosiers were not slow to catch the dynamic spirit of industrial capitalism."(30) It seems that Franklin and Warren Alford were keenly alert to the benefits of capitalism. For example, they owned a relatively large, revenue-producing farm, 422 acres. Secondly, Franklin purchased labor-saving machinery (one of a kind in the county). The machinery was not only used for harvesting his crops, but he engaged in jobs for other farmers. Lastly, the Alfords reflected the "spirit" of capitalism when they frequently borrowed money, loaned money and transferred notes.

During the first year of the Civil War, however, there were many economic hardships for Hoosiers. There was a scarcity of goods, and prices rose dramatically. From Spring to Fall 1861, a barrel of flour went from $5.25 to $6.25. Salt jumped from $1.80 to $2.50 a barrel. Tobacco users were hard hit as a pound went from fifteen to forty-five cents – a Spanish "cegar" went for a dollar. Eggs, on the other hand, held their price at eight cents a dozen. The price for beef, likewise, held steady at from five to ten cents a pound.(31)

In 1861, the prices farmers received for their products were erratic although they would rise sharply by war's end.(32) In December 1861, Franklin wrote of hog prices being "low" at $2.75 a hundred-weight. By 1865, the price was $7.08 a hundred-weight.(33) Franklin wrote he was going to hold his wheat until mid-winter (of 1861-1862) when he thought it would reach $.75 a bushel. In 1864, it went to $1.75.(34) As for corn, the Alfords evidently did not sell their crop but rather fed it all to their hogs. Franklin, however, bought corn in November 1861 for $.50 a bushel; in 1865, corn sold on the market for $.95 a bushel.(35) (It should be noted that farm prices, in general, plunged after the War.)

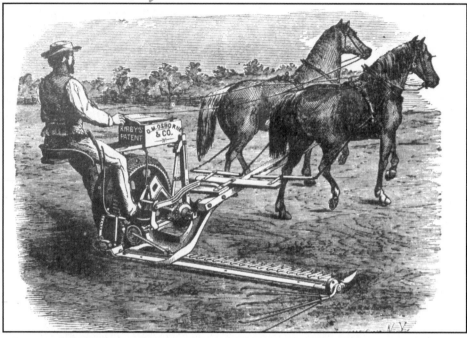

A Mower or Cutter. *(Farm Inventions in the Making of America)*

A Reaper or "Machine" – A Mower with a Gathering Action.
(Farm Inventions in the Making of America)

The Alfords' use of farm "machinery" is atypical for the time. Most agricultural implements for plowing, planting and harvesting were not mechanical. Plow shoes were metal, probably iron rather than steel. Corn and wheat typically were sown by hand although horse-drawn, sulky, mechanical planters were available. A man on foot could plant two to three acres of corn a day, and with a horse-drawn implement, twice that much. The normal corn yield was thirty to fifty bushels to the acre. The wheat yield was about seventeen bushels per acre.(36)

In the Fall of 1856, Franklin took possession of a threshing machine at a rail head in Vincennes, some thirty miles from Alfordsville. On his way home he became engaged in threshing other farmers' wheat for six cents a bushel. His threshing jobs became so overburdening that he protested that he could not get his own work done. The other farmers volunteered to sow his winter wheat, if only he would keep threshing. Franklin did not finish threshing until Christmas. At another point (date unknown), Franklin and a neighbor bought the first mowing machine in the area, the "Ohio Clipper."(37)

In spite of new labor-saving devices coming into use, "the times" were not good in the early 1860s. As the Alford correspondence exemplifies, families were separated, anxiety consumed human energy and death was an unavoidable specter. In Indianapolis, coffins lined the streets near the Union Station as corpses were transferred from train to train. Gambling, drinking, brawling and prostitution became commonplace. People became hardened to death and the lessening of moral standards.(38) Everywhere the abnormal became normal.

Perhaps later, life returned to "common" for some, but not for the Alford family. Before the War, they seemed to be effectively preparing for the future, but all that changed. The War had a catastrophic effect on their worldly paths.

Endnotes

(1) A chapter title from Shelby Foote's *The Civil War A Narrative* (New York, 1958) v. I.

(2) *ORs*, v. II, p. 202. For a full and detailed description, refer to Jack Zinn, *The Battle of Rich Mountain* (Parsons, West Virginia; 1971).

(3) Frederick H. Dyer, *A Compendium of the War of the Rebellion* (reprinted Dayton, 1979), p. 970.

(4) Thomas L. Livermore, *Numbers and Losses in the Civil War in America* (reprinted Dayton, 1986), p. 77.

(5) *Ibid.*, p. 78.

(6) E.B. Long, *ibid.*, passim. Two illustrated histories of the War in western Virginia are of interest, both by Stan Cohen, *The Civil War in West Virginia (Charleston, 1985) and Pictorial Guide to West Virginia's Civil War Sites* (Charleston, 1990).

(7) Baxter, *ibid.*, p. 49. Also, quoted in Tim McKinney, *Robert E. Lee and the 35th Star* (Charleston, 1993) p. 63. Lambert's description of the situation on Cheat Mountain was dated August 7, 1861 and appeared in the August 14, 1861 issue of the *Indianapolis Journal.*

(8) *History of Greene and Sullivan Counties*, *ibid.*, p. 125.

(9) *ORs*, v. V, p. 187.

(10) Quoted in Zinn, *ibid.*, p. 16.

(11) Quotation found in Baxter, *ibid.*, p. 64. This was the order given by Colonel Kimball to Captain Brooks of Company C at the Battle of Greenbrier River, October 3, 1861. The order was remembered and documented by Isaac Crim, Company C, 14th Indiana Infantry.

(12) *History of Greene and Sullivan Counties*, *ibid.* Quote from E.H.C. Cavins, written and published in 1884 as an excerpt from his diary.

(13) Jack Zinn, *R.E. Lee's Cheat Mountain Campaign* (Parsons, West Virginia; 1974) pp. 146-170. Also McKinney, *ibid.*, and Richard Blair Boehm, "The Civil War in Western Virginia: The Decisive Battle of 1861" Doctoral Dissertation, Ohio State University, 1957. All provide excellent detail. Broader reporting may be found in general Civil War histories; e.g., Boyd B. Stutler, *West Virginia in the Civil War* (Charleston, 1966).

(14) *ORs.*, v. V, pp. 186, 187.

(15) Dyer, *ibid.*, p. 971 and Boehm "The Civil War in Western Virginia: The Decisive Battle of 1861" p. 101. There is still a controversy about the numbers involved. See Zinn's summary and analysis, *ibid.*, pp. 149, 150.

(16) William Landon, "Letters from Cheat Mountain," *Indiana Magazine of History* (Indianapolis, December 1933), v. XXXIX, n. 4, p. 365. These letters were first printed in the *Vincennes Western Sun*.

(17) After the battle, Reynolds described this operation as (only) an "armed reconnaissance of the enemy's position." See ORs, v. V, p. 220 for the full report.

(18) A quote of an "Indiana soldier" in Stutler, *ibid.*, p. 111. Also found in *The Soldier of Indiana*, *ibid.*, pp. 90, 91.

(19) ORs, v. V, p. 222.

(20) The "Return of Casualties" table found in the ORs, v. V, p. 223 is incorrect for the returns of the 14th Indiana. Warren Alford's accounting, and Colonel Kimball's report found in ORs, v. V, p. 222, are consistent.

(21) Judson Kuppenheimer diary entries. Unpublished typescript in Vigo County Library Archives, p. 11. Kuppenheimer had been troubled when he learned that Germans were serving in the opposing army, "I am ashame of such a country men," he recorded.

(22) ORs, v. V, p. 229. When it came to reporting casualties, high-ranking officers were as prone to exaggerate as the enlisted men. The opposing generals in this battle reported the casualties as follows: Union General Reynolds estimated the Confederate loss at 300. Confederate General Jackson put the Union losses at 250 to 300. The actual total losses, killed, wounded and missing, on both sides, was less than 100.

(23) ORs, v. V, pp. 221, 222.

(24) In June 1863, this region became part of the "northern" state of West Virginia.

(25) From the title of a Leonard P. Curry book entitled *Blueprint for Modern America: Non Military Legislation of the First Civil War Congress* (Nashville, 1968).

(26) James M. McPherson, *ibid.*, pp. 452, 453.

(27) Thornbrough, *ibid.*, p. 192. Only one-third of Indiana land (approximately) was under cultivation. There are no precise "cleared land" figures available for Daviess County in 1860. It is possible, however, to get an appreciation for the general terrain features through some government surveys published in 1875. Martin County, to the east of Daviess, was 59.1 percent timberland and Dubois to the south was 56.7 percent wooded. See note, p. 365.

(28) *Ibid.*, p. 406.

(29) *Ibid.*, pp. 369, 381 and William O. Lynch, "A Glance at Indiana History," *Indiana Magazine of History* (Indianapolis, March 1937) v. XXXIII, n. 1, p. 60.

(30) Kenneth M. Stampp, "The Impact of the Civil War upon Hoosier Society," *Indiana Magazine of History* (Indianapolis, March 1942), v. XXXVIII, n. 1, p. 9. Also see Steinson, *ibid.*

(31) Unpublished essay in the Community Affairs, Special Collections section of the Vigo County Library. No citation for author or date.

(32) Thornbrough, *ibid.*, p. 390.

(33) *Ibid.*, p. 392.

(34) *Ibid.*, p. 391.

(35) *Ibid.*, p. 390.

(36) *Ibid*, pp. 374-380.

(37) Houghton, "Memoriam," eulogy of Franklin Alford, *ibid.*
Threshing machines were essentially a large rotating, horizontal wheel pulled by a team of horses. Thornbrough, *ibid.*, p. 377. The "Ohio Clipper" probably utilized a vibrating sickle bar and merely cut the wheat. Thornbrough, *ibid.*, p. 376.

(38) Stampp, *Indiana Politics During the Civil War, ibid.*, p. 187

CHAPTER

3

[From Father and Mother to Warren :]

Loogootee Oct 14th J Warren Alford

Dear Sir

This morning I have taken leave of your Brothers Wayne and Lafayette and also your Uncle Bill Gilley and your cousins John W and James M Alford . . . and Clem and some others. [They] are Recruits for Co C [actually Company E] of the 6th Reg of Ind Volunteers under (Col) Critendon [Thomas Turpin Crittenden from Madison, Indiana] and (Capt) Charles R Vantrees [Van Trees from Washington, Indiana]. The (Reg) is stationed in the advance in Ky on the Road leading from Louisville to Nashville beyond Elizabethtown. I will give you further particulars as fast as I get them. I think they will right to you at the earliest opportunity. I must bid you adieu for the present hopeing to be remembered to all our friends and that you will . . . wright often and that you will Pray oft and earnest [for] us all and rest assured we will do the same for you. nomore but remains your kind Father and Mother until death.   F Alford and Mary Alford

Brigadier General Thomas Turpin Crittenden, First Colonel and Commander of the Sixth Indiana Infantry. (Briant's History of the Sixth Indiana)

★

[From Father to Warren:]

Home Oct 18th 61
James Warren Alford

Dear Sir
I am happy to be able to say to you this Morning that we yet
enjoy common health and the hope of immortality beyond the grave
where we will have no aching hearts on account of the absence of
friends and relatives if we all act the Christian part in the great
chance of this life. And also that we received your very kind and
also verry interesting letters of the 6th inst. All of which came duely
to hand at the propper time and very much revived us in our lonely
condition to hear that you still survived the perrils incident to A campaign in the valleys and on the rugged Mountains of Western
Virginia. I do not think you vain enough to think I am useing flat-
tery when I say to you that it gives me pleasure to know that your
Letter is received and read with interest by the friends generally.
You will have heard before this comes to hand that your Brothers is
gone into the service in the 6th Reg under Col Crittendon [regimental
commander Crittenden] and Capt Charles R Vantrees [company commander Van Trees]. [The boys are] now in the advance of our Army
in Ky. I have not heard from them sinse they left. I hope they have
written to you before now. I think I shall get A letter from them
tomorrow and I will then be able to give you somethng more satisfactory. I am glad you have not forgotten your duty to the Bible union
but I fear they have forgotten you for we have not had A Quarterly
sinse you left home. And I am of the opinion it would not be verry
likely to go safe [in the mail] if I sent it but If you think It best we
will attend to It when we hear from you again. Capt Bryant [of the
18th Indiana] is at home on Furlough. He is not verry well and says
a good many of his men has been sick. Your aunt Eliza and Susan
Goldsmythe was up to [see] him yesterday and got back their for last
night. I think they were all (the Alfordsville boys) able for duty
when he left. They were about 50 miles north of your Uncle
Harmons [in Missouri]. I have not had a line from him sinse about
the time you left home. I am sorry that I connot wright but it is
about Mail time. Give my love to all the Boys also to you officers but I
must bid you adieu for the present.

F Alford

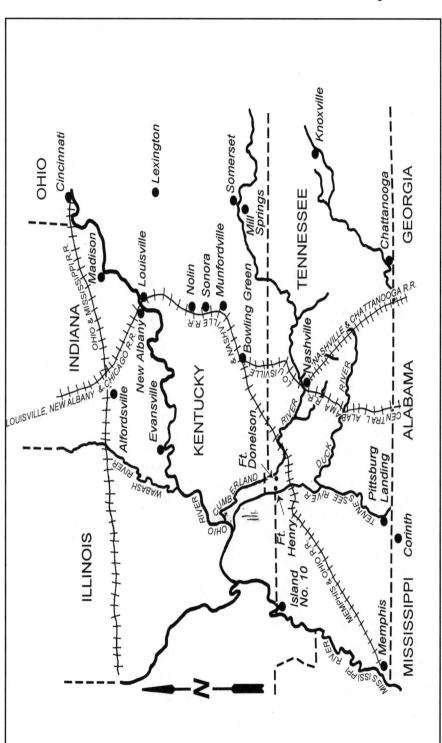

Kentucky and Tennessee, Wayne and Lafayette Alford's Area of Activity, 1861-1862.

★

[From Wayne to Father:]

Camp Nolind
Oct 15th 1861

Franklin Alford. Dear I embrace the first (Father) oportunity of
informing you that We have arived Safe. And So far as I Have
experienced yet I think I shal be Well pleased. One of our men
slipped off at Albany [New Albany ?] and the Captain had to Stay
untill this eavening to hunt him up. But I look for him Down to
Night. The Regiment are on Dress Perade While I am Wrighting. I
Have but little time to Wright this eavening as We are to Be Mustered
into the Service as Soon as Dress Prade is over and are uniforms are
ready. ... I suppose We will get them this eavening. ... We only
arived about one Oclock. Our mess is those who went with us from
Home and Clem Reily.
[Writing the next day, October 16, 1861:]
I must commence to Complete my letter this Morning. We were mus-
tered in yesterday and have received our Cloths our uniform Consists
of 1 pair pants, 2 shirts, 2 pair of Drawers, one under Coat, one over
Coat, 1 Rubber, & one Heavy Woolen Blanket. We will get our caps
and our guns today. I suppose as for our Socks and Shoes we will Not
take them. I Suppose our [new] Drawers is far much better for
Winter than ours. We will Send ours home. I suppose it is quite
Likely that I will come home in the course of 1 or 2 weeks for Some
More recruits. But it is Not certain yet Benjamin [Gilley, a cousin, also
in the 6th] Rote to his family before we got our uniforms. So you
Can just tell them how we are fixed and he Will Write the particulars
in A few Days. As We came Down on the Cars I Brought the ...
Navy revolver and Let Lafayette have mine. I shal Bring My letter
to a close but I must tell you that We had a fine singing Last night
and Several of the boys Came to hear us Sing. As ever Your Dutifull
Son. Wayne Alford I Cannot Write the particulars now as we are
fixing up our things. I will Wright you in a few Days. Ben Sends a
few Stamps home in his letter. They are old Stamps and they wont
go in Ky. ... When you wright Direct your letter to Camp Nolin
Hardin County Ky 6 Indiana Regiment in care of Captain C R
Vantrees [Van Trees].

★

[From Warren to Father and Mother:]

Huttonsville [Va.] Oct 16th 1861

Dear Father & Mother

It is with pleasure I embrace the present opportunity to once more drop you a few lines. I have received three letters from home since I have written all of which gave me great pleasure to hear from home and friends once more. I should have written before this time but I have not been well for a few days and thought I would not write until I got better. I am better now and think I will be able for duty in a few days. The Dr Said I had a slight attack of the Camp fever. We have left the mountain and dropped back 13 miles to a litle vilage called Huttonsville. We are situated in a beautiful valley Called Tigargts valley [Tygarts Valley] on a small River of the same name. There has nothing of importance transpired since the fight at Greenbriar [except that] we have got our new Cloths and received our pay up to the 1st of Sept. I expect to send mine home by Mr Long and you can get it and use it to the best advantage. Long has not reached here yet but is looked for today. Our brigade is all together for the first time since we have been in the service. The post we left on the mountain is now under Command of Gen [Robert] Milroy [from Rensselaer, Indiana]. He had 4 regiments, the 24th and 25th Ohio, and 32nd Ohio and 9th Ind. There is great rejoicing among the boys since they got their money. It jingles around as if every one was ritch. I was glad to hear that the boys about town were so patriotic as to undertake to rais a company there. I wish them great success. The amount of money I will send home will be $70. As I have nothing new to write I will close for the present. Hoping to hear from you soon. I am as ever your affectionate Son. J. W. Alford

Franklin Alford & Mary Alford
Alfordsville
Daviess Co.
Indiana

[From 12-year-old Hellen Alford to Warren:]

Alfordsville Davies Co indiana
Oct the 18 1861

Dear brother. I now take the opertunity to wright you a few line to let you know that i am well at present and hope these few lines will find you well. This is a rainy day here and it is a bad day on the poor soldiers. Warren we herd that the soldiers that is their had to stay their all winter and i am afraid you will all freez to death. I am at school today. Wayn and lafayette and john william and madison Alford is gon to kentucky with charley vantress. And we expect to get a letter from them tomorrow and we are verry lonsom now at home. I went up to loogootee to see [?] last Saturday night. Doctor mitchel made a speech down at the union meeting house and he pretended to be a union man but i dout his being a union man very mutch myself. We herd yesterday that math stafford kild cap brooks but i dont believe it. Wright to me soon. So good by.

James Warren Alford
from hellen Alford

★

[From Lafayette to Father:]

Camp Indiana [near Nolin, Kentucky]
October 20th 61

Dear father   I take this oportunity this good Lords day morning to let you know that I am well [and] hoping this will find you enjoying the same heven favord blessing. Father I am enjoying my self very well. The boys were allout on picket for the last twenty four hours but have just arrived. We [are] going to fit up our camp to day. While I writte the offisers are staking out the goand [grounds] for it. The oficers apointed me sixth Corporal. We had fine battlion drill yesterday evening and [there] was A fine lot of sitizens out. Colonel Critendon [Crittenden] tis A very fine looking man. And allso Lieutenat Colonel Prather [from North Vernon and] our adjutant [John Earnshaw from Madison]. [All] are fine looking men. ... I understand the sesseh have... A strong [position] at Bowling green [Kentucky] on green river. [Actually, the Big Barren River.] I [heard] they have blown up the gariston bridge there. Our pickets and [the Confederate pickets] are in site of each other. ... General Sherman [William Tecumseh Sherman] was here once. ... [This is some of the roughest country I have seen] since I left home. ... We came through A tunnel one nite. ... We have some hard times but we have plenty to eat. It is very fine wether now. We have beaf some times, pork, we have potatoes, Rice, Coffee, ... Crackers. We have soap to wash with. We have daily males. I will express our Cloths home. You can pay the expressage among you when it gits there. I have directed Clement

Reily [to] write soon. Tell all of the friend to write. My love to all. [Pray] for me often. Nothing more only Remains your affectionate son. Lafayette Alford

★

[From Warren to Father:]

Huttonsville Oct 20th 1861

Dear Father

    I embrace the presant opportuinty to write you a few lines in answer to your kind and ever welcome letter which reached me in due time. It gave me great pleasure to hear that you were all well and in as good circumstances as the hard times will admit of. I am not very stout but am mending some since last I wrote. Mr Long has reached here and I got my things you sent me which I was very glad to receive although I guess our condition with regard to clothing was not so bad as it has been represented to you. I [sent home] $20.00 with Mr Long $5 of which is Virgels [Virgil Alford] for you to hand to his Mother. I send a Receipt against a note that Brooks held against virgel. . . . I want you to get the note first opportunity. . . I want it to be [made] right for fear of accident.

As ever Your Affectionate Son.
J. W. Alford

F. Alford

★

[From Wayne to Warren:]

Home
Alfordsville Ind
October 25/61

    Mr Warren Alford   Dear Sir

I am Hapy to have another opportunity of Writing you a few lines from our old and pleasant home. We are all Well So far as I know at present. I suppose you will be a little Surprised when I tell You that Lafayette & myself are in the United States Service With John William [and James] Madison [each an Alford and each a cousin] & B F Gilley [Benjamin, an uncle]. We volunteered Last Monday. [We have been] 1 week in Capt Charles R Vantrees [Van Trees'] Company [E] in the 6th Indiana Regiment. It is now in hardin County K Y. We started Last Monday 1 week for the Camp and arived Tuesday at

1 oclock P.M. And the same eavening We received our uniforms, Blankets [etc.] & Could have got our guns if we had time. We get the Belgian Rifle. The Best guns it is Said in use. It throws [?] ounce Ball level 1000 yards. I think that the 6th Indiana is the Best equipped of any Regiment in the Service and I think our Captain is hard to beet and our company is very Civil. But you May Be ready to inquire How I Hapened to wright from home. Well I will tell you, our regiment ocupies the advance post of General Shermans Division . . . . She [was] reorganized after the 3 Month Service [for three year service.] Several of the Companies Were not [filled]. I & the Captain Came in after recruits and we went out with him and When we got their the Company was not yet full & they Sent me Back for [more] recruits. I Shall Start for Camp again Next Monday. I was at Loogootee Last eavening When Captain Brooks arived. You can Scarcely imagin How glad we were to Se him and to Have News Direct from your Camp. We received your Letter By his hand and will get your Money as Soon as He can get a Little rest & time to count it out. Capt Briant [Bryant of the 18th Indiana Infantry] is at home at present. He has Been unwell But since His arival His health has improved. His boys have [been sick a lot] Since they went to Missouri. But they are all Better at present. Robert Porter is at Home also. He has been laying at the point of Death for Some time but is able to Walk about Now. He has a furlow till the 20th of Next Month. I would Like verry much to see you & be with you if we had not got into the 6th Regiment we would have Certainly have gone with you but it was so Cold Where you are that one Not Being used to the Climate would Certainly Be Sick & besides that we get a good chance where we are. The Company was Dated the 14th of September and we get that Months pay the Same as those who were out. I think from the Signs of the times your Regiment will be apt to Come K Y to winter. If So we may get to see each other. I Hope you will come to K. Y. for it will be more pleasant than in Virginia. As I told you before I expect to Start for Camp Next monday & Dr Laverty, William A Inman, William Stafford, Wm Reily & Some 2 or 3 others that you do not Know. L R Stuckey Says he is going but I dont believe a word of it though he may be Next. I Suppose I will wright from Camp. I Believe I Have Nothing more that would Interest you Much. At any rait I will Defer it for the present. I think if you do Come to Kentucky you Would fair Much better than you Do in virginia. I have Nothing More of interest to Wright. I Believe the boys all as well Satisfied as [can be] expected. . . . I hardly know Where to tell you to Direct your Letter for I expect the Regiment will move before I get Back but you may Direct your Letter to Camp Nolin Hardin County K. Y. 6th Regiment Indiana Volunteers T. T. Crittendon [Crittenden] Colonel in Care of Captain Vantrees [Van Trees]. They say the Letters are More apt to go if you Wright the Colonels Name on them. Father Said put

in a word for him but I Hardly know what to Say only that they are all well & He & Mother are going up to see Capt Brooks. Give My love to vergil [Virgil Alford] and all the rest of the Boys and tell them that I would Be glad to see them all. This leaves me all right. I remain as ever your affectionate Brother unill Death.

Wayne Alford

★

[From Wayne to William R. Houghton:]

Home October 26t 1861

William Houten   Dear friend

For the third time Since you Have been in Virginia I am seated to Wright to you. I answered your Letter & Have Watched the post office Since. Verry anxious to hear from my old friend but as yet have not received one word & I am fast coming to the conclusion that You Did not get my letter or else you were foregetting your old friend and associate. And as I Did not know when I would have another Chance to wright from Home I thought I would Let you know I had not forgotten You. Nearly 5 Months has passed away Since I have Saw you and several [of the] Dear[est] friends as I have on earth. It is unnessessary to go into the Details particularly of what we are Doing as you can see from Warrens Letter that I am in the army trying to Help the friends of our country in their time of Need. I tell you William that Boys are very Scarce around here at this time. Those who stay are Not much for fight any way you take them. We are greatly lifted up Down in K. Y. at the Idea of your Regiment Comeing Down their for we think if any Regiment Needs rest it is the 14th Indiana. It is also Said that the 18th & 24th Indiana regiments are comeing from Misourie. If So it may Be that we may Meet our friends at Last. I hope it May be so but we cannot tell for a while. Having written Warren a Long letter I have Not much to wright unless I Should wright the Same to you. I tell you Will it is Sum [something] to go to Church in this Country Now and Just see 25 or 30 Girll their and only 3 or 4 Boys. . . . The girls say they are Not going to Marry untill the war is over. I tell them I guess they wont be apt to for there is No Boys left except a few who are afraid of _____ and [the girls] wont have them. . . . It Seams to be the opinion of a great many people that the war will Soon be over. As for my part I cant tell. I Hope it may & if So we may enjoy many pleasant hours together yet I must Bring this to a close. Excuse my Bad Spelling and Bad Grammar. This Leavs me well. I remain as ever you sincere friend and Brother.

P. S. When you Right direct you Letter to Wayne Alford Camp Nolin Hardin Co K Y 6th Regiment Indiana Volunteers Colonel T. T. Crittenden care of Captain Vantress [Van Trees].

[From Warren to Father and Mother:]

Huttonsville va.
Oct 28th 1861

Dear father & Mother

I received your kind letter yesterday which gave me great pleasure. And now embrace the oppotunity of answering it. I am not very well yet but so as to be going about a little. It appears as if I mend very slow But it is easy to account for that considering the exposure a sick soldiers has to under go. I am not dangerously bad by any means So you need not be at all uneasy about me. I will try to write as often as once a week and if at any time I should get worse so as to require my removal you shall know it immidiately. It is the general suppostion here that we will not stay here this winter whether there is any certainty in this or not I cannot tell. We are not making any preparations as yet for wintering here. But they have their winter quarters almost complete on the mountain and are laying in supplies for the winter. I received a letter from Lieut. Mc[?] & Aunt Emily and also one from Hannah and will answer them as soon as I can but cannot answer them at present. I do not think you have received my letters regular as you should. I have not received any letter from Wayne yet. If you have let me know how he is getting along in your next [letter]. As for you sending my quarterly pay for the Bible Union I dont know as it would be prudent to do so. If they stop the paper on the same principle. I have a right to stop the pay. I suppose you have seen and conversed with Capt. Brook[s] before this time. And he can tell you a great deal more verbally than I can tell you on paper. I long for the time to come when this unholy rebellion may be put down; and peace may prevail thoughout these once united and happy states and when friends may be permitted to meat again and enjoy the society of those we so dearly love.   I am ever your affectionate son.

J. W. Alford

F. & M. Alford

[From Father and Mother to Warren:]

Home Oct the 29th 1861

Mr J Warren Alford   Dear Sir   We are all well but rather lonesome on account of the absence of your selfe and your equally Patriotic Brothers but whilst in our lonelyness we cannot but Mourn your absence yet on the other hand we are rejoiced to know that our boys is not likely to disgrce the patriotic names of Revolutionary sires which they were. We received your verry kind and affectionate let-ter which gave us great pleasre to hear from you again. And that you were even as well as you were and we hope by this time you may be quite well. I received a letter by the hand of Capt Brooks and also your Money. I expect to use it in payment of the Note which I gave to the men of whom Prater bought the Iron in consideration of which I got yours. If he does not redeem it I shall make $25 in the transaction. Hedrick has traded Hannah Moran about Ten dollars on you. I have not saw him lately. When I see the wrightings I will examine the work and I will be able to give you more satisfactory information about how he is progressing. If he does the work accord-ing to the contract I will try to perform your part. I havent Collected but about 40 cts [percent ?] of our Thrashing accounts since you left. We are feeding 55 Hogs. They have Eat all the old Corn and the 10 Acres nearest your Aunt Sarah Anns and have been in the long field about Four days. They are doing verry well and I think they will be fit for Market about the first of December. What the price will be we cannot tell. Wheat is quite brisk and advanceing. T Brooks says hold on till the middle of winter and he will inshure 75 cents. . . . Clem had charged you with $3.00 at Brookses and he paid me the three dol-lars you sent him. I suppose you forgot that Receipt you spoke of but I have the Note.   Frank Noland [recently discharged from the 14th Indiana] is verry low and it is thought he will hardly ever recover. Warren we had fasting and Prair on the 26th of last month accord-ing to a proclamation of the President [Lincoln] and the solemnity that was manifest on that occasion and the fervency of the Prairs of the brethern on that occasion is never surpassed and seldom if ever equaled. I want you as heretofore to be Careful to observe all that the Lord has commanded so that if you should fall we may be in posses-sion of A well grounded hope of your [admission to] the spirit land and as we are not secure from the dangers incident to a Travel through this world of trials I want you to go oft to the throne of Grace and when you ask blessings for yourself do not for get your affectionate relatives and you may be shure they have and will con-tinue to do the same for you. We are going to see Brooks again this 30th morning of Oct for the last time till he sees you again. Your Mother and I have through the kindness of Cap Brooks sent you a few things to Wit, one Pair of Drawers, one shirt, 2 pairs of Socks, one pair of Gloves, and one set of Combs. A pair of Socks and Gloves or mits to Virgil [Alford from] his Aunt Lucyann. Warren you cannot tell how anxious we are to hear from you again. We had a letter from Lafayette last Saturday and he was all right. But I must Close by saying give my love to all the boys likewise Brother Houghton and (Col) Kimball. Wright often and tell us what you have made since you have been out. Yours respectfully. F & M Alford

[From 15-year-old George to Warren:]

Alfordsville Oct the 29th 1861

Dear brother   I am seated at the stand this morning to write you a line to let you now that I am well and hope this [finds] you well. Warren your mule is as fat as a bare and I ride him evry where I go. He is like andys mare. He is kind of a makeshift but he will push down the fense and come home some times and sometimes he runs off but not often. The secesh gits down in the mouth till they thought they had gained a parshiel victory at edwards ferry [referred to as the battle of Ball's Bluff, in Virginia] and they git sorter saucy again. But they had better watch or they might get there selvs into business. Ira Allen was in bartls store and heard Bartl and Jackman talk and he said he was never so mad in his life. James Alford got a letter from John. He said that George and Bill was in the service. Calven and William Alford has gon to (K Y). They are in the Co with Wayne. That only makes 11 of the young Alfords in the Federal army. I believe that I had better go and make out the 12.   150 of Gen [Charles] Fremonts body guard maid a Charge on 2000 Rebbles which was in the battle of Springfield Mo and put them to flight and hoisted the Stars and Stripes in the town that eavning. I am going to chop would for Mrs Seay tomorrow. I would like to have you help Warren. I have not received a line from you yet. I must bring my letter to a close. Write to me soon.   George W Alford

[From 12-year-old Hellen to Warren:]

Home Oct the 29

Mr J Warren Alford   Dear sir   I am now seated at the stand to wright you a few lines. I have nothing much of importance to

wright to you. George and father has rote about all the particular. I
went up to loogootee to see the boys start yesterday. When isaac [?]
started lavina Alford made a geat to do. She sais Oh he has hogs and
Oh he has put up black berrys. Oh ... if you go i will go to and Mrs
seay sais she heard her up to her house. Oh i had like to forgotten
Elizabeth Helen and Clard mcrackin is going to git married tomorrow.
Warren if you do not wright to me i will ... quit for i have wrote so
often and not receiving any answer that i am getting tired. It is not
because i have wrote so often to you but because i have not received
any answer from you. Enough of this i am now going to wright out
a song and send to you. I will bring my letter to a close. Wright to
me son.

From Hellen Alford to J Warren Alford

[From Wayne to Father:]

Camp Ind
Oct 29th/61

Mr Franklin Alford   Dear Father
I am happy to have the privilege of informing you that I arrived at
camp [in] safety and found all the boys well. The boys all Were so
glad to see us come and Learn that all Was right that they all most
[went to] Holloring. We got along first rate on our trip and I find
that they Have been Subjected to verry Severe Disciplin and I find
that they [have] made a great Deal of improvement in Drilling. They
have moved their quarters a little further up on the Hill and
[enlarged] their Camp and we are not Crowded at all Now. We were
out on Dress Parade this after noon & I got to come out for the first
time with the Regiment. When I reached Camp Lafayette Was out of
picket guard & he Does Not get [back] till tomorrow Morning.... he
has charge of a squad & he had Came in for the boys Dinner & I got
to give his Letters. He Likes Camp Life firs rait & is as heavy as ever
he was. It is reported that we are to March tomorrow but I Dont
believe a word of it as their is more tales afloat than is true. Mother
you Need not be uneasy about us as the boys have got along fine
Since I left.... Our mess has the name of the best mess in the
Company. I must bring my Letter to a Close so Nothing more but
remains Your Affectionate Soon untill Deat.   Wayne Alford

[From George to Warren:]

Home Oct the 31st 61

Mr James Warren Alford   Dear sir I now take the opportunity of writeing you a few lines to let you know that I am well and hope if this comes to hand in due time it will find you well. We have got our loft full of hay. I suppose we will get to gathering Corn in a few days. The Boys have all left but the Girls says that they will help us gather our corn. The Boys that went with Capt Mccarty [Eli McCarty of the 42nd Indiana] or most of them that went here have come back on Furlow of six or seven days. Warren the men have most all gon to war but the secessionist and they will nevver go without they can help old Jeff. [Jefferson Davis, the president of the Confederacy]. Father has sold Waynes Horse to Grandfather Alford. Old ton is dead and he had to have another one. Father got the promise of $80 for him it was thought that Frank Noland was dying yesterday morning but he was not. They are looking for him to dy every day. I would not have written this but I thought you would get tard of waiting for a letter. I rote one and gave it to Capt Brooks and he was going to stay longer than he thought. So no more but remains your affection-ate brother untill death.

George W Alford

[On the same paper, Franklin to Warren:]

Warren   We have put Two of Three letters into Capt Brookses hands and he has not returned as soon as we expected and I fear you have become anxious to hear from home again. We hear that there is some probability of you getting to come to Kentucky. I hope it may be so we are verry anxious to hear from you again. Do not think it strange if you do not get as many letters from home as you have heretofore for I shall have to wright to your Brothers occasionally. And you know I am verry slow but I will wright as oft as I can. I think as often as once A week. Brother Seay rote to his Wife to have Prair meeting at his house on the Night of the 30th of Oct for the spe-cial benefit of the Soldiers. Your Mother and I were there and A fine Congregation of Interesting young Ladies. Yes and I believe I should have said interesting Christian Ladies for they acted there part nobly on that Solemn occasion. Your uncle Wayne and Slater were both there and engaged with the congregation in solemn Prair for all mankind and especialy for the brave soldier Boys who have volun-teered to our rights. I shall have to close this letter for the want of time hopeing that you will pardon me for not filling my sheet and wrighten soon. Give may love to all the boys and rest in hope of my Prairs for your health and success dureing your absence from home.

If you should chance to get to come into Kentucky I will try to come and see you if I can get off. Ever your affectionate Parent in hope of eternal life.

Franklin Alford

[From Lafayette to Father:]

Camp Hosier
Oct 31st 1861

Mr F Alford   Dear Father   I take this opportunity of Wrighting you a few lines in answer to your verry welcome Letter wich I received by the hand of Wayne. It found me well and I was glad to hear from you & to Learn that you were still well and getting Along as well as Could be expected. Our Chaplain Came on Last Lords day. And our Mess had been Singing Some since we Came in Camp.   And our Lieutenant Colonel Prather brought him up and gave us [an] introduction to him & he invited us to Sing for him. So we went Down and Sung for him & he made a verry good preach and he gave out that he would Distribute testaments to all the boys & at 8 in the eavening he organized a Regimental Church. He Said . . . the Apostale Creed. I will give it Near as I Can from memory. We believe in the Supremacy of our Savior & that He was Born of the Virgin Mary & that He was Crucified and buried & arose from the Dead for our Sins. After He Had received Some 40 or 50 Members from all denomina- tions and Some from the World He Received them allowing them to retain all their peculiar Chucrh views But were to Lay them aside for the time and Live together as Christians untill the Close of the war. In taking them in He Was to place opposite their Names the ini- tials of their Different Chuches & then He would wright to the Pastor of their Congregation stating [their] Behavior as Christians & those He received from the world he would Baptise any way they Chose and at that time 2 Universalists Came forward & for their special benefit He Struck out the Reserection & Received them on their terms. But as for our mess we Didnt feel Disposed to go in on them terms & so we just Stayed out. I did not think you would . . . approve of it & so I thought I would write to you about it. I was very thankful for the good advice you gave me and will try to [use] it to the best advantag possible. We pulled up stakes yesterday and Moved back on the North side of Nolin Creek about 1/2 mile East of our old Camp. The reason for Crossing the Creek was because This Creek in time of Hy Water Rises over the face of the earth & we were the only regiment that were across the stream & we were afraid that in time of hy Water

we might be Cut off. . . . We are still in the Advance of all the other
Regiments. We Can Look North Allmost as far as we can See and See
Nothing but Soldiers tents & to the East we are allmost in Sight of
Rousaws [General Lovell Rousseau's] Brigade. I suppose their is 20,000
Men in a few miles of us. Tell Charley and Minerva that I am all
right and that I should Like to have Him along With us but I Suppose
that It is best for Him to Stay as it is Coming Winter fast now.
Wayne sends His Love to all the friends. Especialy to the relations and
take a double portion for your self. Nothing More but remains your
affectioante Son until Death.

Lafayette Alford

Direct to Camp Hosier Near Nolin Hardin County K.y. 6th Regiment
Ind Volunteers Colonel T. T. Crittenden in Care of Capt Vantress.

Wright often Let us know How you Do.

Wayne

[From Dr. Laverty to Franklin:]

Camp Hoosier Hardin Co Ky Nov 5th

Mr Franklin Alford
My Dear Friend

According to previous promise I now avail myself of the
presant opportunity of writing you a letter. My health at this time is
not very good at presant but I do not feel like complaining when I see
so many laying around me that seems to Suffer from the Pawley
hand of Disease. And I hope when this reaches you it may find you
and family all Well and the enjoyment of good health. I beleive I
have no news that will intrest you in Particular only that we are
Camped at Hoosier 'and it may be [we] will stay heare some time.
Word has come into Camp today that we will probably go on down to
Bolder [Bowling] Green but I have my own opinion about it for the
presant at least. I found Camp life just as I expect to find it. So you
find my old Friend . . . I have not been Disapointed. I have just came
from the Boys quarters and found them all well and in fine Spirits
[except they were complaining] that their allowance [food] was rather
short tonight. But it was the fault of their Ordily. Some of them wer
giving him particular fits about it. I have been apointed first
Phaysian of the Hospitle [whose] duty it is to go around twise a day
and procribe for the sick. [That is,] At 6 ock in the morning and at 6
ock in the evening. Then we have a Surgeon, also. Their has been
no apointment made, as yet, for assistant Surgeon and I have got the

promise of Promotision as soon as practiable. And then, I [will be] Satisfyed. I am [satisfied] now but Still a person Desires to climb as high as possible. We have 17 Cases now in th Hospitle. I reported all Better but one young man by the name of Roggers. I think he will die. His Sands of life are fast ebbing out and soon he will go the way of all the Earth and die away from home and among Strangers With no kind hand of a Mother to Soothe his Dying Pillow or Sister to administer to his Dying Wants. Poor fellow I pitty him from my heart, and when I See so many come into the Hospitle that it is hard to tell wheather they will ever come out again or not. The [scene sickens] me when I think of it. Well Friend I must Stop writing and go to bed not that I am tired [of] writing to you but I am So tired to night. . . . The whol camps seemes Cheereful tonight and I hope that you are so tonight. The Boys all went out on Scout yesterday and all came in This morning all write. All that happens on the Scout [was] they Brought in three Negroes & one very fine nice hog. I do not know how they happened to get holed of it but they Brought them in. They all send their love to you. Wane Told me he would write to you soon. John Williams [Alford] Send his love to his folks as well as youns. Layfate is well . . . Wm Riley send his compliment. But I must Stop. Farewell my friend. Give my love to Jos McCord & Wife . . . [?] Winter, Chester Camps & Wife and I will stop. Write to me Soon. Farewell. Pray for me & I will ever Remain your Sinceare Friend. Well wishes.

J. L. Laverty

Direct your letter to Dr. Laverty Camp Hoosier Hardin Co Ky 6th Reg In Vol Medical Department in Care of Surgeon Schusler [Charles Schussler from Madison, Indiana]   Remember me to your wife.

★

[From Warren to the family:]

Nov the 5th 1861
Huttonsville Virginia

Dear Father and Mother and brothers and sister. I now take this opertunity to drop you a few lines to let you know that I am still on the mend. I am so as to be up all the time and I hope when this comes to hand it will find you all injoying good health. I have bin looking vary anxious for a letter from you for the last few day. I have not had a letter from Wayne or Lafayette yet. I got a letter that Wayne was at home on the twentieth after Recruits. I Supose you have saw Cap Brooks and talked with him. I supose you did not understand that letter that I sent by brooks to you concerning that

note. I supose you did not get the Receit as we neglected to put it in
but I did not know it till this morning and I do not think it would
be proper to send it in a letter by mall. I see this Morning in the Ind
State Sentinel [an Indianapolis Newspaper] that Secretary Cameron
[Lincoln's Secretary of War] is going to have our brigde [brigade]
Changed from Western Va to Kentucky. I have now Wrote as much
or more than I expected to When [I] Comenced. I shal have to bring
my lette to a close. . . . I hope I we get to kentucky [and] we may get to
come home some time this winter. The weathe [has] bin vary bad in
the valley. . . . Hellen I red your let and liked it vary well. Green I red
your letter and it was vary nice. You and george mus learn fas
when you go to school and you mus work good when you do not go
to school. So I must bring my letter to a Close for the present by saying that I hope we will all Return home safe when [we] may lif the
rest of our time in peac so lon as the good Lord let us live. So nomore
at present but remains affectionat sone in the one hope.

James Warren Alford

[From Father to Warren:]

Alfordsville
November the 7th 61
Dear Sir   We received yours of the 28th by Tuesdays Mail and was
glad to hear that your health was still improving a little. We hope
when this comes to hand you may be quite well. We are enjoying
common health except that I have the Toothache. I have been at
Loogootee to day and send your money to [New] Albany to pay the
Note I gave when I lifted yours of Proctor. I had a letter from
Lafayette bearing date of 31st of Oct in which he gave me the program of the organization of methodist Church in Camp. . . . He said his
mess [mates were] not in [the camp church]. He said he would see
what Father would say about it first. I heard a letter from Wayne
today and they are all right and have about 30,000 soldiers almost in
sight. F Noland is better today I hear. Tell Bro Houghton his folks
were well and that I was much pleased to hear the letter which he
sent to his Cousin F Brooks. Tell Virgil [Alford] his Mother stayed all
night with us last night. When one gets a letter we are all anixious
to hear it. Dr Laverty is with the boys in kentucky and about to get a
position in the Hospital. We have been gathering Corn at Wm Allens
and are about half done. I think we will get about 16 loads [with]
the side boards on [the wagon]. I believe the hogs will eat near 30

acres of that at home before killing time. I think I will try to swap a mule for A good Mare. It is said Fremont [General John C. Fremont] got in sight of the Rebel Army and was preparing to give them Battle when his Command was taken from him. I think it A verry bad move and at the worst time it could have been done.... You must not expect me to be verry lengthy as I have to wright so many.

[Back side of same sheet - Thomas Green Alford is writing:]

Dear brother. I now embrace the oppertanity to inform you tha all is well and hope when thes few lines come in to hand it will find yo well. We received yore verry kind letter on the twenty eight and was glad to hear that you was mending. [I] will have to git hellen to finish my letter for i have to [start] gathering corn now. Warren i made my half hand in the corn field. Charley is helping us gather corn and we make three loads a day and mother and hellen has to do most all the feeding but they do not feel hard of it. We herd [General John C.] Fremont has bin removed when he has bin making preperaton for a battle for four day and night.... [Father now takes over the writing:] I want you to give my love to all the boys of my acquantance and wright as often as you can and let us know how you are getting allong and how all the boys is getting along and how it happens that you sent so much more money home than any of the rest of the boys. The great federal Fleet sailed from Hampton Roads on the morning of the 30th of Oct but her destination is not known yet by us. We hope to be excused for not doing better. So nomore but remains your kind Father & Mother.

F & M Alford

[Now Hellen writes:]

Warren this is Sort of a scrap letter.... We will try and wright you a long one a Sunday. Florian barth came back on a furlow and got sick about the time he was to go back. If you want to wright to wayn and lafayette you must Direct your letter to camp hosier, Near Nolin, Hardin county, Ky, 6th Regiment Ind volunteers Colonel T. T. Crittendon [Crittenden] in care of Capt vantrees [Van Trees]. Wright often. No more.

Hellen Alford

★

[From Wayne to Father:]

Camp Hoosier Hardin County KY
November 7th 1861

Mr. Franklin Alford
Your verry kind and welcom Litter Came to hand & found us all
well. We were verry glad to hear from you & to Learn that you
were getting along So well. I have nothing of importance to wright to
you their has [been] nothing of interest transpired Since Lafayette
wrote you. Only the regiment was on Picket guard Last Monday.
Their is several regiments encamped Close around here & instead of
Each regiment Sending out their own Picket they just Send out a
Regiment at a time & So our turn will come about one every ten
Days. The weather is fine here at this time though we have had one
Rainy Day Since I came in Camp. The Last time I was glad to hear
that you were getting Ready to gather Corn. Hellen Said in her
Letter that Grandfather had taken my Horse & that He was wonder-
fully Pleased with him. Well I think He has a right to be proud of
Such a Horse as He is. Wright to me about how you traided & if
Braxten had Paid you that for me & if Gilbert White Has paid that
He Owes. If he has not & you Need the money tell both of them you
must Have it without fail. I expect the pay master will be around
[as] Soon [as] Our pay Roll is maid out & as Soon as he comes we will
get our money. Yesterday we got the news in Camp that (it was from
the Louisville Journal) General Fremont Has been Superceded by
General hunter [David Hunter] and that He received the Documents
Releving him of his command & that... Right on the Eave of a battle
the rebels Had advanced & Fremont was making preparations to
march out & meet thim. It also stated ... His entire Staff & Body
Guard are to Leave with him & that Several Companies throw Down
their armes & Swore that they would not fight one Lick under any
other General & it was Not untill Fremont Had urged them for the
Sake of their Country Not to Abandon their Country in her time of
need that they could be persuaded to take them up again. You Could
not imagine how it Struck our Camp & Especialy our Company.
Their was Scarcely any thing else talked [about] that evening. Some
Just Swore that they Did wish the whole of the western army would
Lay Down their arms & Not touch them again until Fremont Was
placed back in this position again. But this morning the excitement
has Somewhat abated. The School of instruction of officers both
Commissioned and Non commissioned commenced yesterday (the 6th)
and I had to Stop Writing & Go and Drill & Consequently I am
Somewhat Nervous [today]. But what [you] cannot read you must
guess at & take the Will for the Deed. I Have Nothing more of interest to wright you. Benjamin [probably Private Benjamin F. Gilley]
Wants to know Whether Stafford Has given that Noat Yet or not. Tell

george that Uncle Ben [Benjamin Gilley] Will Send that pistol Home the first Chance. Tell Him & green & Hellen that I Havent time at the present to answer each of their Letters But they must wright as often as they can & you must wright us all of the particulars as they transpire. We are Drilling Verry Steady at this time & I have to wright whenever I can get a Chance. Tell Charles & Minervia that I will wright to them as soon as I can & they must wright to us. I have nothing more of importance to wright to you. The Louisville Legion [officially, the 5th Kentucky Infantry, with artillery and cav-alry] is encamped in Sight of us & while I am writing they are out Drilling with their artillery. They work six horses to each gun and 5 Riders. They go as fast as the Horses can run. It looks right fine you had better believe but I must Close this as this leaves us well. Your affectionate Son.

Wayne Alford

[in the margin]

Direct to Camp Hoosier Hardin County K.Y.   6th Regiment Indiana Volunteeers   Colonel   T. T. Crittenden Care of Capt Vantrees [Van Trees].

★

[From Father to Warren:]

Home November 10th   61

Dear Son   I am again seated to drop you a line to inform you that we still enjoy common health and a very great anxiety to hear of your haveing regained you usual health and vigor. We hope howev-er when this comes to hand it may find you much improved for I feel more concern about your health than any other one thing to which you are exposed. I have writen so often lately that I have nothing new to wright to you. I have just return from Prair meet-ing. . . . The Cumberlands have a meeting of [?] days in progress at the union house and we have to regret that the few brethren and Sisters who are left are so easy drawn off from the place where they should meet and worship according to the Bible. But we believe we could claim the promise of the Lord that where Two or Three are met in my name there am I. When I look around and view the vacant seats of those whose melding strains used to [cheer] me but whose absense now fills my heart with grief and mine eyes with tears. But I still hope the time is not verry far distant when this unholy rebellion may be put down and the society of those whose absense we now

mourn may be to us all a sourse of enjoyment that will be as lasting
as life and joyous beyond description. I had a letter from our friend
Dr Laverty yesterday in which he informs me that he and all the
boys [are] well and he thinks he is shure of a position on the surgical
staff. Wayne and Lafayette should have ritten to you before this and
I hope they have. I swaped your Mule to Wm Lane yesterday for a
bay Mare about fifteen hands high [She will be] Eight next spring.
Very well turned but how she will work I cannot tell you now. We
have heard that [?] and George Gilley were both sick but have not
heard from them for nearly Two weeks. I heard from F Noland last
Thursday and he was better. I hope he may get well yet. I read A letter from your Uncle [?]. He was well and South of the Osage not a
great way from your Uncle Harmons. Tell all the boys that their
folks are all well and [it has been a long time since we have heard
from them,] particularly Virgil [Alford]. Our Cooperation Meeting
commences next Friday but we dont expect such a turnout as we had
Fifteen [a] Month ago. I wish you could be here to swell the audience
and enjoy a season of Religious service with us and observe the [fer-
vor] of the devotion of the Brethren for the protection of the union
troops in their eforts to protect the people in the enjoyment of the libertys garanteed under them by the Constitution. When you wright
again donot neglect to say whether the boys are all well. I donot
think times are quite so dull as they were some time ago. The money
sent home by the soldiers has given some relief and the bouyancy of
the wheat market has left some money in the Country. And all the
good Horses that was in Country has been sold for money at an average of about Seventy five Dollars. I fear that I am doing injustice to
the other boys by wrighting so lengthy to their Elder and much
[longer] absent Brother. But of necessity I am bound to come to a
close but not with out entreating you to wright often if you cannot
be lengthy. So ever remaines your kind Father until death.

Franklin Alford

[From Warren to Father and Mother:]

Huttonsville
Nov the 14th 61

Dear Father and Mother
I Received your vary kind letters. One on the 8th & those by the
hand of Cap Brooks on the tenth which gave me much pleasure to
hear that you was all Well but lonesome. I hope that it will not be
long before we Can be at home agane. We got a dispatch that our

fleet had bin vary sucessful and that the stars and strips flotes agane over [Fort] sumpters walls. You said you wanted me to tell you how much I had made. I drawed 50 fifty Dollars and thirty three cents and I had of the money I bought with me aboute Eleven Dollars. After paying him three Dollars for Clem Reily which you said you got back of Clem. . . . I sold my pistol and [?] for Eighteen Dollars but only got tenn Dollars down. This is how I sent Sixty five Dollars two you. I alowed you needed the money and I did not need the revolver. . . . The eight Dollars is on a mighty good man to be pid now in a few days. Five dollars of that money is virgles [Virgil's]. He wanted you to give it to his mother. I Rote to you in the letter I sent by Cap Brooks but perhaps you did not under stand me. Thomas Brooks Wrote to me that he had paid you the money I sent you and he said that he saw an omitted account on the books and he said that . . . the only way to get money was from them that ode them and Wanted me to send him an order to you for the money. But as [he] told when I was doing the trading that I could [wait] till Christmas. . . . I have made my Calculations to pay at that time and not till then and that I ned all the money that I shal be able to rase. Father you will see him the first Chance you have and tell him how it is with me. He said for me to attend to [it] immediately. I am mending. I think that I shal be able for dewty be fore many days. The rest of the boy are well. I shal bring my letter to aclose as I must write some to the children as they have bin writing me some nice letters. So no more at the present but Ever remain you affectionate son in hope of eternal life.

J. W. Alford
To his Fater and Mother

[Same letter, Warren to brothers and sisters:]

Dear brothers & sister
I now take the presen opertunity to answering you letters. George you said you rode the mule evry place you went you said he was a kind of a roge. . . . You said you was going to gathering Corn in a few days and you would like to have me to help you. I would be glad to help you but as it is I cannot. George you must be a good boy and help father all you Can till we get back home. You must write to me often. I cannot write any more at the presen. Hellen you must not think hard of me for not writing to you. I rote a few lines to you [and] a few to george in my last letter to father. I hope you have it be fore this time. I received you letter and the verces you sent me. I read the lette wich gave me much pleasure. I see from your letter that you are going to School you must be Careful not to idle away your time but make good use of your time as it passes by. For a

moment once gon never returnes. I will not have time to write any more at present. You must be a good girl and help your mother all you Can. Green a word to you. Are you big enough to do big work since the big boys are not their to help you. Do you go out... ofter to see your fetening hogs or is it to fur for you. You must learn fas wen you go to school and you must help father work like a little man and you must be a good boy. I Shal have to bring my letter to a close for this time. You must all wright to me as often as you can so no [more] for the present but ever remains your brother.

James Warren Alford

I Recived Wayns letter by the hand of Cap Brooks and answered it on the twelth. Writing lafayette in the Same. I shal hav to close for want of space and it is nearly dark. Good by

[From Dr. Laverty to Franklin Alford:]

Camp Hoosier Harden Co Ky Nov 16th 61

Mr Franklin Alford
My dear Friend

Having received your kind and ever welcome letter, I seat my self this evening after the labours of another day to answer it. I can assure you, Franklin, that its quite a favour you confer upon me by writing to me and I will try and answer it in Such a way. I am tolerably well, but I do not enjoy as good health as I would like to But then I have no reason to complain. And I was glad to heare that my old friend and family was Well. And I do hope you may still enjoy the Same degree of health and happiness.

I have nothing of news... for you so far as war matters are consirned. Only that we have heard this evening of a Battle neare Bolding [Bowling] Green. Wheather it is so or not I cannot tell But it is courant [current] in Camp tonight. It is said that our Boys done it up to them in the right kind of Stile. I hope it is so. How long we will Stay heare is more than I am able to Say. Report Says not many hours, hence, I give it no Credit The general health of the Regiment is good, we now have about thirty case prescribing for. The old Surgeon [Charles Schussler] has gone to head quarters to make his report and as I understand [it, he is] to be the guests at a Tea party. He is a very fine man, a great Surgeon and a perfect gentleman. But, a perfect Tyrant when his anger is once up. Go to Watson, or Chester Camp and you will find out how the Steward of the Hospitle makes vinegar. I wrote to them and Told them How it was done But I am off My Subject. I do not Care how Tyranical he may be, so that, I get along. He has promised me that he will make me a Surgeon before I leave him, that I nead not be afraid to Show myself among the Faculty. He Frankly confesses that I am hard to beat in the practice of Medicine, But, says he can do it to me in Surgery. While he mite. As I have often told him after an experience of over 40 years He [was] in the Army in Mexico and in the Crimenian [Crimean] War and has attend all the Hospitles of Surgery, he could get to. He says if I . . . get through the War, I shall weare home My Sash as emblimatic of my Station. But this may seem foolish to you and I expect I am Wearing your Patience. Our Boys are all gone out on picket to day and our quarters look rather lonesome But they will be in tomorrow morning. And I can assure you, I will be the first one to see them. I told them this morning before they went out to be carefull of them selves and get back safe. The Boys are all Well, and in fine Spirits. Always in fine Spirits longing for something to do. I begin to heare some of the Boys say that they would like to get home. After I get through with my labours in the evening, I always go up into the Boys tent and we have a rite good time of it, I can assure you. Well Franklin how do you get along anyhow. Is it now verry lonesome at home now. I supose that old Jackman is gassing as he pleases. But his day is comeing I will yet let him know that he has got to [find] some other hole to go into. I have got the promise from the old Surgeon that I shall come home on furlow about the Hollidays. But that will Depend on curcumstances and how we are situated and What we are doing. If we are Buisy in the Hospitle and have had fighting to do I will not get to come home. But, If I never have the priviledge of comeing to my home any more or seeing you all I will try to live so that We may meet in a happier clime. I often think Franklin of the pleasure I have had at home among my friends But those happy day are over with me. No more in all probability will I ever have The pleasure at home I once of had. But I did not come heare to get Killed. I have never regretted the Steps I have taken when my Poor Suffering Country needs my aid. And if I have to die I will endeavour to [live out] my life as dearly as possible. All hail the day that brings peace to our once happy country. But, I must Stop Franklin and get to an oister Supper Prepared for us at the House of a union Lady neare to Camp. My love to all my Friends and reserve a portion for your self. Write to me soon and I will close for the preasant. And now Farewell. My love to Jo & Emmily and nan Winters. Good by. Your Friend

Dr J. L. Laverty

Direct you letter to Dr. Laverty Camp Hoosier Hardin Count Ky 6th Reg In Vol in Care of Surgeon Schussler Medical Department (L)

★

[From William Houghton to Mary Alford:]

Huttonsville Va,
Nov. 17th, 1861

Mrs. Alford
Dear Sister
  I received your welcome but rather unexpected letter this
Morning. [I] was truly glad to get a letter from you as it is the only
one I have received from any Members of the Alfordsville Church
except Wayne, and he, now, is in the field. As regards Warrens health
I suppose you have heard me mention him in my letters home which
led you to suppose that he was worse than he represented himself to
be   However, I can ease your mind from all disquiet - regarding his
present health   He has had a severe attack of Camp fever, which
always prostrates a person very much - causing weakness, general
dibility [etc.] without causing the Patient any suffering. The fever
commonly last about 10 days and renders a person unfit to perform
any service for two or 3 weeks. Warren was taken sick about the time
I recovered from the same disease and was very sick for over a week,
after which he did not seem to gather any strength for several days.
But for a week past he has been gaining fast and looks nearly as well
as I ever saw him look. As a matter of course, he would make the
most favorable report to you that he could. . . . One would rather suffer here alone than to have his friends and Family Suffer along with
apprehension for his safety without any chance of alleviating this dis-
tress - I am happy to say that all the boys from the vicinity of
Alfordsville are in good health - at present - and as a general thing
they have been the best soldiers in the company. I dont think that
Warren even was Sick an hour before this attack since we came into
the Valley. John McCord is out on a scout at the present time, all the
Balance of the Alfordsville Boys are here. All are in fine health and
all hard at work building pens to hold us in this winter. Bolivar
[Gold] & Steph Collins look better than they ever did at home, Virgil
[Alford] has never been sick an hour during the Campaign. We have
been feeding ourselves on the hope that we would be removed from
western Va., and placed somewhere nearer the borders of our Native
State. But the last link was broken this Morning by the news that
the Ohio troops are ordered back to Ohio while the Indiana Troops,
who have suffered all the hardships, toil & suffering of this whole
Campaign are compelled to stand another five months seige of Storm
& cold. No matter, Indiana Troops are made of Iron and of course
must take the hardest places. There is no news of importance going on

at present - The Snow is about five inches deep on the Mountains. The mud about two feet deep in the Roads. You can imagine what an agreeable location we have. On the whole, we are doing as well as Soldiers ought to do, If we are not ordered to Cheat Mountain again which we very much fear. Excuse this desultory and uninteresting letter. I am in a very poor condition to write to day, haveing more to see about than I can easily attend to. If we are permitted to live here this winter after we get settled in our winter Quarters, I would like to hear ofter from my Friends at Home, and shall take great pleasure in writing. Give my best Respects to all inquiring Friends Accept My Kindest Regards for yourself. Hoping this May prove Satisfactory. I subscribe myself your Brother in the one Hope.

Wm Houghton

[From Warren to Father and Mother:]

Huttonsville Nov the 19th 1861

Dear father & Mother
It is againe I embrace another opertunity to in form you that I received your letter dated the 10th yesterday which gave me much pleasure to hear from you and hear that you was all well. I am not vary stout yet but the Doctor says that I only nead time to gaine strength I feel as well as one could expect being as weak as I have bin. Though I have not been so [sick] at any time but what I Could walk a quarter of a mile and back and their has not bin a day but what I have bin up and about more or less. And if I had bin at home I do not expect I would have went to bed unless I had felt worse than I have here. It is true I have bin sick for some time but you know that persons some times have lingering spelles at home. If I should get bad sick you shal know it as son as possible. I have wrote my condition in every letter as nearly as posible. So enough of this you wrote in your last letter that you had traded off the mule. I guess you have got one trobble off of your hands. I hope you have done well in the exchange. I am going to try to get to come home about tenth of next Month but I do not know how well I will succed. For the present Gen Roscrance [William Rosecrans] has ordered no fur lows to be given. I am going to try to get to come. If I do get disapointed it will not be the first time I have bin disapointed. I have not had a word from Wayne or Lafayette yet. Only the letter Wayne Wrote . . . home. I answered it on the next day after I got it. Virgle [Alford] hear [has] been peuny for the last four or five days but is about well now. The rest of boys are all Well. William Houghan is not vary

well at the present time. . . . I shall have to come to a close as I wan to get [this] in todays male. I would have bin glad to be at the [meeting] to [have] joined with you in Worshiping the god of salvation though we Can pray for each other. . . . But remaines your affectionate. Son

                                                    . . . Alford

★

[From George Alford to Warren:]

Mr J W Alford esq

                                        Alfordsville Ind Nov the 20th 61
Dear Sir I am seated to drop you a line to let you no that I am on the Land and with the living yet. And to let you now that I have not forgot you yet nor do I expect to forget you. Uncle Wayne [Alford] got a letter from Wayne on the 17th. He stated that he had a brash of the Colery morbes [Cholera Morbus] the day before but was well at that time. He stated that it was snowing there at that time. I guess there ears will ketch it for they have little caps. I said that Wayne rote to uncle but I believe he has forgotten us for we havent got a letter from him for a good while now.   Warren it is snowing here and I cant write verry good but if you cant read it just whistle and I will come over and read it for you for I would like to be over there any how. There was some Seamen went through Loogootee a few days ago and had like to have tour up the town. They went through Gibsons store and took all the clothing they could find then to Brookses stoar and dun the same then to H Hubtners shop and took all the Boots and shoes that he had then to a grocery there and roold out three barrels of whisk and nocked the head out of to of them and drank what they wanted and took one with them. I dont no whether this is true or not. I suppose it is. There was said to be about 4 or 6 hundred [who] Telegraphed to Loogootee for them to shut up but they did not do it. Give my love to all the Boys and keep a doubel portion for you selfe. Write soon. Write often. Tell virgil [Alford] that I rote to him not long ago and I want him to rite to me soon. Goodby.

                                        George Washington Alford

[On the other side of the same sheet - from Thomas Green to Warren:]

Dear brother   We reived yore kind letter of the 14 and was glad to hear that you was getting well and it found us all well. It was fine weather until last friday and it turned coald. Warren i se in the

papes . . . part of your brigade is cuming to indiana. I would be glad
if it was you. I guess yu will be destined someplace soon. I hear
McClellan [General-in-chief George McClellan] wants you on the potom-
ic [Potomac River]. I hope you will knot go enny farther from home.
Men that preten to know think the thing [is about] to a close. God
speed. . . . Some of the friends received a letter [from] Wayne and lafe
and they was well and Wayne said that thare was a report in camp
that they was to start to bolingreen [Bowling Green] in the morning
of the eightenth. He did not give it much credit. We also received a
letter yesterday from you of aug the 28th. Fathr mailed a letter to
you the day before we recived yurs. He will wright soon. Warreen
mother sent you a pair of drawes, 2 pair of socks, [?], shirt, a pair of
glovs, and hankerchief by mr brooks, 2 combs, and some pins. Did
you receiv them?

[Now from Father:]

I see according to the Commercial [Cincinnati newspaper] that the
union Sentiment is beginning to trouble the cesesh in Virginia, North
Carolina, and Tennessee. And the report is Three Virginia Regiments
have layed down their guns and are returning home and say they
will fight against the government no more. God grant that this may
be true of them and all other rebels soon. Warren I received yours of
the 14th which gave us great satisfaction to learn that you was getting well. But as I sent you a letter on Friday and received yours on
Saturday I will try to answer about next friday. So fare you well.
F Alford

[From Father to Warren:]

Home
Thursday Evening Nov 21st 1861
Warren I am determined to drop you another line to try to comfort
you in your affliction. I have been gathering Corn till my hands is
too sore and stiff to wright but I suppose you are anxious to hear
from home again. We are all in good health and so are all your
friends and relatives. But they are all verry anxious about your
health and I am proud of it. We received your feeble Letter of the
5th Inst on the 19th and you see we were waiting a long time but it
was a verry welcome message. When it came we was doubly glad to
hear that you was mending but I am anxious to hear from you

again. If you are not likely to be able for service soon and wish to Come and rest till you get better at home I will give you all the assis-tance in my powor as you know I would not spare any panes to make you comfortable. Your Brothers are still in Hardin County Ky. I received A Letter from Laverty last Tuesday and he said the boys were all well and in fine spirits. I believe I told in my last that I had swaped the Mule for a Mare. If we are not hindered we will get our Corn in this week. We want to Butcher in about Two weeks. And we will have about 1150 [?] bushels of Corn left. It is time to go to prair and I must quit till morning. We have enjoyed the kind Care of our Heavenly Father in [?] repose through the night and through this Morning [which] finds us in the enjoyment of common health. Warren I have thought for some time that I would go over to your farm and see what Hedrick was doing and wright you all about it and I think I will soon. He is teaching School and I think he would be gald to get along with out clearing the ballance but I will see him and the obligations between you and I [?]. . . . I will then wright to you again on that subject. Our County Meeting came off here last Lords day. We had the labors of Brothers Wilson [and] Trimble and Mathes and you cannot be mistaken when you immagine the [?] with which the Gospel was Preached. The next Meeting of the kind we have will be at Bethany the Second in August. I hope that the pre-sent difficutys may be settled and the Brethren privileged to exchange the toils of the Campaign for the quiet enjoyment of the House of the Lord and all the hosts of God on earth. Cousen James and I have sent on for the dayly Commercial [the Cincinnati *Commercial*] and I hope we will be a bit the better posted for time to come than we have been. When I commenced wrighting the weather was fine but it is now Raining but we do not complain for we have had us a fine A fall here as you ever saw. John & Wm Alford has got back [from the 6th Indiana] and John is going to work at his trade in Alfordsville. The last we heard from . . . [Alexander ?] Camp he was sick some where in Missouri. George Gilley Died at Georgetown about the 20th or last of last Month as did Lawson at St Louis on the 3rd of this Month. Rice Burris, Albert Patrick, A Robertson, John Gold, and Joel Goldsmyth were all sick the last account. And a many more in their Company [which is under the command of] Capt Bryants [All these men were in Company E of the 18th Indiana Infantry.] Milton Jackson died some where in Mo [Missouri] and was brought home and buried this week. Robert Porter is at home on Furlough to recruit his health. [These men were in Company D of the 24th Indiana Infantry.] I want you to wright regularly and if you cannot you have friend who can and in every letter you can say the boys are all well if it be so. My love to all the friends. I have neither time nor space for wrighting more so. . . . Yours truely. Franklin Alford

[From Warren to Father and Mother:]

Huttonsville Nov the 24th 61

Dear Parents
It is agane I am permitted to drop you a few lines to in form you
that I have nearly gained my former state of healt. I am well but am
not so stout yet as I was Before I was taken sick. But I am gaining as
fas as I can expect to. . . . We are tolerable comfortable now we have a
fine plase two [put up] our tent and it makes it a tolerable comefortable. I hope this may find you with all of the friends and Relations
well as it leaves all of Alfordsville boys well but Conolly [Private
Richard H. Conolly]. He has had two Chills thoug he is able to go
about most of the time. The rest of the boys that was sick in the company is now on the mend. Thier is none but houghten [Houghton]
that you are acquaintd with. Houghten is on the mend. He has not
bin much sick, Mathew Stafford is sick. I guess he is not dangerous.
He is at beverly [the town of Beverly in western Virginia]. I will
state some thing of McCords [Private John McCord] and Matheus
[Mathew] Staffords Adventure. I suppose you will hear of it before
this will come to hand. In the first place that you may understand it
their was tenn men taken wit some fifteen or twenty others [and]
went out on the scout and as they went along (the scouts was commanded by a man by the name of Anderson this is the generals aide
camp he has the rank of Lieutenant) and as they went out Stafford
got a little sick and was not able to go with them and thay left him
at a house where they staid over nite. . . . John McCord staid with
him and the next day [they] would have started but for a heavy
Rain that fell that night. The man told them that they could not
Cross the River but if they would go up on the hill they could kill a
deer directly. They went out and was not gon long before it began to
Rain and a heavy fog sprung up and they began to [think] they had
gon far enoug and they began to try to get back to the house and
after they had wandered out for some time they concluded they were
lost. After trying to get back to the house for two days they then
aimed for the tigart [Tygart] valley (this is the valley we are in) and
after wandering about for four days they came in sight of the valley.
. . . After going for six days and five nights without any thin to eat
but one bit of a feasant that one of them killed with a rock. They
just had the hide off and they eat it raw. They left evry thing at the
house but there gunn. They were with out blankets and the snow
fell on the mountain one foot deep. They had now matches the last
night but they hapened on the same fire they had bin by the night

be fore. This was all that saved there lives. The next day the sun
shined for the first [time since] they were lost. By the sun shining
they tuck acros and came to the Valley. If it had not bin clear that
day I supose they would not have got in at all. John McCord joined
the church last night. He thinks that it was only the mercy of god
that saved him. He conclided that God had his life in his hands.
From this time on we will have one more in our mess for preaching
Christianity. From every apearance this Ware will not last long thoug
If it does we are going to try to live as Christians and not as our
brothers have done. They are playing cards evry day. They say for
amusement. His name is barney [possibly Sergeant Barney Berry]. I
shal have to bring my letter to a Close. Hoping to hear from you soon.
Ever remember me in your prairs while I pray for myself.

J Warren Alford

[In the margins:]

I intende to Wright to georg in this letter but I can not Wright for a
few days.

[From Wayne and Lafayette to Father:]

November 24th/61
Camp Wabash Lerue Co Ky

Mr F Alford   Dear Father
Through the mercies [of] a kind Creator I or rather We Will attempt
this Lords day morning to inform you of our Where Abouts & what
we are Doing. We pulled up Stakes at Camp Hoosier on the Morning
of the 21st and Started on a March. We Did not know at that time
[where] we were going. Neither Did it concern us. We were Marching
[and] that was enough for a private to know but the fun of it was
we had not proceeded 1 mile before it began to rain though their was
no Stopping then. Well we Marched about 4 or 5 miles and encamped
but it rained right Strait Down on us all the way & continued to
rain all Day & at night. It turned cold and froze relly Sharp but we
are fixed up now & feel just as well as if we had been Dining at
Some kings parlor & we are all hearty & so you need not be uneasy
about us. Well enough of this. The other Day ex Govenor John
Crittenden [of Kentucky] visited us at Camp Hoosier and we were
called out and the rest of General Rousaws [Lovell Rousseau's] brigade
except the Cavelry & artillery came over and the regiments all formed

Kentucky Governor John J. Crittenden.
(Filson Club Historical Society)

*Union Major General Lovell
Harrison Rousseau.* (Miller's)

in Seperate Colums and the governor Drove along in front of the 6th
& General Rousaw [Rousseau] Got out & introduced govenor
Critenden [Crittenden] of ky [Kentucky] to the Soldier & he
(Critenden) made us a speech & encouraged the Soldiers in the Cause
of the union. Well I belive we have Nothing more of interest to
wright to you. It is supposed that we will Not Stay here Longer than
this week & the Colonel Says that we will have our pay tomorrow
though We Cant tell. Dr Laverty Send you his respects. He is all
right & the old Dr has been promoted to Brigade Surgeon & the first
assistant took his place in the Hospital here & Dr Laverty is promoted
to first assistant & Surgeant. I will now bring my Letter to a close.
Give my Love to all the friend & reserve a Double portion for yourself. With much respect I remain you Dutifll Soons until Death.

                                    Wayne & Lafayette Alford

George W Alford in your Letter to Lafe you . . . [wrote] that We had
not Written to you before this time but if you knew anything about
the facilities for writing here you would not complain. But as I have
a chance this eavening I will wright you a few Lines. Well george we
have Some Verry good times & then we have some verry hard times

though all in all soldiering is reather a hard life though not any harder than I looked for nor hardly so hard. Their has been No verry Cold Weather here as yet though I Dont think it gets as Cold here as it Does in Indiana. George We would Love to have you here for a few Days but if you want to make a Man of yourself Just put in your time well and Spair No times or pains in Learning & when you grow up you will never regret it. Well George when we write home remember that it is to you and we will wright to you Specialy as often as we can. When you Wright Direct your letter to Camp Wabash Lerue County K Y 6th Regiment Indiana Volunteers Colonel T T Crittenden Care of Capt Vantrees [Van Trees]. Well George While I am Writing I received Mothers & fathers & Hellens Letters and I will Just answer them along with this. Tell green to try & improve as fast with his Studies as he can & if We get home I want to See you and him advanced as much as possible. I recieved a Letter from Warren & one from Wm Houtin [Houghton] & they Say that they are getting along verry well. Warren thinks he will be able for Duty in a few Days. I remain your Brothers Wayne & Lafayette Alford. Wright often.

★

[From Lafayette to Mother:]

[Written under a letterhead with image of Colonel Elmer Ellsworth, an early martyr of the Civil War, and the following Ellsworth quotation: "I am perfectly content to accept whatever my fortune may be, confident that He who noeth even the fall of a sparrow, will have some purpose even in fate of one like me. My darling and ever loved parents, good bye. God bless, protect and care for you." Elmer]

Camp Wabash
Lerue Co K.Y.
November 24th/61

Dear Mother . . . I attempt to write to you this eavening & I thought these Lines [above] would express my Sentiments. These words were expressed by Colonel Elsworth in his last letter to his parents. I was Sorry to hear you Complain at me for not writing to you. Specialy [after you sent us] Some Nice things in Laverties [Laverty s] trunk. I did Not have time to right you a Letter & I just bairly had time to wright what I Did. I realy thought their was Some feeling or Some accommodation in people that pretend to be my friends but I find their is no Dependence to be put in Some friends unless it is Something to their own interest. I Did not Send word for you to

Colonel Elmer Ellsworth, an Early Hero in the North.
(USAMHI)

Send me Something because I was realy Suffering. . . . We get plenty although it is rough but I Sent Simply because I had a chance to get Something & I new that Nothing would give you more pleasure than to get a Chance to Send us Something Nice but never mind that. I will no who to expect favors of next time. You wanted to know if we had heared from Warren. I received a Letter from him and one from Wm Houtin [Houghton] both Dated November 11th Houghten was well & warren had been Sick as you know & he Says he thinks he will be able for Duty in a few Days. The rest of the boys were well I think. From the way he wrights that he is out of Danger. It greaves me Sorely to hear of So many Deaths amongst our own boys in Misourie. You Said it grieved you to hear me wright So much foolishness. Well Honestly if I rote foolishness I Dont remember it. I am as much oposed to be writing folishness as you Can be Mother. I am afraid you Cause yourself many Miserable Hours. Hours that Cannot prophet us in any way and this troubles me Mother. I try to Live Just as Strict with regard to christian Duties as I can & never expose myself any way unnecessary. You Said Something about a cover for our caps. We get oil cloth Covers for our caps at the Sutlers but we Dont need them Much yet. But anything that we need to make us comfortable or Healthy we will Certainly get. But we Dont Spend money for anything foolish or unnecessary Mother. I must bring my Letter to a Close by Saying remember your Children at a throne of grace. Direct your letter to Camp Wabash Lerue County Ky 6th Regiment Indiana Volunteer Colonel T T Critenden [Crittenden] care of Capt Vantrees [Van Trees].

Your affectionate Sons. Wayne & Lafayette Alford

[Note from Wayne:]

Hellen I would Like to Wright to you & green but I have to answer Warrens Letter & I Cant get time Now. I Want you One and all to write as often as you can and Studdy & improve as much as you Can.

Wayne & Lafe

[From Hellen to Warren:]

Nov the 25th 1861

Mr Warren Alford Dear brother I take presant opertunity to wright you a few lines in answer to your lines which I recieved with gladness. You do not know how glad I was to get a line from you. You said you did not want me to think hard of you. I do not think any ways hard of you but did think when you was well that you mite have wrote to me. But now you have got sick I will not look for a line from you very often but a line onse and while. We herd that you was going to winter there. And if your mess need any bid cloaths send word home and we will send them to you. Oh Warren how I long to see you and be with you once more. It just seems as if I could not stand it no longer but I will just have to stor

it till you come home if you ever do come home. I think of you may
times and think of you. . . . At home on your good warm beds instead
of laying on the cold ground. I will tell you what I am studdying at
school orthography [or spelling] reading, writing, geography, english
grammar but I must close for it is a bout school time. Wright to me
as soon as you can. Good by

Hellen Alford

Union Brigadier General Henry Washington Benham.
(*USAMHI - MOLLUS Collection*)

Confederate Major General John
Buchanan Floyd. (LC)

Union Major General John
Charles Fremont. (Miller's)

[From Father to Warren:]

Nov the 28th 61

In the quiet enjoyment of home Dear Sir   I am seated by the
light of a Candle to drop you a line to inform you that we are still
enjoying our usual health and we hope we may soon hear that you
enjoy the same blessing. We receive your of the 14th on Saturday last
and when we learned that you was regaining your health we leave
you to immagine how glad we was to hear It. And at the same time
we received one you had ritten the 28th of August to your Friends at
home. We had A letter from Wayne & Lafayette just Saturday & two
from B J Gilley on last Tuesday and they were all well. I saw a very
fine letter from James Kellams to his Mother to day. He Is well in
the 42nd Reg at or near Henderson Ky. And I think the Signs of the
times warrents the conclusion that there will be A forward move in
front of Washington and some point on the Southern Coast and also
in front of Louisville. And great preparations are being [made] to
start the Gun Boats down the Mississippi with a strong forse. I am
Reading the dayly Commercial [Cincinnati *Commercial*] and I see
there Is great activity in the moveing of troops to Ky from Ohio, Ind,
and Western Va. Even the half of your own Briggade. I would like
to know the strength of the huttonsville quarters and how you are

situated for comfort and whether there is many Rebels in that vicini-
ty or not. For I hear than Benham [Union Brigadier General Henry
Benham] has run Floyd [Confederate Brigadier General John Floyd]
off and took nearly every thing he had to fight with and Fremont
[Union Brigadier General John C. Fremont] Run Price [Confederate
Brigadier General Sterling Price] very nearly If not quite out of Mo
[Missouri]. But when he was removed his Army was scattered and
Price returned and the last I hear of him he was about [on] the line
of the Pacific Railroad. Well sir after the quiet Nights repose we are
finishing our letter I visited your farm on last evening to see how
things was going on. Your Aunt has A small patch cleared but is
doing nothing more. Hedrick has five Acres under fence but I connot say It is Cleared. . . . He says he expects to chop it off for fire wood
this winter. He Is teaching Scool and he says he cannot get but Ten
Acres in this winter and he will have to hire that done and he will
be glad to get off from clearing the other Ten but if you are not willing he will have to try to do it. But [he] cannot do it all this winter.
He has Ten Acres deadned. The Five Acres that he has fenced is
Twenty Rods wide [110 yards] by Forty long [220 yards] and the fence
is Seven rails high and A few pannels may be eight including all the
rails that was there. Now you know the contract and I have given
you A pretty correct account of how matters stand and you can
wright to me what I shall say to Hedrick or your Aunt. I have got
about 25 bushels of wheat to word the Payment for the Machine.
There is 150 bushels behind of good clean White Wheat and if I do not
get It I shall contend for at least 75 cents per bushel. I paid your
Uncle one Dollar 64 cent the balance on an order he held against you
for Hedrick and 2.60 cts on Book. I let [my brother] Wayne have the
Braxton note and he gave you credit for your part of the same. I got
Forty Dollars of it A few days before Wayne went away and the balance is yet unpayed but I will try to get it as soon as I have time to
go after It. I thought I would have killed the Hogs next week but
there is nothing settled about the price and I bought 100 bushels of
Corn for 20 dollars and I can feed till Christmas. I saw Brooks and
told him I would pay him when I sold my Pork and he said it would
be all right. The Children were verry glad to get [a] line from you
and they will wright again soon. Minerva and Charley and Enoch
are all well and all the rest of your friend[s].

[In the margin:]

My love to all the Boys and also Capt Brooks and Col Kimball and do
not neglect to reserve a portion to your self. So you see I must close
by begging you not to forget to wright at least once a week and oftener if Circumstances Calls for it. . . .

F & Mo Alford

★

[From B.F. Gilley, Mary Alford's brother, to Franklin:]

28 Nov 1861
Camp Sixth Ward, Hardin Co. Ky

My dear brother   With much pleasure I take a seet on the straw in our tent to drop you a few lines in answer to what you hav request-ed to settle my business. And I want it settled soon so that I can pay J. B. Gilley. I want him paid pretty soon now. Brother Franklin I want you to goad him up a little if you pleas as I think it will have to be dun. Now br. F. I must say to you that the boys behavs them selves admirabley. By now Bro F. I supose from wat you said the morning we left that [or perhaps it was] siter Mary that she thaught that Leafayett would not conduct him self right but he seems to con-duct himself firts rait and all of the bouys that is with me. I think that thair is no danger but what the boys will do first rate. You must know that we ar not so well fixt as you ar. I must close so good knight. B. F. Gilley

[From Wayne to Father:]

Camp Sixth Ward K.y
November 28th/61

Dear father   I received you verry kind & ever welcome letter yester-day Eavening which found Lafayette & myself with the rest of the boys well and enjoying all the pleasures incident to A Soldiers life. Hereafter I shal write for Lafayette and myself in the Same letter. We have moved as you Can see from the heading of this letter. We wrote to you on Sunday last from a Camp we Called Camp Wabash but that was Not a verry good Camp & so yesterday P.M. we move about 3/4 of a Mile to a Verry nice Camp & So we have got back in Hardin Co. I have heared a great Deal of talk [about] Kentucky & especialy Hardin Co positively [but] if this a Specimen of this County I honestly would Not give the old homestead for all I have Seen. Now you may think this a hard story but it is Nevertheless true. I think this will Cure Lafayette of wanting to leave home to find a good Country. I tell you one Cant See the beauties of home being used to them all the time but I tell you just let them come to Kentucky & then they can see the

Contrast verry forcibly. If their is any fighting to be Done this is the Country to do it on for it is actualy good for Nothing else. We are still verry well Satisfied here for if we have to fight lets meet them on their own ground and not Have our own state overrun with the two Contending armies. We have a beautifull place to encamp but I heard General Rousaw [Rousseau] remark to the Colonel [Kimball] last eavening that we would not stay here many Days. I think it wont be long before we move down to green river. We are 15 or 20 miles of it now. The ladies of Louisville have made A fine flag to present to the 6th Regiment & they are to be here today. About 100 of them to present it but is is raining So today that I hardly think they will Come. We have received No pay yet. They are looking for the pay master every Day but we Dont Care whether he Comes Now or not. We have had No weather that was verry cold yet. It Spit Snow a little one Day but None of any account. I Dont think that it is near as cold here as it is at home. I beleive I have writen all the news. You Semed to think that we ought to wright oftener. [The problem is] we had nothing to write but I will write oftener I think in the future. I received a letter from warren & one from Wm Houghten [Houghton] and was very hapy to learn that warren was getting along so well. Our Spiritual health is as good as it was when we left home. The wickedness in Camp Disgust me. Pray for us that we may still do our Duty to god & to our Country. We remain as ever your afectionate Sons in the Army. Wayne & Lafayette Alford All of you write often.

[From Angeline Stafford to Warren:]

November the 29 & 61
Dear [Church] brother I this ugly morning seat my Self at the table with my three little children. . . . I have nothing of any importance to write. I must write about our big meeting. Brother mathes and old uncle Joseph wilson and uncle trimbe was with us. We had the best of preaching and I wish you cold have bin at your good home soe you could have bin with ous but the way thing are arrange you could not but I hope you can bye and bye when the wars are over. There is nothing of eny importance a going onn. Joshua want to tell you that he as still trading yet. He owns four horses. We have hade beautiful wather all Alonge till now. It is whirled cold and is snowing. You dont know how I pitty you when I think of you and that is ever fifteen minuts threw the day. I must bring my leter to A close. Write to us as soon as you get this and let us know whether you have suffered with cold or not. Give my best respects to the boys.

Save a double portion for your Self. So no more at preasent but remains as ever your brother and sister. Angeline Stafford to J W Alfford

★

[From Wayne to George:]

Camp Advance
December 2nd/62 [sic]

George W Alford
    Dear Brother   I embrace this opportunity of Writing you a few lines to let you know how we Do & what we are Doing. Well George we are just Doing Nothing at this time. Their is Nothing for us to Do here only Stand Picket once in a while. I Dont know of any Rebal troops in force Closer than Boalingreen [Bowling Green] & they are about 40 miles off & Manifest no Disposition to interupt us Since the German Regiment [the 32nd Indiana Infantry] gave them Such a round. My health is improveing as fast as Could be expected. The Workmen are Still working away on the Bridge & are getting along verry Well. I believe before we came Down here they had constructed a bridge for infantry to pass over So as to picket on the Side but this bridge was Not thought Safe for the Artillery to pass over So they went to work & Built what they Called a pontoon bridge. It was made of boats that Lay Side by Side on the water and was anchored above so as to hold them Secure. George the reason of our not writing to you Sooner is that we had So Many letters to wright that we could not get time but I want you to Wright as often as you can & when we Write home it is intended for all. We would love to know what is the reason Charley [brother-in-law] Dont Write for we rote to him so long ago that we have almost forgotten it. But I must Close. May the Lord bless & Save you in Heavin is my prair.
Wayne & Lafayette Alford

[Same letter, new sheet of paper - Wayne to Hellen and Greene:]

By Permission Hellen & Green Alford   I take this opportunity of Expressing to you our thanks for the many kind & ever welcome letters We have received from you since We have been away from home. We have Nothing New to wright you only we received your letters this Eaevening & Believe me they were thankfully received by us. We want you to continue to wright & tell us all about the farm & any other news you may Chance to have. We would be verry glad to See you and have a long talk but as we Cannot. Right to us What father got for his park and how Much he Sold. Be good Children & obey your father & Mother and you will never have cause to regret it. I must Close. Yours till Death. Wayne & Lafayette Alford

[From Wayne to Father, Mother and family:]

Camp 6th Ward K.Y.
December 5th/61

Mr Franklin Alford & Family
Dear Father & Mother
Your verry Kind & ever welcome letter Came to hand yesterday Eavening & found us well with all the rest of the boys. Dr laverty has for some days been pestered with a Severe cold though he is better now. Their is nothing of interest gowing on in Camp at this time. We were out on picket Last Sunday & had a verry good time of it though it Snowed Sunday Night and all day Monday. We came in Monday Morning & the boys Killed Several rabbits and Had a stew when they got in Camp. I had like to have forgotten to tell you that Lafayette & myself were on the [same] post. I was Sergeant & Lafe was Corporal. We had no Disturbance only all day Sunday were anoyed by reading passes. But at night the out posts of pickets were anoyed Some by a man making his appearance along there lines. They halted him & he paid no attention to them and they fired away after a while he made his appearance again and they fired at the gentleman again though they did not hit him. As they [?] he took the hint and did not try to pass again. Lieutenant Solomon [Alanson Solomon from Washington, Indiana] Sent out more men & doubled the guard at that post. As for our post it was right on the Turnpike leading to Nashville. All we had to Do was halt every one that Came along and See if they had a pass from General McCook [Bigadier General Alexander McDowell McCook] or Rousaw [Brigadier General Lovell Rousseau]. I Suppose we examined 50 passes in the Curse of the Day. Well I believe their is no news that is relyable. The paymaster was to have been here for the last two weeks but he Hasent Come yet & I dont now when he will. Though I heared our Chaplain Say the other Day that from the best relyable information he Could get he heared that the man that was paying the Indiana troops was on the way & he had about 3 Regiments to pay off before he got here & it took him two Days to pay a Regiment. He said he thought this was about Correct. General Rousaw [Rousseau] Says that we have got to have a fight at Bowling green (that is if they stood) before Christmas. Though the General is in poor health at this time he has a Slight attack of qunaza [quinsy,

an inflamation of the tonsils] though I think he will be well in a few
Days. We are looking for Captain back today but We cant tell
whether he will Come Captain or not. Father if you trade that
Lumber to Baw for the watch Dont give him more than forty Dollars
for it Unless He will give you Such a trade in the Lumber as to justi-
fy you & what he owes. You can take of my money to pay yourself.
I think when the paymaster Comes we will Have Some money to
Send home. If we cant get a Chance to Send it by Some good fellow I
will fix it up and Send it by express. Father them fellows that ows me
if you need the money just Make them fork it over. For you had as
well have it as them. I want you to Send us the presidents message
as soon as you can. Lieutenat Halls [Henry C. Hall, Sr. from
Washington, Indiana] Health is very poor. He thinks he will be able
for Duty tomorrow but the Doctor Says he cant stand it & their is no
use trying. He Says if he Dont get well Soon he is going to Resign. I
will bring this to a close by Saying I rote to Warren Some time ago
and must write again Soon. Except of my best regards for you as
Dear Parents & believe me to be your affectionate Sons. Wayne &
Lafayette alford

PS George & Hellen & green I want you to let this Do for you as I
Cannot wright at the present. Wright to us all about the farm and
Stock & how things are Doing. Wright as often as you Can. We
remain your Brothers untill Death. Wayne & Lafayette Alford

[In the margin:]

Remember us at a throne of grace for it is in & through the blessing
of god we Live move & have our being.

[From Father to Warren:]

Dec the 5th 61
Home Thursday Evening
Mr. Jas Warren Dear Sir I take pleasure in addressing you a few
lines to let you know that we are still enjoying our usual health and
we hope that you may be able to boast the same. We received your
verry kind letter of the 19th which brought to us the welcome
inteligence that you was almost well. It is not necessary for me to
warn you about being careful your Self for I feel assured that you
will do that the best you can under the Circumstances. We will all be
verry glad if you succeed in getting to come home at the time you say
you intend to. . . . I want you to wright as soon as you make A trial

and let us know what success you have and when we may look for
you Home if at all. And if you chance to be disappointed I want you
to be reconciled to your lot without A murmur and we will try to do
the same. But our Prair is that you may succeed. I believe I told you
in my last that I expected to Butcher this week but on account of the
unsettled condition of the market I have bought an Hundred bushels
of Corn and I intend feeding till about Christmas. We have one load
of Corn to gather and we will be done. We have had a small skiff of
snow and pretty sharp weather for about A week but it has moderat-
ed today and bids fair for Rain. I sent you [?] Numbers of the
Reviews on last Monday. So goodnight.

Good morning Sir with my usual health except I have quite A Cold
and hoarseness but suffer no other Ill convenience from it and now
proceed to finish my remarks to you. I received Letters from your
Brothers last Saturday and one from your uncle Ben [Gilley] on
Tuesday last and they are all well and in fine Spirits. They have
made two short advances which I suppose brings them within about
Fifteen miles of the Enemys Camp near Bowlingreen they are still in
Hardin County Camp sixth ward. We was sorry to hear by the latest
nuse from your Camp of the misfortune of John and Math but
while we sympathise with them on account of there misfortune yet
we are glad that it is no worse. Give my love to all the friends and
Brethren and reserve the same to your self and be careful to adorn
that confession that you have made before many witnesses. By your
Christian deportment in this time of trial which I feel confident you
will do and if you fall during the Campaign I may have no cause to
sorrow as those who have no hope. But I must Close by subscribing
my self your affectionate father.

Franklin Alford

Say to Brother Houghton that we received his very kind and interesting letter and we fully appreiate his affection manifested through the
[?] and will answer in due form soon. But I must close for the want
of time and space.

F Alford

[From Warren to Father and Mother:]

Philippi, Virginia
Dec the 8th 1861

Dear Parents
It is with pleasure I agane embrace an other opertunity to drop you a
few lines [and] to in form you of my were a bouts and [announce]

that I am well a gane and hopin that you may be bless with the
same. I have not had a letter from home for some tenn days but the
reason of this is we have not had a male for that length of time. We
are now quartered in Philippi a little town about twelve miles off the
Railroad. We will [get] Mail about two days Soner than we have bin
geting it. We are quartered in houses we will have a vary nice place
when we get fixed up a little. It is a town a bout as large as
Loogootee. Our male went through this place going to huttonsville yesterday eavning. We will not get it before the 10th. I have got some
money that I would send home but I thought I would [wait] and see
if [I] could not get to come home for if I do I will neade it. If I do not
Come I will send it when I draw agane. If you nead money to settle
any of my dets Boliver Gold will let me have it. James Gold has some
fifty Dollars of his money and he says that I can have it at six percent. I will have him to rite to James Gold so that you can get it. I
Received your letter dated the 20 of Nov that was the last. I shal
have to bring my note to a close for this time and will right a gane
in a few days. The Boys are all well and harty. So I shal have to
bring my letter to a close. Hoping to hear from you soon. Ever yours
in the one hope.

J Warren Alford

[From Wayne to Father:]

Camp McCook Hart Co Ky
December 12th / 61
Mr Franklin Alford   Dear Father This is to inform you that we
received your verry kind Letter yesterday Eavening and it found
[us] verry well. We have [been camped at] Bacon Creek and expect to
move on to green river this morning. Their is no Orders yet but the
Colonel thinks we will move this Morning. Father I Cant write much
this Morning. We were paid off yesterday & I received $10.00 and
Lafayettte received $7.00. We are going to Send home all we Drew
and Some that we brought out with us that we Dont need. I will
Send $15.00 Dollars & Lafe will Send $10.00. Old Colonel Vantrees [?]
Colonel Kimball or Captain Van Trees] Said if Captain would have all
the money from the Company expressed to him he would Distribute
it. We had ours put up in a package to itself & marked from me to
you. Our Chaplain is gowing to Louisville to express it so it will go
perfectly Safe as Soon as Old Colonel gives you word that it has come
you go Down and get it. John Williams [Alford] also sends $10.00. I
must Close. I will write to you again as soon as we stop. Wayne Alford

★

[From Father to Warren:]

Mr Warren

Home Thursday Night Dec 12th/61

Dear Sir   I have sought the present opportunity of penning you a few lines to inform you that yours of the 24th Came to hand on Last Saturday and found us without cause of Complaint and we feel our selves under revered reason to Prais the Lord for his kind Care over one that we feel so much Care for in restoring of such an one to health. We rejoice in the hope that these lines may find you quite well. We had the happy privilege of Reading your Aunts letter of the 29th last Tuesday and enjoyed It verry much. You may be ready to ask why it is almost A week from the time I receive your letters before I answer. It is this. I must wright Two letters each week and I have it so arranged that yours starts on friday morning and Lafayettes & Waynes on Monday. We had a verry kind Letter from them Last Tuesday. They stated they were all well but Dr Laverty ... was ... suffering from a Cold. I am glad to hear that you have got A little nearer the [rail] road and I suppose you are quartered in A much better place. I suppose you have heard of George Gilleys & Lawsons Alfords Death. The former at George Town & the latter at St Louis. And we learn that Alexander Robertson Died in St Louis also about a week ago. I read letter from Wm Gold and Kenny Edwards this Week and they were well and also your Uncle Elen. Your friends are all well as far as I know. Your Grand Mother Gilley excepted but she Is able to do her work. [Charley] Donaldson put up a good Stable today. We are dayly Expecting to hear of the rebels being Routed from Bolingreen [Bowling Green]. I see from yesterdays Commercial that our Troops are advanceing on them there with about 60,000 troop and It Is thought indcative of A general Forward move and it is generally believed if our Armies are successful when they do make A general move the whole thing will be wound to a close very soon. And I Pray the Lord It may be so but time can only tell the events of tomorrow. From the best information we can get Prices [Confederate General Sterling Price] and his rebel forces are gone into Winter quarters in the County your uncle Harmon lives in. At or near Oceola [Osceola, Missouri]. Your Mother wants to know what sort of beds you will have for the Winter and if she Can do any thing for you in the way of bed or Bedding. I think It altogether likely that Edmund will be hard up to pay you but I will try to get Hedrick to take a part of the note. And If I can I will try to get

him to devide It and get his fathers name to it. Camp has A fine lot
of Hogs and [?] started to kill them by today and I must help him.
Pork is verry low only worth $2.75. I still hope It will be worth
Three but how It will be I cannot tell. But I shall not kill for Ten
days or Two Weeks. If you had time to wright A line to brother
James Gilley & Aunt Cis It would be received verry gladly. Give my
love to all whose love would reciprocate. . . . Wright soon and give us a
description of your new home. So nomore but ever yours. Good by.

F & M Alford

★

[From George to Warren:]

Alfordsville In   Dec the 13th 61

Mr J Warren Alford

Dear sir   I am seated this morning to drop you a line. I am well.
I have first been makeing a fire and I thought I would write to you.
I have been going to School for a while here lately and I think I am
learning very fast. We had a very good spelling last night and I am
tolerable Drowsey. Oh I had like to have forgoten one thing. We had a
great Polemic here night before last. I tell you we had fine speaking.
You art to have been here and heared us speak. It was very interesting Warren. The mule come back last nite. He dont look so well as he
did when we let him go. Your mare that we got for him is geting Fat
as fast as I ever saw. You no how spunky pidge was. You can guess
how spunky she is when you git on hur and the other horses run
on. You cant hold hur. Mr Camp is going to Kill hogs to day. He has
a fine lot to kill. About 63 i believe. He has got the fier started now.
I dont guess we will Kill till between Christmas and newyears. Give
my love to all the Bous and keep a double portion for your selfe.
Write to me as soon as convenient. So no more at present. But
remains your brother. Goodby.

George W. Alford

[On the back of the same sheet - from nine-year-old Thomas Green to Warren:]

Mr J W Alford
Dear sir We received you kind letter of the 24 and was glad to hear
that you was well [and] that [you] dont [have] time to writ. George is
going out to feed the fatning hogs. They are geting tolerable fat.
Minerva says that you might wright a letter to her. I will have to
close for the want of time. Wright soon.

Thomas Green Alford

[Now, Hellen's turn:]

Mr J Warren Alford   Dear brother I take my seat by the stand to wright you a few lines. We had a fine spelling school last night and I wish you and Wayn and Lafayett had bin here to help us spell. Cousin James Gilley comes down evry time we git a letter from you to here it read and he says he would rather here from you than any body that has gon to the war. . . . But I must close for father is hurry-ing me. Wright soon. Good by.

Hellen Alford

[From Warren to Father and Mother:]

Philippi Virginia
December the 15th 1861

Dear Parents It is with pleasure I now take the preasent opertunity to answer your kind letters. One of November the 28th and the one of Dec the 5th. One from Minerva & one from George an Hellen. All since I last rote to you and [I] will indeavor to answer them in this as I have not much time to rite. As the Weather is fine we are drilling most of the time. Their has bin another fight about 25 Miles from Cheat Mt [at Camp Alleghany] but our Reg did not get to take a part as we are about Sixty Miles from Cheat Mountain. Their Was about four Reg that had a hand in the figh. We have not heared the partic-ulars yet but Col Kimble [Kimball] said this morning that [we] Whiped them with a Loss of 30 of our Men While the Rebles Loss of 200 Kiled and 70 prisoners. They run Like Turkeys. Col Kimble [Kimball] [starts] for home this morning. You will posibly get to see him While he is at home. As for my Coming home I can not say as yet as I have not made inquiry yet only of Cap brooks and he did not know any thing much about it. But he sayed he was [willing to do] his part. But I do not now how Long We will stay here. The Col said he was going to use his in fluence to have us removed to Kentucky and if we go their I will not get to come home at the time I calculated to. But I sill calculate to come home this Winter but I do not know at what time that will be. You stated in your lette that you had bin over to see Wm Hedrick and to look at that Work. I want him to do the work as it was to be done and I will try to come up to my part of the contract. The pay will be as much at this time as though he Went on with the Work and I think by the time the second payment is dew I shal be able to meat it. When he get the work done acording to contract then

[I will] try to pay him and not tell then. T H Kyle holds the article of agreement Between Him and me. [Check] to see that he does cut timber out side of the Clearing and see that Aunt Kelms does not have the timer Distroid off her Leace. I will proceed to answer a few questions and then I am through. We are quartered in a house and are tolerable Comfortable. We can have blankets when we need them Cheaper than we can get them from home. This is a vary pleasant place to stay and if we stay in winter quarters I would as soon stay here as any place this far from home. As to the number of secesh I have kiled. I do not know that I have kiled any one. I have saw several cesh and my old Musket would go off. This leavs all the Boys With my self Well. I shal have to bring my letter to a close for the presant. Hoping god will bless us and save us all is my prair. Ever your Son.

J Warren Alford

★

[From Hellen to Warren:]

Home Dec the 15th 61

Mr J Warren Alford   Dear Brother
I this pleasant Sunday morning seat myself to drop you a few lines to let you know that we are all well and hope when these few lines come to hand it will find you well ... off. The folks have gone to meeting but Green and Enoch and myself and I had just bin thinking of wrighting you a few lines. We received you letter of the 8th and was glad to hear that you was well. Warren I wish you was here to eat some Walnuts. I have just bin out eating some Walnuts. Your letter stated that you still thought that you was comeing home. I hope that you will succeed in getting off for I want to see you very bad. Worse than ever I did before.   Minerva and Charley has came back from meeting.   Joseph Murry preached to day and he mad a pretty smart sermond. There was a prety smart congregation out for the people is few. When there is ten or fifteen [of] us we [consider] it is a large congregation. Aunt Hannah recived a letter from John William Alford [in camp with the 6th Indiana in Kentucky] and thay are all well and they are in Hardin county. Yet he sayd they had built them a smal cabin four round high and they streached there tent over for a cover for it and it was eight by ten feet. Charley and Minerva is about [to] start home and are well. Now Minerva Says She is going to give you a Scolding if you donot wright to her for She has wrighten to you and has not recieve any answer.

Now She says she think you might wright to her.   Good by. Good
evening. Sir Jam now [I am] seated to finish my letter. Now Warren
John William [Alford] rote that Rewsaw [General Rousseau's]
Cavaldry [in Kentucky] went out on a Scout and came onto a body of
Cecession trops and they had some prety sharp fighting and they
killed buckers son [probably Confederate General Simon Buckner's
son] and the Secession men sent a flag of truce to our men they
wanted to go through our lines to go up to louisville to bury him but
Rewsaw [Rousseau] sent them word to go to hell. Warren your mule
cam here and we put him up and this mourning. To dirty boys came
after it. I do not think it was a very suitable day to be hunting
mules. Uncle Joseph Mcord has just come back from cincinnatti and
he brought a letter to Charley from Lafayette and it had bin down to
Washington city to the dead letter ofice. It was the 3rd of November.
I think Warren we have had to the finest foul [Fall] and winter so
fare that i ever Saw and the medow has growed up so that we have
not had to fead the cattle any yet. Wrigh to me how you git your
washing don and how often you wash do you ever shave any and I
would like know what you look like if you dont shave and how did
it happen that you got in them houses. Did the Secessions run from
them or not. Answer all thes questions if you can. Father is a going
to wrigh on this So I must close. Wright soon. Good by

[Next page written by Franklin:]

Mother wants to know as soon [as possible] whether you [are coming
home] and if [not] she wants you to wright. Warren your Mother
wants to send you some fruit if you dont Come home. If you Cannot
Come wright as soon as you find out and let us know something
about the probable Chance of getting anyting from home. Hellen has
written you a long letter and it is not worth while for me to wright
the same things. I have written you A letter every week for serveal
weeks and some times Two. I Mailed one last Friday and this on
Monday and we will try to wright so as to Mail regularly on
Monday. There is A strong indication of A general move in the
Army in Kentucky and on the Mississippi this Week. First on
Bolingreen [Bowling Green] and then on to Nashville. Ther is fifteen
Gunboats about ready with the Aid of A number of Steamers to
Carry Land forces and land them were they will be able to asist in
the sujugation of . . . first Columbus then New Madrid. Thence to
Memphis and soon down the Mississippi till they intercept the great
Southern expedition. Not having had the opportunity of wrighting
last night and haveing to wright a few lines to the other Boys this
Morning and Consequently will have to Close this hasty scrall to get it

in this Mornings Mail. The health of the neighborhood is verry good
and the weather fine. My love to all the friends and reserve a good
share for your self. So no more but still remains your affectionate
Father until Death.

Franklin Alford

[Father to Warren:]

Home Sunday Evening Dec 22nd 1861
J Warren Alford   Good evening how do you do. Dear Sir   I am
well and hope you Enjoy the same blessing and Since Circumstances
forbid us the Enjoyment of Each Others Company or the privilege of
enjoying the Pleasant bright Fireside and the society of those whom
we all so much love. But we feal happy that Circumstances are as
favorable with us as they are. We are still blessed with Mail facilitys
and the privilege of keeping up A Correspondence. Theyby we
received yours of the 15th Inst and was verry glad to hear from you
again and particularly to hear that you and all the Boys were well.
We were all verry glad to hear that you got to Phillippi [Philippi] and
had got Houses to winter In. I hear that Col Kimball is on his way
home to his residence in Loogoottee and if I hear when he gets there I
shall be shure to go to see him if the Lord [is willing]. For you may
be shure I would take pleasure in converseing with the Lowest private in your Company or any one who has shared with you in the
toils on the Mountain Summit. I suppose you got the nuse pretty
often since you got to where you are now. We had Two letters from
the Boys in Ky yesterday. They were all right. John Wm [Alford of
the 6th Indiana] says they slept on the Ground where the 32nd Ind
and about three thousand Rebels had A bloody little skeirmish Killing
80 Rebbles and several Prisoners. [Reference to an engagement at
Rowlett's Station, near the Green River and Munfordville, Kentucky.]
The No of Wounded not known. The Federal Loss [was] Eleven killed
& 25 or 30 wounded. He said they was about two miles off when the
Cannonadeing began and Capt Vantrees [Van Trees] walked up to the
head of his Company viewed his Command and said there was but
one scared man among them. The reason I give Johns account of the
(Green River) skirmish is because he gave some of the particulars
more at length than Wayne. I think the Bridge over Green River
will be done tommorrow and then I think they will move on down
to Boling [Bowling] Green without delay where there is a prety Strong
Rebel force said to be 25 or 30,000. I think from the best I Can learn
Gen Buel [Union General Don Carlos Buell] will be able to Concentrate

at least 75,000 troops around Boling Green in A verry short time and
I feel verry shure he will have possession of it in ten day. Good Night.

Good Morning Sir   Well Warren after the enjoyment of A quiet
Nights rest we enter upon the dutys of another day and verry near
the Close of most eventful Year that has ever marked the Pages of
American History.   An It [comes to] us in view of the Goodness of God
In spareing and Protecting our Lives through the many dangers trials and aflictions that we have been Called to pass in the present year.
And when we view our dependence upon Him and His Loveing
kindness manifest towards us let It Stimulate us to A doubling of our
diligence to arise in the Scale of Christian Perfection dayly and if it is
possible make better progress in the devine Life than we have done in
any previous year of our lives. Now let us love Mercy and walk
Humbly before God that our days may be long on the Earth and be
them many or few let us spend them all in accordance with the
word of truth. ... God may be Glorifyed and our profession Honored.
We have Just partook of our Morning repast and tied it on with A
Mince Pie. We have had about Three weeks of as fine weather as I
ever saw at this time of year but it is Cooler now with A litle snow. I
must settle with Kelso this morning and pay him off. I will settle with
Wm Hedrick soon and see what you owe him and if I Cant raise the
money otherwise I will sell some wheat. The Friends of Alfordsville
Boys are all well so far as I know. This leaves us all well but I must
Close by bidding you an affectionate Farewell. Yours Truely.
Franklin Alford

[From Warren to Father and Mother:]

> Phiippi
> > Virginia
> > > Dec the 22nd
> > > > 1861

    Dear Parents
This good sabath day as my Twenty third birth Day.   Just as the
Church Bell is tolling the Hour of two for preaching I commence my
letter in order to answer your request of the 15th which came to
hand yesterday and found me well with the exception of a vary bad
Cold. I was glad to hear that you was all well. The Reg left here on
the Eighteenth and they thought they was going to romaney
[Romney, western Virginia]. But I heard to day that they was in bell

air [Bellaire, Ohio] on the 20th but I do not know whether it is so or
not. I am left at Philippi in charge of a party of men that was not
able to travel and I do not [know] when I shal get to follow the Reg
but I do not think it will be long. So I can not tell you where you
shal hear from me next. You nead not direc any more to this place
when you hear where the Reg Stops at you can wright to me. I got a
letter from Wayne yesterday dated the 15th and they was all well. I
do not expect to get to come home this Winter but I in tend to make
an other effort be fore I give it up though. If I do not get to come I
whal content my self. Mother spoke of wanting to send me some
Peaches as it is uncetan wher we will be and I can get any thing I
want. I would say I [am still] trying to live So that wen I come to
dye I can look on my past with Joy and not gief having a concience
a void of offence to ward God and man. I must bring my letter to a
close for the preasant.   Ever hoping [we will meet] one day.

   As Ever
    Your
     Sone
      in the
       one
        Hope
         James Warren
         Alford

★

[From Thomas Green to Warren:]

Mr J W Alford
       Alfordsville Ind dec the 22 61
Dear brother We received you verry kind letter of the 15th and was
glad to hear that you was well. It is raining now and we had quit a
sleet last night. I cant wright fast enoug and I will get hellen to
wright for me. The fatning hogs looks fine and we are going to kill
them about thursday next. Yore mare that Father traded far is a
spunky as old pidge was. Father and mother has gon to meatting
[Mother continues the letter:] Warren i have returned from meeting
& as green was trying to wright i thought i would scrib a little. Do
you know wat happened 23 years ago today. An american soldier
was born and also one [on] the 15th and one [on] the 6th. Their
names is warren wayne and lafayette alford. We had two lettrs
from the boys yesterday. One [written on] the 15th and [one on the]
17th. Wayne said he rote to you some tim since he thougt woul
wrigt again. That day he said he had but litle time to wright as they

ware on the march. Your father will tell more abut them. The tories
of daviess county and martain [Martin County] met at high rock
thusday night in convention. They chose mitch white, kyle jackman,
old luke slicr, madden and more. . . . They say thay are going to send
men to congress to make peace. I want them to go to cheat mountain.
Those has several of their tribe made peace their now. Cut dobbins,
tom brown, wish hedrck, wer in the mess. They thank God rather
[than] the devil that union men ware put down. I long to see the sol-
dies come home. I think such scamps will have to leave hear. I have
thaut i cold not stand to see anny boddy kild but will tell you what i
hav wished it. . . . I get so [mad] sometimes i feel like i coud do it my
self. I guess i hav some of the blood of my Grand parens. They had
to fight toris. When i think of childen and friens being deprivevd of
home and its enjoyamens a kind mother can not enjoy it. There is
but few left here that is worthy to live in indiana when they hear
of the toris killing some of our men they get vary saucy. But i tell
you they know who to talk before. If them old scamps see any boddy
come where they are they will run like scared houns. Enough of this
warren. Strange said their was a talk of giving bud a discharge next
spring on on account of being disabeld in his feet. I did not think he
could stand it. Their is a report that your lungs was affected and
you would get a discharg. I did not believe it. If bud can not go
threw it [it] would be a fin thing for him to come now [as] his mother is verry lonesome. I mus come to a close. As ever your affectionate
mother. To warren alford in the one hope. We do miss thee at home.

[From Father to Warren:]

Home
Dec the 29th 1861

Mr J Warren Alford
Dear Sir
I am Comfortably Seated by the fire side this beautiful Lord's Day
morning to Inform you that we still enjoy common health and an
anxiety to know that you enjoy the same precious Blessing. We have
not had A letter from you since the one you rote the 15th. I saw A
Letter from [John] McCord which Informed us of your orders to
March and another since he arrived at Romney [western Virginia]
written the 22nd. In [the latter] . . . he gave A description of the trip
from Phillippi [Philippi] to that place and that the Alfordsville boys
are all well and you was left at Phillippi to attend the sick. [After

reading the McCord letter] and [hearing] the word brought by some
who have lately been discharged . . . from your Company . . . relative to the condition of your Lungs [leads me to ask] why. (If you are
as well as I hope you was) you was left to discharge that service that
might be perfromed by some person who would not be half as able to
do or perform any laborious service as your self when in good health.
But I suppose It Is all for the best for If you are not stout It Is fortunate for you that you are not more Exposed. And if you are ever so
well I suppose you are In no danger of an invading foe and [you are]
Housed up were you Can take good Care of your self. Now warren I
want A solution of those difficultys. John [McCord] says they had A
hard days March over A bad Road to Weston [in western Virginia]
and then A pleasant ride of 100 Miles on the Rail Road and then A
march of about 16 Miles over A fine Road to Romney where they
have the finest prospect he had seen sinse he left Indiana. I took
7200 lbs of Pork to town on the 17th but I Cannot tell you what I
shall get for It . . . . I saw Col Kimball and had some Conversation
with him. He agreed to give us A speech In Loogootee on towmorrow
night If he was not called away before that time. I think I will hear
It If not Providentially hindered. I thought I would have sent this
by the Col but when I learned that you was still at Phillippi [Philippi]
I . . . determined to direct as before. I have A little Money belonging
to Wayne & Lafayette that I Can use for our benefit. I will settle
your Account at Brookses with Pork and Hedrick has traded out
$5.00 In the store and I can pay that with Lard and I have some
wheat on hand that belongs to you and If I Cant get along without I
can sell that. And you may be shure that you have A friend at
Home that will spare no Pains In trying to attend to your Interest In
your absence. And I hope your affairs will Cause you no uneasiness
this Monday Morning and the goodness of God still Guards our path-
way with belssing almost inmeasureable and I proceed to finish my
Letter. We still have verry fine weather. I have not had A letter
from Wayne and Lafayette since last Saturday A week ago but I saw
one from them to their Aunt Hannah last Saturday and one from
your Uncle Ben [Gilley] at the same time and they were all well then.
And your uncle says a few of our men in the vicinity of the Green
River Encampment was attacked by A body of Rebels and the union
Boys baged 400 of them with out loss of A man. It has been but A
few days since Jefferson [C.] Davis [from Indiana] with about 300 of
his Command Captured 1300 of [Confederate General Sterling] Prices
men and 60 heavy laden Waggons of Army Stores and 1000 Horses
and 1000 Stands of arms and A great deal more that I cannot now
recollect. This was done by Jef Davis but not the one that gave . . .
Ind the Good name in Mexico. [Ed. note: Father is being facetious;
Confederate president Jefferson F. Davis, while in the Mexican War,

gave Indiana troops a bad name.] [The recent fight] was done in Mo
near your uncle Harmons with the loss Two men. The Alfordsville
boys were hardby but not in the Engagement. Our Navy Is recieving
about 30 long range dalgreen [Dahlgren] Guns and mounting these
each week. But I must Close tho I will not neglect to tell you that
Elizabeth Stafford was Married yesterday to Jas McGeehee. Your
Aunt Hannah, Nancy Allen & Marthy Alford went to the wedding
but have not got back and therefore I cannot tell you any thing. . . .
And I would like to know if virgil [Alford] is becoming disabled in
his feet so that there is any talk of his being discharged. Ever
Praying the Lord to bless and protect you in all your trials.
Affectionately your Father Franklin Alford

[From Warren to Chester Camp:]

Romney Virginia
Dec 31st 1861

Mr C[hester] Camp [in Alfordsville]
    Dear Friend
I received yur vary welcome letter 28th Dec which found me in good
health boat spiritual and temporal. I am some times vary much at a
loss to know how to enjoy my self. As in the armey is a vary
unpleasant place for a Christian to live though when I look for word
to the promise of our Lord who says my grace shal be suficient for
them that put their trust in him and allso to our glorious as it once
was. We can fais all the toils with pacients for if we do not bair the
Cross we can not wair the crown. And if our Country is a gain
restored to peace and we get home we will be well paid for all our
privations. All of the boys are well and in fine spirits. I will now
procede to answer the part of your letter that was concernin that
dowery of Mrs Cooks. You sayes that she wants to sell and that you
think that now is the time to by. . . . You think that she is likely to
out live Cook. I hardly know what to say for I do not know whether
the land will be worth more in five years than it is now. For I am
not going to make any improvements til I come home and I may not
then for some time after. But as I have left all my business in
fathers hands I do not know that I can do better than to say for you
to tell the circumstances to him and what ever he does is all right
with me. If he thinks best to by her dowery. What ever he is willing
to do will [be] all right with me. This is the plan for me as I am not
their to see to it and he can do just as well as my self. So I shal have

to come to a close for [now]. Hoping to hear from you agane. I ever
remain your friend.

J Warren Alford

Captain Brooks said to say to you that he was much obliged and that
he would be glad to have a letter from you his self. Col Kimble
[Kimball] is on a tower home. You will probably see him before I shal.

Good by.

J Warren Alford

★

3
BACKGROUND

"I think our Captain is hard to beet
and our company very Civil."[1]

IT WAS QUITE A LEAP. ON OCTOBER 8, Wayne and Lafayette were home,
excited about their involvement in the Alfordsville militia company. Six days
later, they were on a train headed for Kentucky to join the 6th Indiana
Volunteer Infantry for three years. It can be presumed that Captain Charles Van
Trees, a veteran of the three-month 6th Indiana Infantry, and a resident of
Daviess County, had made a successful recruiting visit to Alfordsville.

Earlier, on September 15, 1861, the three-year 6th Indiana Infantry had
been partially organized with 500 men at Camp Noble on the old fairgrounds at
North Madison in Jefferson County.[2] There was a great urgency to fill the volunteer unit and dispatch the recruits into the border state of Kentucky.

Confederate forces had moved into "neutral" Kentucky on September 4 and
immediately, Northern troops, likewise, tried to garner control of the state by
military occupation.[3] In Indiana, Governor Oliver Morton was anxious to
help the cause – and to assure that the Confederates got no closer than
Kentucky.

Unlike the 14th Indiana, the 6th had little time to train before moving to
the front. On the morning of September 19, the half-filled 6th Indiana Infantry
was marched down the hill from Camp Noble and loaded on a paddle wheeler,
the *City of Madison*. By late afternoon, the steamer had plied the forty-five river
miles to Louisville. Upon disembarking, the troops proceeded to the Louisville
and Nashville Railroad (L & N) station and boarded trains which hurried them
to Lebanon Junction, Kentucky. Three days later, they were marched to
Muldraugh Hill. Another move occurred on October 10 when the demi-6th
Indiana was transferred to Nolin, Kentucky, and "Camp Wabash."[4]

Lieutenant Colonel Hiram Prather and a collection of about 400 new men
caught up with the regiment on October 15.[5] Wayne and Lafayette were part
of this contingent. After leaving Loogootee on the 14th, the Alfordsville boys
evidently went by train to New Albany where they crossed into Louisville.

At least 100 of the latecomers were from Jefferson County and they became
Company K of the 6th Indiana. This brought the volunteer regiment up to a full

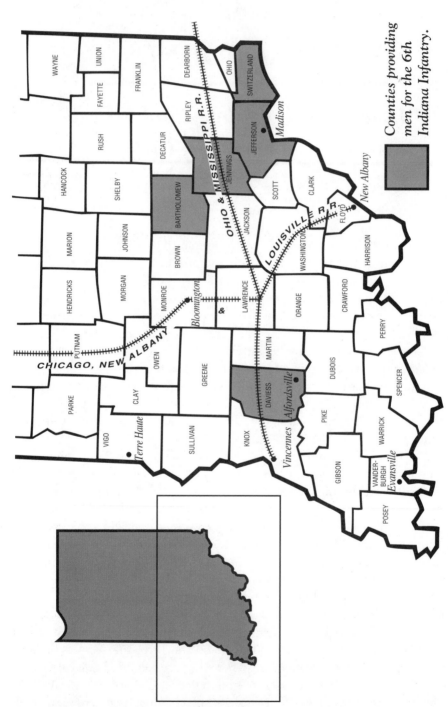

The Indiana Counties Significant to the Alfords and the 6th Indiana Infantry.

Counties providing men for the 6th Indiana Infantry.

The First <u>City</u> <u>of</u> <u>Madison</u>, Built in 1860. On August 18, 1863 She Sank near Vicksburg, Mississippi, as Result of a Gunpowder Explosion. The Estimated Loss of Life Ranged from 63 to 156. The Owners Received a $45,000 Damage Award. (The Jefferson County, Indiana Historical Society.)

complement of ten companies. It also resulted in the unusual circumstance of four companies having been raised in Jefferson County (A, D, F and K). Wayne and Lafayette Alford fit into Company E, all Daviess County men. The other companies were from the counties of Jennings (Companies B and I), Bartholomew (Companies C and G), Switzerland (Company H).(6)

The commanding officer of the 6th Indiana Infantry was Colonel Thomas Turpin Crittenden, a well-travelled Madison, Indiana, attorney. Crittenden was born in Huntsville, Alabama, reared in Galveston, Texas, educated at Transylvania College in Lexington, Kentucky, and served as a second lieutenant in the Mexican War with the Missouri volunteers. Thomas T. Crittenden was a cousin of future Union Major General Thomas L. Crittenden and future Confederate Major General George B. Crittenden. Colonel Thomas T. Crittenden had commanded the three-month 6th Indiana Infantry from April 27 until August 2, 1861 when they helped clear western Virginia of Confederate forces.(7)

Nolin, Kentucky, the new camp site for Colonel Crittenden and the 6th Indiana, was south of Elizabethtown, Kentucky, near Nolin Creek, on the L & N

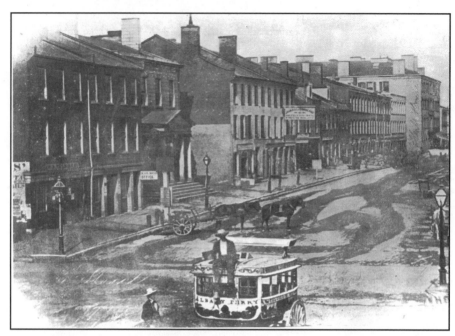

Louisville, Kentucky – 1850's Street Scene, Third Street Looking East on Main. (University of Louisville Archives)

A Portion of the 1856 Louisville and Nashville Railroad Passenger Station, at Ninth and Broadway in Louisville. Date of Photograph Not Known.
(University of Louisville Archives)

line. It was here Wayne and Lafayette learned the finer points of soldiering. A regimental historian from the 6th Indiana boasted, "more men were...educated in the art of war, in the winter of 1861-2 than will ever again be called upon to take like lessons, in the history of our country." The same proud historian thought the resulting military discipline was "one of the wonders of the civilized world."(8)

The 6th Indiana moved farther south on the L & N to Sonora, Kentucky on November 22, just in time for a Thanksgiving Day celebration. A group of 200 ladies and gentlemen from the Sixth Ward in Louisville arrived by train with "sumptuous" food, a glee club, a political orator and a flag to be presented to the regiment. In appreciation, the camp immediately was designated as "Camp Sixth Ward."(9) Neither Wayne nor Lafayette commented about the gracious ladies or the Day of Thanksgiving.

During the winter of 1861-62, tens of thousands of American soldiers lay in camp and anxiously waited to battle each other. By November of 1861, Warren, in the East, already had "seen the elephant," having been in two battles; Wayne and Lafayette, in Kentucky, were eager for the opportunity.

we soon...presented the appearance of warriors(10)

To be a soldier, of course, a young man had to have all the garments of war. Wayne wrote that they received their uniforms on October 14: a pair of pants, two shirts, two pair of drawers, one under (or frock) coat, one overcoat, a rubber poncho and one woolen blanket. Shoes, socks, caps and guns were to come later.

In the early days of the Civil War, there was not a standard issue of clothing for the soldiers. Each state provided their own in the best way they could. In Indiana, the first twenty-five infantry regiments and a few cavalry and artillery units were supplied by the state. After August 1861, the federal government took over the responsibility for clothing the new recruits. This arrangement created much turmoil. At first, the federal clothing supply was inadequate. Something had to be done, so Governor Morton initiated his own procurement system and sent the bills to Washington. This bold stroke, however commendable, resulted in the state and federal agencies bidding up the price of goods much to the chagrin of the Washington authorities. Nevertheless, Morton continued the practice.(11)

There were many variations of what constituted military dress. A few units, in their attempts to be distinctive (and war-like), went to extremes and were later characterized as scarecrows and circus clowns. Most regiments modeled themselves after the regulation U.S. Army uniform of the day.(12) Volunteer soldiers in the Union Army were given a clothing allowance of $3.50 per month,

*Uniform of the Sixth Indiana Infantry – Worn by Sergeant
Major Ed McDevitt, Company F.* (Doll's History of the Sixth Indiana)

or $42.00 a year. In 1861, this money was spent on whatever was available. Wayne's uniform was typical for the day, for example: his one pair of pants (about $3.00), the two shirts ($1.75), two pair of underwear ($1.00), one waist coat ($6.75), one overcoat ($7.25), one rubber poncho (?) and a woolen blanket ($3.00). Shoes, socks and a cap would drive the initial outlay to approximately $30.00, thought to be the average cost for outfitting a soldier.(13)

The 27th Indiana Infantry, in September 1861, was attired in the same uniform as the 6th and their historian remembered they "cut a figure . . . close to ridiculous." "Imagine," he wrote, "a thousand men . . . clothed in little coats the length of an ordinary vest and wearing diminutive skull caps, barely large enough to perch on top of their heads." There was the hint that one size would fit all, resulting in undersize coats which did not extend to the oversize pants.

C.C. Briant, Historian of the Sixth Indiana Infantry.
(Briant's History of the Sixth Indiana)

Belts were of little help as they sagged under the weight of cartridge boxes, bayonets, knives, etc.(14) Similar scenes, in October 1861, may have contributed to
"jollity and fun which prevailed in the camp" as reported by a 6th Indiana historian.(15)

The manual of arms instruction and marching drills also may have contributed to the "jollity." The average young, formerly independent, soldier in
1861 disliked the idea of drilling – and any discipline. A private in a
Pennsylvania regiment made the now-classic analysis: "The first thing we do in
the morning is drill. Then drill, then drill again. Then drill, drill, a little more
drill. Then drill and lastly drill."(16) Another "trainee," in another camp,
became impatient with doing the same routine over and over and suggested to his
drill sergeant, "Let's stop fooling around and go over to the grocery."(17) In later
years, C.C. Briant of the 6th Indiana painted a word picture for his old comrades:

Boys, go back with me to your first effort at squad drill – do you remember how that other fellow used to step on your heels, and cause you to lose step, and in an effort to "catch the step" again, you would step on some other fellow's heels, throwing him out of gear; then he would stumble on some other fellow here we would go hobbling along like our feet were tied together; until every fellow in the squad had his own step; about this time the Sergeant who is acting as drill-master, and who, by the bye, is about as green as any of us, becomes desperate and yells out, at the top of his voice, "H-a-l-t there! what the devil are you trying to do?" Every fellow has his own halt, but he generally stops when he runs against the comrade in front. After they have all halted the Sergeant orders them to "front," then, "order arms," then the old belgiums [rifles] begin to drop one at a time; about this time some fellow would give one big howl, grab up one foot and go hopping around over the ground cutting the most desperate gestures, and with a face that would seem to indicate cramp colic, but directly the poor fellow would get his breath, and the first words that escaped his lips would be, "by thunder, I believe my big toe-nail is mashed off."(18)

An injured big toe was a small price to pay for the honor of carrying a gun in a war. The Alford boys understood such things. When they left home, they proudly took revolvers. The real weapon of war, however, was the rifle. In 1861 there were many types of rifles being issued to Civil War soldiers, both U.S. and foreign made. Those in the 6th Indiana drew Belgiums, a .69 caliber rifle later to be referred to as "European Stovepipes." However manly to carry such a weapon, it was said the Belgiums would not shoot straight and were unreliable in battle.(19)

Civil War Company. (Miller's)

Civil War Camp Site. (LC)

Civil War Camp Site. (LC)

Civil War Regiment on the Parade Grounds. (Miller's)

Civil War Regiment – Ten Companies. (Miller's)

There were other hazards with the Civil War rifles. In Warren Alford's 14th Indiana regiment, many, if not all, the men were issued Enfield rifles, a reliable .58-caliber, English-made instrument. A correspondent to the editors of the Vincennes *Sun* wrote of several incidents of accidental woundings in the 14th Indiana camps. On August 30, 1861 William Landon told how George Betters from Newburgh had recently blown his right hand "clean off at the wrist." The previous night, Private Paul Truckey, from Knox County, accidentally shot himself in the right leg, requiring amputation. Two weeks later, Lieutenant William Denny, also from Knox County, almost shot off his right hand.(20)

"Mud and rain, snow and sleet, freeze and thaw . . . our first winter as soldiers."(21)

Wayne Alford wrote his father on November 28 that their camp in Hardin County would be a good place to have a fight because it was not any good for

Union Major General Alexander McDowell McCook. (LC)

The Green River Bridge at Munfordville, Kentucky. (University of Louisville Archives)

Civil War Regiment on the Move. (USAMHI)

anything else. The camp was best remembered as "Camp Ground Hog." The boys dug ten by twelve feet rectangular pits ("dirty mud holes"), four to six feet deep, and covered them with their tents. These living arrangements became intolerable as the sickness thrived.(22)

On December 9, the regiment moved ten miles south to Bacon Creek in Hart County. This camp was designated Camp McCook, for General Alexander McDowell McCook, the division commander. The boys received their first pay as soldiers in this camp on December 11th. On December 17, they saw the results of a Civil War skirmish for the first time. Then, once again, the 6th struck their tents and moved south, this time to a high bluff near Munfordville and the Green River railroad bridge. This site, called Camp Wood, for General Thomas J. Wood, was Wayne and Lafayette's home for the next six weeks.(23)

In the eastern theatre, Warren Alford, likewise, was on the move. On October 8, the 14th Indiana departed the Cheat Mountain Summit, the hill they had occupied since the battle in mid-September. As with all soldiers since time immemorial, the next camp, they thought, would be better than the present one. Captain Augustus Van Dyke of Company G wrote of the 14th's impending move and the ensuing elation when the orders came to leave Cheat Mountain, ". . . all was hurry and confusion, cooking grub, packing knapsacks, striking and packing tents. . . . 'Fall in Company G'. . . . Soon the line was formed and, on calling the roll, I found that all answered to their names for the first time since our advent upon the Summit."(24)

The 14th moved on to Huttonsville, (West) Virginia, and then to Philippi; and on December 30 they were in Romney, Virginia. Francis Brown of Company B reported to his family, "Romney was a beautiful place, but the people paid a terrible price for their support of the southern confederacy."(25) By mid-January 1862, the 14th had moved its camp to within six miles of Cumberland, Maryland, near the Baltimore and Ohio Railroad. It is here that William Landon wrote, "better quarters no soldier would ask for."(26)

The "better quarters" were Sibley tents. Each tent, commonly called teepees, accommodated a stove and space for 20 men, one-fifth of the company.(27) The stove was positioned in the center and the men slept like spokes in a wheel with their feet to the fire.(28)

In February, after the 14th moved to Paw Paw Tunnel, Maryland, the boys built small, rectangular huts. Private John Kuppenheimer of Company F recorded in his diary that, "a lumber pile in the neighborhood had to suffer."(29) The captured lumber and logs were erected into simple rectangular boxes with pitched roofs and windows. Mud caulked the cracks and a chimney facilitated an indoor fireplace. The resulting appearance was that of a miniature house, big enough for (up to) four men.

Meantime, the 6th Indiana, in Kentucky, was housed in tents, what specific type is not certain. Whatever the berthing arrangement, the order of the day

A Sibley Tent. *(Civil War Collector's Encyclopedia)*

was drilling, parading and going on picket duty. Overcoming the boredom was a major activity in the camp as many men who "never knew one card from another, learned to play euchre and smoke a pipe. Nothing to do, but to think of home and loved ones left behind. Half sick and discouraged, what else could we do . . . ?"(30) It is doubtful the Alfords ever took up card playing.

Union soldiers seldom suffered from a shortage of food. The daily food rations, as prescribed in Washington, included a pound of bread (or its equivalent in flour), three-fourths of a pound of pork or bacon and one-fourth pound of fresh or salt beef. Three times each week, one pound of potatoes was issued to each man. This was supplemented with beans, mixed vegetables, coffee beans, dried fruit, onions, tea, sugar and vinegar.(31) The rations also included the leg-

Winter Camp. (USAMHI)

Winter Camp. (LC)

*"Hoosier City" – Winter Camp of the 27th Indiana Infantry,
near Frederick, Maryland. (Indiana at Antietam)*

endary army hardtack, a cracker-like substance measuring approximately three by three by one-half inches. Although these biscuits were tough as rocks, weevils were known to penetrate the hardtack. One often-told story relates how one man was eating hardtack and exclaimed he had bitten into something soft. When his comrade asked if it was a worm, the first soldier replied, "No, by God, it was a ten penny nail."(32)

It seems the Alfords, although in separate parts of the country, were well-fed and adequately housed. One uncontrollable factor which did create misery was the weather. The scribe for the 6th told of incidents when the boys slid down Kentucky hillsides on a sheet of ice and how it became too cold to sleep.(33) Wayne, however, wrote that it never got so cold (in Kentucky) that two men could not get warm if they slept together under their blankets and overcoats. Local residents told

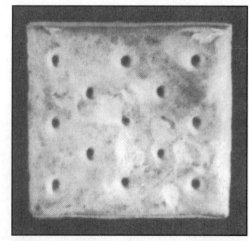

Hardtack. (Civil War Collector's Encyclopedia)

Wayne it was a "common" winter, or normal. Warren and the 14th Indiana fared far worse in northern Maryland. Cold, wind and snow seemed to be the typical weather pattern. A young man in the 7th Indiana, camped on the frozen ground not far from the 14th, recorded that on February 24 there was a tremendous rain storm accompanied by tornado-like winds. Tents and sheds went flying as did kettles, clothes and unfinished letters.(34)

Had it not been the soldiers' first winter, there might have been far more complaining. The conditions could not have been good but that seemed to add to the adventure of it all. Everyone was sharing in the misery.

Endnotes

(1) From Wayne Alford's letter, dated October 25, 1861.

(2) William Doll, *History of the Sixth Regiment Indiana Volunteer Infantry* (Columbus, 1903) p. 18.

(3) Lowell Harrison, *The Civil War in Kentucky* (Lexington, 1975) pp. 12, 13.

(4) Doll, *ibid.*, pp. 18, 19. See also, Charles C. Briant, *History of the Sixth Regiment Indiana Volunteer Infantry* (Indianapolis, 1891) pp. 76, 77. After the War, the men of the 6th Indiana took great pride in the "fact" that they were the first Union regiment to enter Kentucky. No doubt, there were other veterans and historians who challenged this point.

(5) Doll, *ibid.*, p. 20. William B. Fetcher wrote the following description of Prather, partially published in *Indiana of Magazine History* (Indianapolis 1961) v. LVII, n. 1, March 1961, p. 53: "Lieut Col [Hiram] Prather – is a good looking man – with white beard and moustache – both long and full – he is a man of the old school – raised in the woods . . . the father of 15 children – he never swears or drinks . . . he insists upon asking the blessing at the table – and keeping morality in camp. He is about 60 years old. . . . "

(6) Briant and Doll, rosters. Also *IAG*, v. IV, pp. 74-90.

(7) Warner, *Generals in Blue*, p. 101.

(8) Briant, *ibid.*, p. 78.

(9) Briant, *ibid.* pp. 81, 82. Also, David I. McCormick, *Indiana Battle Flags* (Indianapolis, 1929) pp. 36, 37. The flag now should be in the Indiana World War Memorial in Indianapolis.

(10) Briant, *ibid.*, p. 81.

(11) Thornbrough, *ibid.*, pp. 167, 168. Also, *IAG*, pp. 314-320. The government acknowledged that the greatest clothing shortages were shoes, socks and overcoats. The Alford brothers were victims of these deficiencies – no overcoats in western Virginia – no shoes and socks in Kentucky.

(12) Francis A. Lord, *They Fought for the Union* (New York, 1960) p. 137.

(13) *Ibid.* p. 149.

(14) E.R. Brown, *The Twenty-Seventh Indiana Volunteer Infantry* (Monticello, 1899) p. 35. Brown obviously could see humor in the situation.

(15) Doll, *ibid.*, p. 19.

(16) James I. Robertson, Jr., *Tenting Tonight* (Alexandria, Va., 1984) p. 52. The quote was attributed to Oliver Norton of the 83rd Pennsylvania Infantry.

Norton may not have been too far from the truth. The army regulations
were:

6:00 a.m. Reveille	12:30 p.m. Dinner
6:15 a.m. Police call	2:00 p.m. Drill
7:00 a.m. Breakfast	5:00 p.m. Parade
8:00 a.m. Guard mount	6:00 p.m. Supper
8:30 a.m. Drill	9:00 p.m. Tattoo
11:00 a.m. Drill	10:00 p.m. Taps

From Hattie Lou Winslow and Joseph R.H. Moore, *ibid.*, p. 244.

(17) Lord, *ibid.*, p. 26.

(18) Briant, *ibid.*, pp. 80, 81.

(19) Lord, *ibid.*, pp. 140, 141.

(20) William Landon using the pseudonym "Prock," "The Fourteenth Indiana
Regiment on Cheat Mountain" *Indiana Magazine of History* (Indianapolis,
December 1933) v. XXIX, no. 4, pp. 361-365. "Prock" was a correspon-
dent/writer to the editors of the Vincennes *Sun*.

Accidental gun-shot woundings and deaths occurred frequently during the
Civil War but reliable statistical data is not attainable. "Prock" also reported an incident (of what is now referred to as friendly fire), on July 17, 1861
which involved an Ohio unit firing into an Indiana unit, "killing and
wounding several." He explained that because of the various uniform styles
and colors, "'tis hard to distinguish friend from foe at 150 yards."

(21) Briant, *ibid.*, p. 90.

(22) *Ibid.*, pp. 82, 83.

(23) Doll, *ibid.*, p. 24.

The 6th Indiana became a part of the Army of the Ohio on December 2,
1861. In this Army, commanded by Don Carlos Buell, there were five
(later six) divisions containing seventeen brigades. The 6th Indiana was in
a brigade with five other regiments: 1st Ohio Infantry, 5th Kentucky
Infantry and units from the 15th, 16th and 19th U.S. Infantry. The
brigade (designated the Fourth) was commanded by Brigadier General
Lovell Rousseau and was part of Brigadier General Alexander McD.
McCook's (Second) division, all part of the Army of the Ohio. Refer to
Frank J. Welcher, *The Union Army 1861-1865* (Bloomington 1993) v. II,
pp. 192-194.

Or, from Wayne and Lafayette's perspective:

The Alfords were two of approximately 100 men in Company E which was
one of ten companies in the 6th Indiana which was one of six regiments in
a brigade which was one of four brigades in a division which was one of five
divisions in the Army of the Ohio.

The arithmetic suggests there were approximately 96,000 in the Army of the Ohio although 70,000 would be a better guess as few units were ever at full strength. Regardless, the numbers would be overwhelming when considering the population of Indianapolis was 19,000, or that the Army of the Ohio was equivalent in numbers to 1/14th the population of Kentucky.

(24) Baxter, *ibid.*, p. 65. Cited as a Van Dyke letter to "Folks at Home," October 18, 1861.

(25) Francis Brown, *ibid.*, p. 28.
In January 1862, the 14th Indiana was transferred to the Department of West Virginia, a rather unorthodox military organization. The Department was commanded by William S. Rosecrans and composed of four major parts: One, The Cheat Mountain District, was made up of various regiments of infantry, artillery and cavalry, commanded by Robert H. Milroy from Rensselaer, Indiana. Two, The Railroad District – comprised of various regiments of infantry, artillery and cavalry – was commanded by Benjamin F. Kelley. Three, The District of the Kanawha – composed of three brigades of infantry plus unattached infantry, artillery and cavalry units – was commanded by Jacob D. Cox. The fourth major organization was (Frederick W.) Lander's Division. The 14th Indiana Infantry was in Lander's Division. There were three brigades in this division; the First Brigade was commanded by Colonel Nathan Kimball, formerly the commanding officer of the 14th Indiana regiment. In addition to the 14th Indiana, the brigade embodied three Ohio infantry regiments (4th, 8th and 67th), one (West) Virginia infantry unit (7th), and one Pennsylvania infantry regiment (84th). The Second Brigade was commanded by Jeremiah C. Sullivan from Madison, Indiana. There were five regiments in this brigade, one being the 13th Indiana. The Third Brigade was under the command of Erastus B. Tyler and included as one of its six units a regiment from Indiana, the 7th Infantry.

(26) William Landon, a.k.a "Prock," "The Fourteenth Indiana Regiment in the Valley of Virginia" *Indiana Magazine of History* (Indianapolis, September 1934) v. XXX, no. 3., p. 281.

(27) *Ibid.*

(28) Robertson, *Tenting Tonight, ibid.*, p. 45.

(29) Kuppenheimer, *ibid.*, p. 20.

(30) Briant, *ibid.* pp. 86, 87.

(31) Phillip Katcher, *The Civil War Source Book* (New York, 1992) p. 103.

(32) Wiley, *The Life of Billy Yank*, p. 237.

(33) Briant, *ibid.* p. 90.

(34) Skidmore, *ibid.*, p. 103.

CHAPTER

4

[From Warren to family at home:]

Romney V A
January the 2nd 1862

Dear Parents
It is againe I am privoliged to write to you to let you know that I am
well at preasant and [I] hope when this comes to hand it may find
you all enjoying good health. . . . And may our hearts ever be filed
with gratitude to our God for permitting us to live [and] see the end
of the old year and may we commence with the new to love him
more and serve him better. I received your letter dated Dec the 22nd
on the 29th directed to Phillippi [Philippi] but it did not find me thair
but it came dewly to hand and found me about one hundred miles
east in Hampshire Co. Romney . . . is the County seat. We are not
over one hundred miles from washington Citty [District of Columbia].
We are quartered in Court House but we are expecting to get our
tents in a short time. Boliver Gold wrote to James Gold and told him
about geting that Money that I told you [that] you could get. I am
going to send you some Money when I draw again. We was mustered
for our pay on the 31st ultimo but I do not know when we will get
it exactly but guess it will not be long. I think I can send you 50.00
and I will send it as soon as we are paid. I got a letter from Chester
Camp stateing that he had a letter from Cooks Wife. [He] had saw her
[and] she wanted to sell her dowery in that land I got from prater
and that it could be got for one Hundred Dollars and per haps less.
And if I wanted it he thought he could get it for me and would let
me have it at what it cost him. The reason she rote to him she
thought he still owned it. I wrote to him to [say] . . . that you would
tend to it for me. You can find out how the thing is and [then] you
can do as you think best. . . . I will bring my letter to a close by saying the boys are all well. So good eavening.

J Warren Alford

★

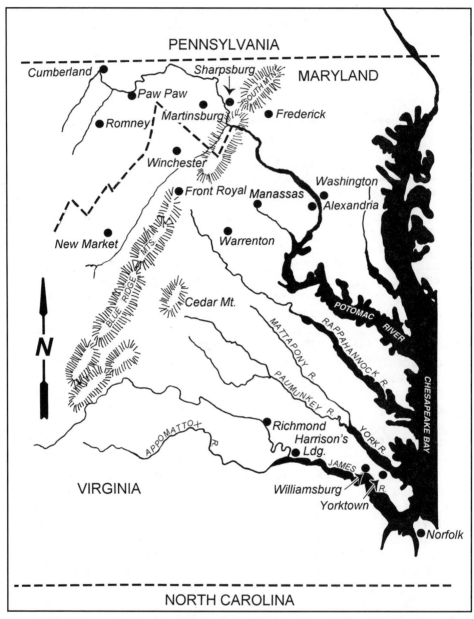

Virginia and Maryland, Warren Alford's Area of Activity, 1862.

[From Father to Warren:]

Home Jan the 5th 1862

Mr J Warren Dear son With Joy unrepressable and A sense of the obligation I am under ... I am proud to be represented In the grand

struggle for the supremacy of the Constitution and Laws that has pro-
tected us In the quiet Enjoyment of the Civil and religious rites
Bequeathed to us by our Revolutionary Sires and those who would . . .
be willing to give their life to ward off the blow that was designed to
parellize all our free Institutions and establish an Aristocracy In Its
place that would deprive us of all that Is worth liveing for. Our
rights have been Disregarded and the emblem of our Liberty has
been ruthlessly torn down by the . . . rebels who have Dwelt secure
under Its mighty Folds from Childhood even to old age. Oh what a
burning shame. I hope you will not think me vain when I say
again that I have three sons in the service of our Country and what
increases my Joy Is there determination to go for the defense of the
Constitution In the strength of God In whom we trust who has said
his Eyes are over the righteous and his Ears are open to there Prairs.
But I have deviated from my purpose. We are all well Enough this
Evening to be wrighting. Hellen & Green has been A little sick for
Two or Three [days] with Chicken Pocks but Is about well again. We
received your letter of the 23rd ult ritten to Minerva and was very
glad to hear that you was still enjoying moderate health. Your uncle
B F [Gilley of the 6th Indiana Infantry] got home last Night [from
Kentucky]. He has been unwell for several Days. He Is getting well.
John William [Alford] has the Measles but he Is doing fine & Dr
Laverty says when he Is able to Come Home he would send him on
furlow till he gets able for duty. B F says Wayne has been sick but
he wants plenty to eat and he will be on Duty soon. Will Riley [Reily,
also in the 6th Indiana] is Home on Furlow to recruit his health.
Your uncle [B.F. Gilley] says Lafayette & Madison [Alford] Is all right
and In fine health. I was in attendance to hear Col Kimball address
the Citizens of Loogootee and vicinity on last Monday Night and was
as well entertained as I could have Expected. I had the pleasure of
Conversing with him about an Hour Tuesday Morning and highly
gratifyed to hear him speak so highly of the Alfordsville boys. I hope
you may have received my letter and the small present I had the
pleasure of sending to you by the Col and [I] enjoyed the privilege of
Conversing with him about home. . . . James Gold received instructions from Boliver [Gold] to let you have his Money but he said he
had an application for it at 20 per cent. I thought I Could get along
by useing what Wayne & Lafayette Could send home and allow
James to do much better for Boliver. If you meet with A favorable
opportunity remit what you may have on hand to spare.

[Continuing the next day or] Monday Morning and all well. All to
gether we have sold very near Eight thousand Pounds of Pork but I
dont expect to get more than $2.75 per Cwt and Could not get that If
It was not for our Store Bill. I have got Wm Hedrick about Payed off
and Wash says If I can pay him A part he will try to wait A while

and I will try to get Along with him Somehow. I think I can manage
that without any difficulty and I hope you will not Caus your self
Any uneasiness about your affairs at Home. If Edmund Could pay
up I would have no difficulty In meeting all your Contracts but I
fear he will fail to some Extent At least. The Children has written to
Wayne & Lafayette for the Likeness and they request the same of
you and I Could enjoy It very well my self. Do as seems prudent
under the Curcumstances. Charles Donaldson has let his part of the
Mill fall back and Charles Allen bought It. He says he Could use the
Money you owe him If he had It but he says It makes no Difference
for he Can get along with out It and when he Cant Do without It I
will try to pay It. Your uncle Joseph A had an order on you from
Hedrick that was not all Paid and [it was such a] small Account I Paid
It. But I must begin to bring my remarks to a Close. Your friends
are all well and manifest great Concern for your well fare. The general Health of this place and vicinity Is As good as you Ever knew It.
It has been so long sinse there has bin A Burying in the neighborhood that I Cant tell the last. Give my love to all the Boys and
Brother Houghton. Also Capt Brooks & Col Kimball . . . be sure to
wright us every week and oftener. If circumstances require It do not
forget to watch and Pray that the Lord may keep you secure from
the power of your Enemmys and the vices of the army and believe
me yours.

F Alford

[From Wayne and Lafayette to family at home:]

Camp Advance
January 9th 1862

Mr Franklin Alford & family
Dear Sir
    Your verry kind letters Came Duly to hand & found us well &
glad to hear from you & to learn that you were all well. Well I have
no news to wright you & can only Say that we are well & the boys
in the Hospital with the measels are getting along verry well. We
received your Christmas gift yesterday by hand of Mr John
Freeman. They were thankfully received not on account of their
worth [but] because they came from Home & we expect to wear them
home if they will last that long & the Lord will that we Should
return home again. The Children Said they wanted us to get our likeness taken with all of our acourterments on & Send them home. Well
we had been thinking about that. Their is a man in the regiment

who takes pictures but he takes such poor ones that I Dont know yet whether we we will or not. If he get to taking them right we will but we Cant tell yet for if we get pictures we would like to have a good one. I learned from Freeman that he had Seen father & that Benjamin [Gilley] is going to start back next week. Well father I want you to get $1.00 worth of postage stamps and a lot of envelps and Send them to us by him. Dont forget to Send us 1 flannel under Shirt a peace & Also Send us Each a pocket Hankerchief & Lafayette a neck Hankerchief. I believe that you may Send us a Small ball of yarn & a Darning kneedle So that we Can mend our Socks. I believe this is all we Stand in nead of just now. I want you to look at my book and See how much ben [Gilley] & james Alford ows me. We will get our pay in a few Days & Ben says he wants to pay me then. Wright to us how you are getting along in the money line. Tell the Children that I would answer all of their letters if I had time but I Cannot at the present but I want them to wright as often as they Can. I reckon we will have Some money to Send home when we are payed off. I must bring my letter to Close. We remain you affectionate Sons untill Death.

Wayne & Lafayette Alford

Give my respects to all friends.

[From Dr. Laverty to Franklin]

Camp Advance Hart Co Ky Jan 9th 62

Much Respected Friend

I seat myself once more to remind you of a promise you made me when I left home. That if I would write to you I mite expect answers. You are due me one letter. But as I am now at leasure I will write to you again.

My health at this time is good for which I am very thankful And hope that you and family enjoy health and happiness. As for news I have none. I believe Only that we are wating for some fun. But as yet have been sadly Disapointed. And I think we will still be dispointed. But some of our officers think that we will have some work to do. Our Picketts shot some four of the rebbles last night and took some seven prisoners. The rebbels came in this morning with a flag of truce to take away their Dead. The Picketts came very neare not paying any respect to them and it was with the greatest Difficulty that Col Willikes [August Willich's] men [in the 32nd Indiana Infantry] could be controlled. They cocked their Riffels and was for shooting But they finely gave up. How long it will be before this

unholy war will sease is more than I can say. I am feareful that we
will have to whip England yet. They have not forgoten New Orleans
and now My friend is a fit time for them to do their Dirty Work.
And I do honestly beleive that they will give us fight. I hope not but
I am afraid. Oh how I would love to see it stop [and] that friends
may once more meet who have long been parted. What happy meeting of friends. I got a letter from Home today and I would give all I
expect to make heare in the army if I could go home and see my Dear
Old Mother. She seams to think that she will not live to see [me] again.
Oh my Mother My Mother [if only I could] see you tonight. The word
home has a depth of feeling about it now that It never has had
before. I am perfectly satisfied heare and would not leave heare [and]
if I had a chance to go I would not do it But I would love to see
friends I never expect to see again. And if Providence spares my life,
to get, safe Back again I will pursue a Different course in life. I don
not know when I will get to come home to see you all. I hope soon.

I would love to see you all once more and shoud I live to come
home I think that I can enjoy a long visit. Give my love to Chester
Camp and family and to old Mother Winters. Tell Mother Winters
that I have not forgotten her. I have written Several letters to Aly
[?] Camp but I can git no wourd from him. Wayne & Lafayette are
well. John William [Alford], George Wheeler & Maddison Alford are
doing fine. Please report. I will look for a letter from "you" soon. My
love to Jos & Wife. Give me the news if you have any. So now
farewell. Hoping to heare from you soon. I will ever remain your
Sincere friend & Well wisher.

Dr. J. L. Laverty

My love to friend and family.

[From Father to Warren:]

Lords Day
Home

Mr J Warren Jan the 12th 1862

Dear sir yours of the 2nd Came duely to hand by saturdays Mail
and found us Enjoying our usual health and anxiety to hear from
you. And we hope this may Come duly to hand and find you enjoying the same incomprehensible blessing. I hardly know how to
Express to you my gratitude to him who giveth Life and health and
all things, for his kind Care over us, In sickness & In health In peace
& In war we are asshured that as Is the tender Grace before [the

throne] so Is feeble Man without the protection of him who
Numbereth the Hairs of our Heads and without whose notice Even a
Sparrow doth not fall to the Ground. I hope I shall not have intrud-
ed upon your patience in Expressing our dependance on god and our
strict adherence to his Council. . . . I heard last Monday that Wash had
gone to Town to Institute A suit against you and I thought If he had
after Talking to me as he had I would be sharp Enough for him.
And I started Early Tuesday Morning and went to Washington and
Called at the Clerks Office Intending to give A Judgment and stay It
before It [ran into a lot of] Cost. But he had not bin there and the
Clerk told me he Could not get A Judgment against you without
Serving A summons on you or makeing out that you had gone and
secreted your self to keep from paying your debts. It may be that he
never talked of pushing you. But I am well paid for my ride [to the
courthouse] and If he acts [like a] man I will try to pay him as soon
as I Can and that kneed [not] be long. If I have good luck I [will] settle with Wm Hedrick and his work was worth $25.74 - Exclusive of
the Rent. . . . I have Paid It and got his Receipt. He has done
Considerable on the next Ten Acres. I have been thinking something
about selling him A Cow on the next Ten Acres. I have Paid Kelso
what you owed him for the use of the Mill and [Charley] Donaldson
will Pay Allen. Wayne & Lafayette has been Mustered for Pay and if
they draw all that Is Comeing to them I think they will be able to
send me 50 or 60 Dollars & If you meet with A Chance to send [home
some of] your [pay] I think I Can square up [with] your Uncle
Wayne. [We] got a letter from Dr Laverty yesterday he said Wayne &
Lafayette was well. John William [Alford] has the Measles about fifteen days. He Is on the mend and Dock says . . . soon . . . it will be
safe for him to Come. He will send him home to Recruit. Madison
[Alford] & [George] Wheeler has both taken the Measles. Since your
uncle Ben [Gilley] Came home [he] has so improved that he Expects to
start back next Tuesday. I see they have the Green River Bridge
[near Munfordville, Kentucky] Complete and the Gun Boats at Cairo
[Illinois] Is ready to sail and the Burnside Expedition [to North
Carolina] has already sailed. And I see that some of our boys have
Routed A Rebel Camp on the road from Romney to Winchester
[Virginia]. Warren I have about $30.00 of the old Threshing Accounts
to Collect yet If I Can Get It. Capt Bryant [of the 18th Indiana
Infantry] Is at home. I saw one of his men yesterday. He left the
Camp at [?] about last Thursday. His name Is [Corporal Ellis] Corn
from Dubois [County]. He said Wm Gold was well but John & Henry
Edwards was both sick. Albert Patrick has been sick but Is very near

well. [Alexander] Camp, Joel Goldsmyth, E[benezer] P Gilley &
[Augustine] Bigham [Bingham] are all well. If there Is Any thing In
my Letters that will interest the boys let them hear It. I have almost
forgotten Wm Allen. He is well and so are all the friends and relatives at home. Old Mrs Hill is dead. Tailor Pottes Son James Died of
small Pox In the Army. James [?] Died also but I cant tell what was
his disease. Now Warren as It regards that dowery right on your
land I will try to find out what will be best to do and I will try to do
[what is best] under the Circumstances. Minerva & Wm Sullivan and
George Kelso has the Measles. Warren I want you to go often to A
throne of Grace and when you ask blessing for your self do not forget your friends and Brethren and Companions in Arms. I will Close
by saying Wright often and may the God of Hosts keep and protect
you through life and save you in death is the prair of your kind
parents. F Alford

[From Mother to Warren:]

home Jan the 12th 62

Mr J W Alford
My son i take my pen in hand to let you know that i am wll but
verry lnsome. I can pay the week tolerable well but i tell you sunday is a lonsome day with me. Yet if i am fond complaning i would
think my self unworthy of the position that i ocupy. Neither do i
wish to hear you complan as i hear some. Their is some yung men of
the adjoining neighborhood that apears to not be satisfied with their
lot. I think like margart keese said they had better be soldier at home.
I will not name them but thank God old reeve township has turned
out some as good soldiers as ever handld a musket. Their is one thing
that gives us great staisfaction. I rad the papers regularly and i see
the tories is getting [flattened ?] on all sids. [I] will tell you somthing
else. Miah rainy come home on furlow. It appard to be short as he
did not get his feet warm. It is said the officer was after him. Their
was another man with him and he escaped. It is a pitty that such
boys were started out. I hope our boys will never disgrace them
selves thus. For if they have to die i want them to die soldiers. We
had a letter from laverty. He said Wain & lafayete was well.
Madison [Alford], George wheeler & John W Alford had the measles.
We ricived his letter yesterday. He rote to you . . . that he would have

john sent home as soon as he gets well enough to come. You uncle B
H Gilley is going to start back next tusday. Gram mother winters
recived a letter from her sister. She said her nephew was taken prisoner at romney. He was a lieutenant in a virginia Rdg. [Probably a
Union regiment.] His name is chester hall. She said he and an other
officr went a cros the line to bye butter. They went into a rebbs
huse. Now warren i want you to watch and never ventur to far but
do your hole duty. The children is going to school. They learn verry
fast. Green is the best in geography for enny in the school. George is
second best in arthimetic. Bud wrote that william kelly messed with
you. What have you done with dick. We want to know it all. B T
says lafayette is as fleshy in the face as Minerva. He said he stood
camp life first rate. I guess he is left alone. His mess is all sick. Will
Riley has come home. I guess he will winter here. Give my respects
to W M Houghton and all the boys. If they have anny friends here i
am one. If i hear one word said against the goverment or soldiers
you had better believe their is somboddy mad. Warren wrigt to us
often. I remain your affectionate mother. To j W Alford. I had forgotten how to wright. I thaut i would try to learn agan. I guess you
think it poor writing. Tell Houghton to wright to us.

[Same letter – notes from Thomas Greene and Hellen:]

Alfordvill Jan the 12 1862

J W Alford
Dear brother   I now take my pen in hand to let you [know] that I
am well and hope when this comes to hand it will find you well. . . .
At chool a man by the name of Holloway had a geography singing
the other night and I answered most all of the questions that he
asked. 1 must close. Wright soon.

Thomas Green Alford

Mr J Warren Alford
Dear brother   I am now seated to drop you a few lines. Green told
you about the singing the other night. I went. When I got ther they
had the Maps all over the house. Now Warren it almost schooltime
and I must close for the want of time and space. Ther as ben three
letters written on this sheet and that is enoug I think. Wright soon.
Good by.   Hellen Alford

★

[From Father to Warren:]

Home
Jan the 19th 1862

Mr J Warren Alford   Dear Sir

I am seated again this Lords Day Evening [to] take the liberty to
address you A line according to promise to let you know that we are
Still Enjoying our usual health and happiness. We have but little to
wright as there has nothing new transpired since I last rote to you.
Only Brother Wm Sullivan died In the Hospital at Evansville the past
week and was brought home by His Brother Manoak. He brought
him to the Meeting House on Thursday Evening and he was Buried
at our Grave Yard on Friday (after A verry appropriate Sermon
delivered by your Uncle Wayne) In the Honors of war. Manock has
had the Measles and Is not verry stout. . . . He left George Kelso In the
Hospital with the Measles & his Father Is gone after him. I had A
Letter from Wayne & Lafayette last Tuesday they were well and still
at Munsfordsville [Munfordville].   John Wm & J M Alford & George
Wheeler has all got the Measles but are all on the mend. Your uncle
Ben [Gilley] started back to Camp last Tuesday. I had almost forgot to
tell you that I had a letter from our Friend Laverty on Tuesday last.
He said he was well and Expresed A determination to devote his time
to the service of God. We had A meeting to day . . . and John
Goldsmyths Wife & James Raney Joined the Church. I settled your
Bill say $17 and I forgot the Cents but I have a full Receipt. Warren
I see that there has been some strange moveing from Romney
[Virginia] over In to the Edge of Maryland. There appears to be general move Just at Hand all along the Union lines and we listen for
stiring nuse from all quarters soon. The Mississippi Fleet Is about
starting [a] quest of something. . . .

This is Monday morning dark and Cloudy and verry muddy but we
have [had] A great deal of fine weather and I will not now Complain.
Tom Brown left Alfordsville about Two weeks ago and last saturday
his Wife got A letter from him stateing that he went to Louisville and
volunteered in A Cavelry Company. I saw and read A letter from
Wm Gold this morning and he said he weighed 166 1/2 lbs. I guess
that [he] Is 20 lbs more than his Common weight. Your Aunt Eliza
had A wood Choping saturday last and George sad she got A fine
chance of wood. Old Brother Joseph Wilson told me yesterday that his
Son Burton was at Frederick [Maryland] In the 27th Reg of Ind vol-

unteers. The Government Troops appears to be gaining Ground at every point. And It looks like king Cotton will soon be dethroned and the Constitution Reign supreme. But I will Close by admonishing you to be faithful until Death and the reward will be Eternal life where you will enjoy the Company of Friends & Brethren to all Eternity. So nomore but remains your affectionate Parents & Brothers & sisters. So Goodby. Ever yours.

Franklin Alford

[From Wayne and Lafayette to Father:]

Camp Advance
January 18th 1862

Mr Franklin Alford   Dear father   It is with pleasue I seat myself to let you know how we are getting along. Lafayette and myself are both enjoying verry good health Since I got over that little brash that I had. I feel better than I have felt for Some time & as for Lafayette he is getting almost pussey. He has fattened ever Since he came to Camp. We received a letter from you just before [Uncle] Benjamin [Gilley] Came Back & owing to Being Very Busy I Did not have time to answer it until we received your letters by the hand of uncle Benjamin [Gilley] & now I will just answer them both in this. The presents you Sent us were thankfully received & Specialy Mothers Sausage & butter & cake. I will just return you our Sincere thanks as we have Nothing to repay you at present. But we Will try and repay you by living as Soldiers & Christian in every Sence possible. Well I have Nothing New to wright you at this time. John William [Alford] has got out of the Hospital this Eavening & is getting along verry well. Madison [Alford] is getting along as well as ever I Saw anybody. . . . He is still in the Hospital but He will be out in a few Days. Their is Nothing Strange gowing on . . . they are Still working away on the Breastworks across the river. They will have it Done in a few Days. I dont see any prospect of a forward Move though I think we will not move untill the roads Settles a little. . . . The rebals Came up the other Night within Eight Miles of our Pickets & burned Cave City a little town & they burned about three hundred cords of Wood & a Hay Stack & a Fodder Stack but they took good care to keep out of the way [of] our guns. Our Regiment was on picket on the out post but we Saw No chance to get a Shot at them. They are Cavalry Scouts & whenever they hear of our being Near they Dont stay to See it. Well father I must Close for the want of Something to wright but Before I close I will return our Sincere thanks for the kindness you Showed us & Sending us those Shirts and provisions you sent us. You may think Strange of my being So busy in as much as we Dont Drill any. Well the reason is that our orderly Segeant is sick & I have to attend to the business for him. Well I must bring my letter to a close I will Wright to you again as Soon as I get any thing to wright. Give my love to all the friends and reserve a portion for your Selves. We remain as ever your affectionate sons untill Death.

Wayne & Lafayette Alford

George I will wright to you as soon as I get time.

W A

[From Dr. Laverty to Franklin:]

Camp Advance Hart Co Ky Jan 21st 62

Mr Franklin Alford
Respected friend

As I am not able to do any labour of any kind all I can do then is to write to friends at home. And as I have always considered you among that number I will now give you a few lines I received your kind and welcome letter day before Yesterday and would have written immediately but to tell the truth I was not able to do so. But I hope this will answer as a sufficient excuse. I was glad to heare from you and home for thrown out heare as I am when I fail to get letters from those who I corespond with it often fills my heart with gloom. So far as news are consirned we are now under marching orders. Whear our place of Destination will be is hard to tell. I hope Bolden [Bowling] Green. The Regiment had orders to cook three days Rashens preparatory to a March. I think it is high time this portion of the army would begin to do something. I may be saying to much by senturing [censuring] Genl [Alexander McDowell] McCook for I suppose he had to obey orders from General [Don Carlos] Buell But I will venture to say this. It is a disgrace to our Division of the army under Buell to let the Rebbels come within gun shot of our Pickets and Burn and Destroy property.

I was sitting in My tent this evening a little after dark talking with some friend who had called to see me When the orderly came running in and said that Rebbels had set [fire] to the Rail Road Depot. ... We get up and went out and sure enough their it was all in a blaze and it within a half mile of our Picket lines. And I suppose they will finish the balance of the town before morning. Its awfull to see the work of destruction. But I hope that the day of their retribution is close at hand and that they will pay for it yet. I presume before this reaches you will have heard of the death of the notorious Zoligoffer [Confederate General Felix Zollicoffer]. He got into the rong pew. . . . This [Edwin McMasters] Stanton who is the Secratary of War Dep I know well. Often have I heard him plead at the Barr. He is from the county seat of Jefferson Co [Ohio,] Steubenville. A lawyer by profesion and a great gentleman I will Tell you an incident that I . . . know Consirning him if I ever see you again if you do not let me forget it. It will make you laugh. I did think I would get to come home once more in Feb to see you all but I am afraid the chance is

Secretary of War, Edwin McMasters Stanton. *(USAMHI)*

poor. The health of the Reg is poor And our first Surgeon told me this evening in my tent he did not see how he could possibly spare me to go. I shall feel very sorry if I should not get to go But I will not complain. I saw Wayne, Lafayette & John William [Alford] this evening. They are all Well. John William is doing fine. He has called [on me] twice a day since I have been sick. He will come home on Furlough as soon as we can succeed in getting them through for him & Maddison [Alford] and George Wheeler. It is the opinion now Franklin of our more popular men or those more acquainted with national affairs that this war will soon be over. For my part I must confess I do not or cannot form any opinion of my own. I do hope that it may soon find an end It is true if they should get a few more stabs such as they got last Sunday they will begin to think that a Southern Confederacy is not the thing it is Recommended to be. It is a good deal like the doctor's pill it will be hard to swollow [and] "It will be awfull bitter." But so it goes. Let them "have it" so. Well I believe I will stop and go to rest as I feel weary tonight and would like to have some rest. Give my love to Chester & wife, [?] Winters, J. A. McCord and wife & Remember me to your lady and family.

"O see heare." Tell James Alford and wife I have not forgotten them altho I have never written to them but tell James I will do it

soon. I mean James that lives out back of the school House. Give
him and wife my respect. I will try and come home If I can But lest
I wear your patience I will bid you good night. Hoping to heare from
you. I will remain Your friend as ever.

Dr. J. L. Laverty
asst Surgeon 6th Reg In Vol

Tell Mother Winters I heard from Alex today. He is well and hearty.
(L)

[From Wayne and Lafayette to the family, with a special note to George:]

Camp Wood Green River Ky
January 22nd 1862

Mr Franklin Alford & Family   Dear Sir
We are hapy this Morning to have the privaledge of addressing you a
few lines through the Medium of [pen] & paper this being the only
means at present. We received your letter by the hand of Dr Laverty
and was verry glad to hear from you again & to learn that you were
Still well. Your letter Came to hand just as our regiment was Starting
out on Picket & consequently I could not answer it untill we
returned home. Nothing to wright that would interest you at present.
We are all well at present. John William [Alford] is in Camp Now
but he Does not Do Any Duty yet. Madison [Alford] is in the hospital
yet He looks about as well as ever he did. . . . Their is room in the
Hospital for Him and it is a better place for him than in Camp. We
have had not very cold weather here yet and the citizens say that the
winter Has been as cold as common. It Has never been So Cold but
what two of us Sleeping together & laying our blankets and overcoats
over us would Sleep warm enough. I received A letter from william
Porter & [Alexander] C Camp. [Both in Company E of the 18th
Indiana.] They are well but the weather is Verry Cold their. They
are still near Otterville [Missouri] & Dont know when they will move.
They Say they think if ever they get a fight they will Have to leave
Misourie. I find they Have the Same Opinion of Misourie that we
have of Kentucky. Father I will Close for the present for I want to
wright Some to [my brother] George & [my brother-in-law] Charley in
this letter. [Letter to Charley not found.] Tell Mother that we
received the Darning Kneedle. She Seamed to be afraid we were getting bare for Socks. You Need not be afraid of that for [I still have]
the 2 pair of Socks that I brought from Home [and] we are Saveing

them & wairing Our Government Socks as they are tolerable good yet. We remain your affectionate Sons untill Death. Wayne & Lafayette Alford

P.S. Well George I would be verry Glad if I Could think of something to wright but I will Declose I Hardly know how to begin. Our Regiment Has orders to Keep 3 Days Rations Cooked ahead and it is thought we will Start pretty Soon on a 3 Days Recanoicence. But I think it Doubtful George. Lafe & I are fat and hearty but I have run out of Soap. So I will bring my letter to a Close. We would be verry glad to See you all again but Cannot at present. George Wright as Soon as you can and believe us to Be your affectionate Brothers untill Death.

W & L Alford

[From Warren to the family at home:]

Camp North Branch Bridge
Maryland January the 25th 62

Affectionate Parents
Brothers & Sisters
It is With pleasure I received your kind Letters. One on yesterday. . . . The one from you and the one from Mother and one from the Children all in the same Letter. But thought I would not answer it till I would get an othe Letter as I had Written you on the day before. I hav had so much Writing to do since I came here. I rote A letter to Wayne and Lafayette day befor yesterday and one to Sam Gilley this Morning and have ritten several . . . more since I came here. We have our New Tents and stoves in them. They are vary comfortable Much more Comefortable than we was in the Old Courthouse in Romney. That was the nasties place I ever saw. It is worse than Cheat Mountain if possible. We could not get Good water that was fit to wash our selves in. But we have pleanty of good Water to use here. We are where the [B&O] Railroad Crosses the Potomac and the canall [Chesapeake and Ohio]. [The canal is] 30 yards from our quarters. The ground is now coverd with snow but it is not vary Cold now nor has their bin any vary cold weather here yet this winter. I am glad to [hear] Mother is tryin to learn to write. Give Grand fathers and grand Mothers My best respects. I would like to hear how they ar geting a long in their old age. Tell Uncle Jim Gilley and aunt Cis that I send them my best Respects and will rite to them as soon as I have a chance. And I want them to Write to me as they have abeter cance to right than I have. But I write a letter

Most every day when we are not on the March and have some that
is not answered at this time. Tell Hannah that I will answer herse a
soon as I get paper. This the last sheet of paper I have on hands. You
sayed you heared that W Hedrick was going to push on that Note. I
hope you will soon have the meanes to meet that note. If Edmund
Trulove meets his prommis which I think he will. . . . As to hedrich
Clearing I want him to try and get it all in next spring if he can and
I will try to save the Money for him but I want you to just do with
my things as if they was yours. But I do not want you to . . . troubl
your self on my account nor do I want you to use the other boys
money for my benefit. I think I can save some money and you can
sell any thing I hav till my debts are paid. I must soon come to a
close. I was sorry to hear of the deat of Wm Sulivan but we all must
dye sooner or later. I am still trying to live so that I may be able to
sustane my Christian caracter and so that if we never meet on earth
we will be sure to meet in Heaven as ever your affectionate son.
  Jas Warren Alford

I receive the small preasant you sent me by Col Kimble [Kimball] but
it was not vary profitable one. If it had been in the shape of a ring I
would have thought none of it. And as to geting my likeness. I have
[not had a] chance . . . to get it and do not now when we will have a
chance to have it done. I must Close.

James Warren Alford
to the Children

[From Father to Warren:]

Home Monday Morning Jan 27

Respect Son   Mr J Warren Alford
Kind Sir again with pleasure I am seated to answer your kind note
of the 16th Inst which came duely to hand on the 25th and found us
all well (and likewise all your friends and also all the friends of
your respected associates about Alfordsville). [We were] verry anxious
to hear from you again as we had not heard from you only rather
Indirectly through the nuse papers since the 2nd Inst and I suppose
you are as anxious to hear from us as we are to hear from you. I
suppose It Is not reasonable that you feel the same anxiety about us
that we do for you as we are less Exposed than your self to the rav-
ages of this unholy Crusade against the quiet enjoyment of the rights
garunteed unto us by that Glorious old Constitution under whose protection we and Even Rebels have Dwelt secure for these 80 years.
But the Rebels like many A naughty boy have grown haughty and
ungrateful and have Justly merited the Chastening frowns of this

mighty Republic. The emblem of whos Honor and mighty power
proudly waves on Every Sea and In Every port where the name of
the Lord Is known. . . . But enough of this. Warren I have been faithful In Compliance with my promise and have written to you regularly every week regularly every Monday morning. I remember my
obligations to one of whose Patriotism we are proud. We had A letter
from Dr Laverty last Saturday he says he Is unable to do anything
but write to his friends. But Wayne & Lafayette was quite well.
John W & Madison [Alfords] and George Wheeler have all had the
Measles. John was out of the Hospital and It was thought that
Madison would be soon but Wheeler was not quite so well. Tell
Bolivar [Gold] that Wm Gold Weighs 166 1/2. I see an account of A
prisoner arriving at Richmond by the way of Manassas A few days
ago wose name Is Wm Redding Sergeant In Co I of the 14th Reg of
Ind Volunteers. Now the reason I have Written this Is because I had
[read] that there was A man A missing from the Reg that Could not
be accounted for. Hillary Seay has Come Home to spend A few days
with his Family & friends and I am going to see him as soon as I am
done writing. And as Mail time Is drawing near I must Close till
another week rolls around. Things Is glideing along In their old chan-
nel without any Change of note. Give my love to all my friends who
would be Interested with A perusual of this Epistle and donot stint
your self. So fare you well. In hope that God In his abundant mercy
may bless us all In time and save us In Eternity for the sake of
Christ Is the Prair of your Humble Father. Just this moment I hear
of the Death of Feilden Gillocks Wife by Measles. Sononore but
remains your affectionate parents and brothers & sisters. Until
Death.

F & M Alford

James Gilley send you his love.

★

[From Dr. Laverty to Franklin:]

Read to friends if you see fit

Jan 30th 1862
Medical Department 6th Reg Ind

Mr Franklin Alford
  Respected friend
  I am seated tonight in my tent to answer your ever welcome let-
ter which came Duly to hand and was read by me with intrest.

Your letter found me enjoying very good health at presant and I hope that now I may see better times than I have saw for the last two months. I was also glad to heare that you and family wer well and the health of the neighberhood was good for I do not Desire that old Gutts should get one call while I am gone. [Evidently, reference to the Alfordsville physician.] I have had but little New for you friend Franklin. At presant as we are still laying heare inactive so far as fighting is concerned but of course still preparing for the bloody work. I have heard for several Days that we will have a battle heare. Our Regiment on picket duty day before Yesterday captured an Indian scout or spy (whichever you choose to call him). I call him nothing but a spy and as I told our Lietenent Col if I had my way I would shoot the good fornothing cuse. However they Brought him into camp and he told us that General Heineman [Confederate General Thomas Hindman] had fifteen days alloted him by the Rebbel Jonston [Albert Sidney Johnston] to attack us heare and that if he did not do it in that time they would have him [replaced] by some one else. Well if they have a mind to try it let them pitch in. I think if I am not mistaken they will meet with a warm reseption from some of the Hoosier Boys. And I also think that they will have the pleasure of Digesting some Galena Pill [cannon balls] before they cross the Green River for I can assure you that their is large Mouth's arti-cles of Merchandise right on the hill above the ford that command a view of two miles both up and down the river and that it is very thickly settled with gentleman cannon which I have heard [speak] in thunderest [sounds many] times long ago. . . . They [will] have . . . to face [the cannons] and do their own dancing besides.

And you cannot imagine how Franklin impudent and saucy the rebbels are. How conspicuous they try to make themselves. I will give you an instance of their impudence. Today the corpse of old Zoligoffer [Confederate General Felix Zollicoffer] and Bailey Peyton [Lieutenant Bailie Peyton, Jr.] his aid [de] Camp Came on the express train to the depot Just above our Camp About 2 ock. Their was an escort of Rebbels came up to our out side Pickett with a flage of truce And in [?] language Demand of the Picketts if this was the advance of General [Don Carlos] Buells army. They wer told by the pickets that they considered it was none of their Business. When the rebbel Cap who had the command told our pickets they had Business with [Union] general [Alexander McD.] McCook and that they wanted through the lines. But their was some of the blood of seventy six about our Boys and they wer told That they could go no farther unless they the Picketts had further order from general McCook. A Runner was sent into Camp And the General McCook and [General Lovell] Rousaw [Rousseau] with guard went out to see what the fools desired. They had brought a flag of truse for the body of the notori-ous Zoligoffer and aid. But they came on a fools errand. They wer politly invited to go back and as soon as we got tired of looking at the old rebbel we would see he got down into seceshdom by an escort of our own men. So we will have the pleasure of going down into the land of Dixie to see for ourselves. I want if Possible to go along if I can get away. I am invited to see the old chap in the morning before he goes off at head Quarters. But to cap the climax he has not got a bit of hair on his head. The place wheare the hair out to grow Our Boys pulled it all out and he is as bare on the head as a Balled eagle. [A rather strange rumor. After Zollicoffer's body was returned, the Confederate officials were complimentary of how respectfully the Union officers had treated the body.]

Confederate Brigadier General Felix Kirk Zollicoffer. (Miller's)

I told some of our officers to night if they would let me have him 6 hour I would Scrape his Bones for him and save them the trouble of sending him off. But I suppose they will not do it. I would love to do it and with a nice grace to. Our Picketts today caught a Texian Ranger splendly mounted and brought him into Camp. The poor Deveil did not like to be disarmed of his side arms and carbine or shot gun but they told him he had to [do] it. They took him to head Quarters. I have not heard what they done with him. I supose they will send him to head Quarters at Louisville. I have saw a goodly number of Rebbels since I have been heare and expect to see more of them if I should be permited to follow the army. I will tell you some fun I had the other day in Company with a first Sergent and the Medical Staff togather with several others if I should live to come home Franklin. If ever a horse run he did that day I can assure you. But I must stop and get to bed as it is now midnight and the camp is hushed in Sleep. Everything Quiet save the sentry who called out 12 ock and all right. I am sending a paper to Chester Camp published at Madison Ind. Notice a peiece I have marked in it Relative to a young man who died on his road home after taking him out of Hospitle. Giv my respect to you wife, Jos McCord and family & Chester [Camp] and do not forget Grand Maw

Winters. The boys are all well and hearty. John William [Alford]
and Layfatte wer down in my tent tonight John is improving nicly.
B. F. G.[illey] send his respect. I will see you all after while if the
health of the Reg improves. . . . Read this to friends if you see fit.
Farewell now my friend Franklin and write to me when ever you
can as I am glad to heare from you. It Does me good to get a letter
from you. I will ever remain you sincere friend.
J. L. Laverty

★

[From Wayne to the family at home:]

P.S. I read [wrote] the 1st & 3 pages & then the 2nd & 4th. I made a
mistake.

                                        Camp at Green River
                                         January 30th 1862
Mr Franklin Alford   Dear father   I am happy to inform you we
are Still enjoying reasonable portion of health. We received a letter
from Warren Last Eavening & he was in Maryland at Camp North
Branch Bridge. He is well as common & they had orders to keep
themselves in ready to march at an Hours Notice but he Said that
had been the orders for Several Weeks. So he Did Not know when
they would move but I learn Since his letter that they have had a
fight their but I cannot tell whether it is the fact or not. We was
glad to hear that you were all enjoying good health. We learned from
Hellens letter that you had the news their that we had had a battle
here. Well it is all a mistake. We have had no battle Nor is their any
Prospect of a Battel. Our men are Still Working away at the
Breastworks and have Nearly completed them and besides this
Captain Stones Battery are throwing up entreanchments on the
Heights on this Side of the river. But what the intention is I cannot
tell. Well father the report is that their is a flag of Truce on the Side
of the river. I will not close my letter untill we hear further. Their
has [been] a regiment or two just went over. Their is no further
News here at present. Our Orderly Sergeant has gone home on furlow So I have to act in his place untill he comes Back. That will be
the tenth of next Month. The Boys that had the measels are getting
along verry well.   Lieutenant [Henry C.] Hall from [Washington,
Indiana] has got back. He is not quite well yet though he is better. I
will finish my letter tonight if I can.

Well I promised to wright more to you tonight. That flag of truce came after the Body of [Confederate] General [Felix] Zolacoffer [Zollicoffer]. It is at Munfordsville [Munfordville] & tomorrow our Men is to take it out to them as they will not be allowed to come inside of the pickets. Our pickets brings in a prisoner or two almost every Day. Yesterday Our Regiments was on Picket yesterday and one of rebals . . . said he was half Indian & that he was in the rebal army as Cook but we took him to be a Texian Ranger. But it was all guess work with us. [When] he come to our Lines he Said he was Deserting from the rebal army. So we took him and brought him in to Camp [and] Sent him to head quarters & I dont know what they Done with him. You must excuse this awkward Letter for Some how in turning over the paper instead of Commencing at the 2nd page I turned over Commenced on the third page & never new any better untill I turned over again. Turn to 4th page.

Dear Mother we received yourn and Greene letters this Eavening and have nothing to wright to you more than I have written to father. You Spoke of Jerry Rainy's Deserting and coming home & you Did not know what they Do with him & then Spoke of his Digraceing himself. Well mother one thing I can assure you that we would love to see you all as well as any body I Suppose but if we never come home untill we have to Dessert and Disgrase ourselves and parents forever you may be Sure we never Desire to go home. We were raised Honorable and left home honorabley & we expect to return honorably or not at all. All our Desire is that we may be Soldiers and Christians while it is ours to live and if we never meat on earth let us live So that we may meat in heaven. This is the earnest prair of your unworthy Son. Tell the children that we would be verry glad to See them all & we want them to wright to us as often as they Can. But My Sheet is full & I must Close. Accept our best wishes and believe us to be your affectionate Sons until Death.

Wayne & Lafayette Alford

[From Franklin and Mary to Warren:]

Home
Feb the 2nd 1862

Mr James Warren Alford
Most Obedient Son The time has arived that I according to promise [must] drop you A line In answer to your kind and affectionate let-ter of the 25th which Came to hand yesterday full of Comfort to your kind relatives and friends and found us all Enjoying Common health. And [we] rejoiced to know that you were blessed with health

and Christian fortitude. Now Warren my Prair to God Is that your
Efforts to secure his favor may be Crowned with the best of
Consequences and the most unmistakeable Evidence of his approval of
your Christian Character. I hear that Capt Brooks has got home but I
have not had the Chance to see him but I shall try to see him soon If
not hindered. Warren your Grand Father & Mother Alford was here
& your Aunt Eliza also and heard your letter last Eavening. Your
Aunt was hunting the Tax Receipt that John Grismore got for her
last winter and I told her that I felt shure I sent It to her by you. If
you Can Call to mind anything about It let me know for the Land is
delinquent in Houghtons name. Warren I fear Trulove will not be
paying anything on that note soon. He says he has It oweing to him
but Cannot get It. And I am at A loss to know what to do and he Is
Talking of going with Brother Sed to drive a Team. But I think It
uncertain he has not paid up for the machine yet. I have about 250
Bu of wheat to sell and It Is worth from 85 [cents] to $1.00 In
Cincinnati and I shall ship It as soon as the Roads get so that I can
Hall It. I have not had a letter from your brothers sinse last Tuesday.
They were well and verry anxious to hear from you. I hope they
have had A letter from you before [you receive] this. There was letters from John William [Alford] & Madison [Alford] and all was well.
Warren I have thought something about that dowery and I Counciled
A Lawyer and he says he would not give more than $25.00 for It at
the present time & I told Bro C[hester] Camp If he Could get her Claim
for that Amount I would Give It. But nothing more at present. He
told me he had written to her and If he got an answer I should see It
and perhaps I will gain some Information. And If I do I will write to
you again about it. But It Is getting late and we have bowed around
the Family Alter which I believe we have done…at Home as regularly
as Evening Shades return. Think O think of Earnestness with which
we approach a Throne of Grace In Behalf of the Dear ones who have
often said amen to our humble Prairs. But I must retire hopeing to
be able to finish my letter In the morning.

Well Warren this Morning hails us In the Enjoyment of health and
Happiness and A longing desire for an Amicable adjustment of the
difficultys that has sundered the ties of our once happy union. The
love of which has Caused many a brave Boy to leave home and
friends and rally around th Emblem of our liberty. And God speed
the time when It will again Float In unmolested triumph over Every
Inch of Coulumbias soil and those who have been engaged In holding
It . . . be returned home In triumpth to Enjoy the reward due to
them on account of their Toils. And that all nations may know that
the Amerian People are Capable of sustaining A republican
Government. Wm Kelso Jr enlisted About the last of Oct In the 58 [th
Indiana Infantry] Reg and It Is said that he is dead and It Is believed.

[Kelso died January 20 at Bardstown, Kentucky.] Well Warren I believe George Is third In Grammer Class and Green Is best In Geography. George Is second best In Arithmetic. Warren I want you to remember me to all our Friends and Especially Bro Houghton. Warren show him this If you see fit and If there Is any thing In It that will Interest him I shall be happy to know that I have pened a line that has Contributed to A Friend and Brother the least ray of Comfort. My love to Col Kimball also. Tell him that A letter from any of them would meet with A hearty welcome and duely appreciat- ed by us. Warren we have A Gloomy looking morning. It haveing snowed and rained last night and the ground Is white snow and Ice this morning but It Is not verry Cold. Nearly all the Dogs in the neighborhood has been biten by a mad Dog last Evening and this morning. But I must Close by Commending you to God. . . . Yours Truely.

Franklin & Mary Alford

[From Lafayette to George, Hellen and Thomas Greene:]

Camp Advance
February 3rd

Dear Brothers and Sisters   It is with pleasure I take the opertunity to write you a fiew lies to inform you that we are well. . . . We received your letter Hellen [which pleased us to learn] that you was well and to lern that you had not forgotten us. . . . I thought being as I had this sheat with the ballad ["Red, White and Blue"] on it I would send it to you. . . . Learn it and sing it when I come home. Well George I would like to sea you all and go to school with you but I can- not but you must be contented til I come back. I think I will come back by and by. You must take good care of the horses but I know you will. Madison [Alford] has came back from the Hospital. [George] Wheeler is getting Along very well. The helth of the Regiment is git- ting Better than it has bin but there was one man dide out of our Company yesterday and he was innbalmed last nite. And they are going to send him home today. His name was John Killion [from Daviess County who died of "disease" at Woodsonville, Kentucky.] It is very Mudy here. It rains nearly all the time. The river rases and falls like the creeks in Indiana. . . . How do you gitalong with sing ing when you goto meating. But I must Close by say ing this leaves us well. Write often for you do not know how much good it does us to hear from you. Nothing more.

Lafayette Alford

Red, White and Blue

Oh Columbia, the gem of the Ocean, The home of the brave and the free, The shrine of each patriot's devotion, A world offers homage to thee, Thy mandates makes heroes assemble When liberty's form stand in view, Thy banner make tyrants tremble When borne by the red, white and blue.

Chorus -

 When borne by the red, white and blue, When borne by the red, white and blue, Thy banners make tyrants tremble When borne by the red, white and blue. When the war waged its wide desolation, And threatened our land to deform, The ark then of Freedom's foundation, Columbia rode safe through the storm. With her garland of victory o'er her, When so proudly she bore her bold crew, With her flag proudly floating before her The boast of the red, white and blue.

The boast of, &c.

The wine cup, the wine cup bring hither, And fill you it to the brim; May the wreath they have won never wither Nor the star of their glory grow dim; May the service united not sever, And hold to their colors so true! The Army and the Navy for ever, Three cheers for the red, white and blue

Three cheers, &c.

[From George to Warren:]

Mr James Warren Alford   Dear Brother
I am seated this eavning to drop you a few lines to inform you that I am well and have not forgoten you yet. I was down at C. W. Dondelson [Donaldson, the brother-in-law] last night. I rode your Mare down and she carryed me high. She is one of the best ridind animels about. While I was down there I went to see George Kelso. His Father braught him home from the Hospittal at Evansville and he has had the Mumps since he got home and it goes very hard with him. I dont think he will be able for Survice for some time. Warren I want to no what kind of land you have in Maryland whether it is good as Ind or not. I want to no whether you ever shave or not and if you dont how long has your beard has got by this time. I will close by saying write to me when Convenient.
Goodby G. W. Alford

★

[From Thomas Greene to Warren:]

Home Feb the 9 1862

Dear Brother   We received your kind letter of the 25th ult and was glad to know that you was well and georg received a letter from Lafayette and they was well. John Gold [of Company E of the 18th Indiana] cam hom Night be fore last. He got a furlough for 30 days and he was very pourly. Hilry Seas [possibly John H. Seay of the Company D, 24th Indiana] is going to start back to morrow and Edman Foulow and Mitchel White and John White & Andrew White is going with him they are going as wagners. I guess they can not make soldiers out of them. I am so slow I believe I will get george.

[Different handwriting as George takes over.] The boys had a polemic the other night and the old War horse went home mad. He proposed a question and the boys voted it down and he got mad over it. He dropped something on the floor and Isaac Camp allowed [he had been dropped]. Remains your unworthy brother   T. G. Alford (the war horse is J W Jackman)

★

[From Hellen to Warren:]

Alfords ville Ind Feb the 9th 62

Mr J Warren Alford   Dear brother

I am now seated to drop you a few lines in answer to yours of the 25th. This is A fine morning. The first day the Sun has shown … clearly for several days. George & me received A letter from Lafayette. He sent us A Union Song and he said the boys were well now. Warren there was a Mad Dog running through the Country and bit most all the Dogs. . . . He bit Bill Williams cow. We put Mitch up as soon as we herd it and Charley just shot Colonel. Enough about the dogs. Dock Laverty wrote A letter to Father. He Said they brought the body of Old Zolicofer [Confederate General Felix Zollicoffer] and Bailey Peyton his aiddecamp on the express train to the Depot just above our Camp about 2 ock. There was an escort of rebbels came up to our out-side pickets with A flag of truce and…demanded of the Picketts if this was the Advance of General [Don Carlos] Buells army. They wer told [by] the pickets that it was none [of] there business. When the Reble Capt Said they had business with General [Alexander McD.] McCook and that they wanted through the lines. But there was some of the blood of Seventy Six about our boys and they wer told that they could go no further till they the (Pickets) had further orders from General McCook. A runner was sent in to camp and General McCook and Rousaw [Lovell Rousseau] with guard went out to see what the fools desired. They had brought A flag of truse after the body of the notorious Zolicoffer and [his] aid and they wer told to go back and as soon as we got tired of looking at the old Chap we would see he got down in to dixie. But to clap the climx he has not A bit of hair on his head. Our boys pulled it all out and he is as bald on the head as a balled egal. But enough of Old Zollecoffer. Now Warren I have bin out to Mr Seays to get him to show me how to Sing A Song that Lafayette Sent me. Mr Seay is A going to start back in the mourning . . . to Mo [Missouri]. Rick Burries is a going to start to morrow. I saw him this evening and he looks very well again. Now Warren Clem and Hannah is here to night. Warren I would like to see you and have a long talk with you. O how I long to See you all but I guess I will just have to wait till you come home Warren. Green Says that he forgot one thing that he wanted [to] wright. He is in Federal Money in the Arithmatic. He does not Cipher at School. He just Cipher at home. But I must close for the preasant. Wright to me soon. I ever remains your unworthy Sister. Goody

Hellen Alford

[From Franklin to Warren:]

Home February 10th 62

Mr Jas Warren Alford   Dear Sir   The Children have all written you A [letter] but perhaps you would not be willing to Excuse me. Well Warren we received yours of the 25th ult which came to hand last Saturday and found us all well and glad to hear from you again. We are all Enjoying Common health up to the present Morning and I hope this may Come duely to hand and find you and your friends quite well. Your Aunt received your letter last Saturday and I was glad to hear again that you was well. We [learned] from Saturdays [newspaper] that Landers [Union General Frederick West Lander's] force have repossessed Romney [Virginia]. We learn also by the same Paper that the Federal Gun Boat fleet have run up the Tennessee River to Fort Henry [Tennessee]. The [Confederate] Infantry run off and after A sharp Contest of about an Hour and A quarter the [Union forces] took the Fort with all the Contents [which included] Twelve or fifteen mostly large bore Cannon and about Twenty

Mortars & about Sixty Prisoners. But I hope you may have had the full particulars of the hole affair before this faint picture Comes to hand. I believe there Is an Expedition up the Cumberland River but that Is all I know about It. Well Warren I will tell you who talks of going with J. H. Seay to drive teams. Edmund Trulove And White McWhite & Son, Alf Patterson. . . . I wrote to you In my last [letter] I hardly knew what to do about what Edmund owes you but I finally Concluded that the best I Could do would be to get his father to put his name to the note which I did by agreeing to wait Six Monthes and took his note for $37.12 the amount behind on the machine. I have not got the Corn Debt yet but the sale Money Is Comeing due and If I dont get It before I think I Can manage to get It then. I have not Payed our Tax yet but I have the most of the money. Yours and mine together Is about $42 and If paid against [before] the middle of March It will be all right. We had A letter from Lafayette & Wayne last Saturday and they were well and so were all the boys. I heard that Bolivar [Gold] Wrote that virgil [Alford] had had A Chill. Warren I am writing regularly Every Week and I shall Expect the same from you. Without [a doubt] you have A reasonable Excuse. I Commenced my letter last night but there was Company Came In and I had to pospone It till this morning and I have written twice as [much as] I Expected but I must Close by Exhorting you to be faithful In the discharge of the duties you owe to God and to [man]. And If we meet nomore on Earth let us meet In Heaven. So fare you well. We subscribe our selves your truely.

Franklin & Mary Alford

[From Wayne and Lafayette to Father:]

Camp at Green River
February 11th 1862

Mr Franklin Alford

   Dear Father   This is to infom you that your verry kind letter Came to Hand on yesterday Eaveining. [I was] anxious to hear from you again. Yesterday was a verry busy Day for Soldiers. Not particular for our regiment as we Done nothing but Stand by and look on all the troops that were at Bacon Creek passed by our Camp & crossed over the river into the land of Dixie. Their was about twelve hundred Cavalry & about thirteen regiments of infantry with Some Six batteries of artillery. Among which was Loomises [Colonel Cyrus Orlando Loomis' First] Michigan Artillery. Our brigade has not

Union Brevet Brigadier General Cyrus Orlando Loomis. (USAMHI)

received Marching orders as I know of. We have orders to keep too Days Cooked rations on hands though it is thought we will be left here to Guard the Bridge. One of our Boys by the name of Killion [John Killion from Daviess County] Died in the hospital of Measels (but at this time all of the Soldiers who Die or are killed in this Division have to be embalmed & Sent home if the friends desire it). I Was present and Witnessed the . . . [emblaming]. It was Done by our Doctors [Samuel H] Charlton [from Seymour, Indiana] & [James] Laverty [from Alfordsville] & after one is embalmed he will keep for weeks as natural as life. We then dressed him up as well as circumstances would admit & Got him a Coffin Made [out of an old] box and expressed it home. The Health of the Camp is Getting Smartly better than it has been formerly. The Clerk of the Weather has been Giving us plenty of rain for Some time. The weather has been Just about warm enough to rain. Well Green river has been verry high last week but it is Down now. It Just raises and falls Just like Shugar Creek. In the high water they had to tear out the Pontoon bridge for to let the Drift through. But they have floored the Railroad bridge So that all the troops that passed yesterday passed over it [and] So that if the Pontoon bridge Should Go Down we Could [still] pass over [the river]. I Sent you a Louisville Journal by to Days Mail which has a Correspondence from a member of our Company, Viz. Wm S Gaffney the old School examiner in Daviess. It is Headed Camp at Green river. He Wrights tolerably often to the Journal and as often as I find anything from him that is interesting I will Send it to you. I Have nothing more of interest. I will keep you posted So far as I can. Wright as often a you Can. This leaves us well I remain as ever your Sons untill Death.

Wayne & Lafayette Alford

★

Pontoon Bridge over a Small Stream. (NA)

A Temporary Bridge over the Flooded Big Barren River at Bowling Green, Kentucky. (USAMHI)

[From cousin John Kellams to Warren:]

Alfordsville Daviess County Ind
february the 16 1862

Mr James W alford my Dear cosine It is with the gratest of peasure
that I embrace this presant oppertunity of informing you that i am
well and cincerly hopeing these few lines may find you well. I have
not got any answer for that letter I wrote you last . . . but I suppose
you have not got it yet. I cant think of any thing to write Just now
but I thought that [since] uncle franklin was [writing you, I would
send this with his envelope and] I would let you know that I am
Well and harty. They are a singing geography now and I cant think
of any thing but that. . . . Will Close for this time but remains you
affectiont cosine until Death. May the good lord bless you and awl
the good soldiers. Excuse bad Writing and an awkward hand for the
scribe. You may write A few lines to me if you please.

Good By For This time.
John Wesley
Kellams
to
James Warren
Alford

[From Wayne and Lafayette to Father:]

February 21st 1862
Camp on the L & N RR
86 Miles South of Louisville

Mr Franklin Alford   It is with Some difficulty that I get this oppertunity to answer your letter which came Duly to hand & found us
well. We Started on the Morning of the 14th and have been marching untill the 19th. Only Stopped then to repair the R. R. which the
rebels had torn up So that we Could get provisions along. We are
under marching orders at this time & yesterday Eavening we Sent
half of our baggage on 11 Miles to where their was stone pike. We
expect to go on today. The rebels are retreating & it is Supposed that
we will push on to nashville. . . . General Mitchells [Ormsby
MacKnight Mitchel's] Division is in the advance at this time & he has
left Bowling green for nashville. Several Days ago the rebels did not
Stand at Bowling green just as I expected nor do I think they will
Stand any where. We received news that the Rebals were leaving
Columbus [Kentucky] & that the Governor of tenesee [Tennessee] had

ordeed the Confederates to lay Down their arms & fight nomore
against the union & that the Stars and Stripes were now waveing. . . .
As it is my opinion that we will never get into a fight but it is hard
to tell. But Everyody thinks that in the Course of 2 months the job
will be completed & I am of the opinion that we will be Mustered out
of the Service against [before] the 4th Day of July next. I could tell
you a great many things if I had time and Space but I have neither
at this time. You must not be uneasy if you Dont git letters very regular for a while. I expect we will be moveing for a while at least you
need not be uneasy about our getting into a fight & we are all able
for to stand the tramp. Madison [Alford] & John William [Alford]
were left in barrax at Munsfordville [Munfordville] as they were not
able to Stand A hard march. I heared from them yesterday & they
were getting fat & Saucy & I think they will bee with us in a few
Days. We have not Received a letter from Warren for Some time. We
would be glad to hear from him. We have each bought us a pair of
boots the march was so hard on boots. That is marchng on the pike &
we Did not have a Chance to Send home for them. Give our respects
to all the friends and tell them the reason we Dont wright. Direct
your letters to Sixth Regiment. Yours as ever. Wayne & Lafayette
Alford

★

[From Father to Warren:]

Home Feb the 23rd/62

Mr J Warren Alford
Dear Sir   I am happy to have the privilege of Informing you that
we are still Blessed with health and strength of body and mind. A
disposition to Glorify God with our bodys and our spirits which Is his.
I hope these few lines may Come to hand In due time and find you
Enjoying the same blessing for truely they are blessings without
which Even life Its self would be loathsome and would pass slowly
away. I have not been greeted with A letter from you since the one
you wrote on the 3rd of this Month. I saw one from John & one
from Steve of the 12th. And I saw one to day from Bro M[athew]
Stafford [of the 14th Indiana]. And I am glad to hear from you Even
that way. I am still writing to you Every week. I have not had A
letter from Wayne & Lafayette for several days but I suppose they
are on A march perhaps to Nashville. I think they struck tents last
Friday morning. . . . Warren we have A great [deal] of war nuse that
Is verry Cheering In deed yet I suppose we have but little If any that
would be new to you. I will give you A paragraph from the

Commericial [the Cincinnati *Commercial*] that will give you a general
view of what has been done by our Army In the last Month between
the 19th of Jan & the 16th of Feb. The Federal Armies have made the
following records (viz) Battle of Mill Springs [Kentucky], Battle of Fort
Henry [Tennessee], Battle of Roanoak [Roanoke] Island & Capture of
Edenton [and] Hereford [probably Hertford] & Elizabeth City [all in] N
C, Evacuation of Springfield Mo [Missouri] and Bowling Green &
Russelville Ky, Capture of Fort Donelson [Tennessee] & reported
Capture of Savannah [Georgia]. General [Felix] Zollicoffer was Killed
& [Confederate Generals] Lloyd Tilghman, S. [Simon] B. Buckner,
Bushrod Johnson & Edward Price [?] captured besides A Score or Two
of Colonels. Commissioned officers by the 100s & Privates by the 1000.
Between 20 & 30,000 small arms have been taken or destroyed.
Neary 200 Cannon have been taken. Over 4000 horses and Mules &
Immense quantitys of Commissary Stores and Camp Equipage. Seized
all the Rebel Gunboats in Pamlico Sound [North Carolina] and on the
Tenn River have been destroyed. And A number of valuable Prizes
Captured by the Blockadeing fleet. It has been A Month of Glorious to
the Army and Navy. Since the Capture of Ft Donelson our Troops
have Pushed on up the River and took possession of Clarksville
[Tennessee] with provisions Enough to last our Army 20 Days. And
the Land forces under Gen [Ormsby] Mitchel was only 30 Miles from
Nashville on last Tuesday. And there are various Rumors about the
Capture of Nashville and New Orleans and the Evacuation of
Columbus [Kentucky]. [Confederate Generals John] Floyd & [Gideon]
Pillow were both at Ft Donelson but they succeded In getting away . . .
Wise was wounded at Roanoak and afterwards died. [The son of
Confederate General Henry A. Wise.] Warren we have had . . . bad
weather In this Month. Your Mare Is getting In fine . . . and she is
all life. I have not worked her yet. The roads have been to bad to
hall off any Wheat yet but It [wheat] Is still rising at the river. It Is
now 98 to 1.10 cents. I saw Capt Brooks last thursday but have no
Chance of talking with him. He Is [enticing] several recruits. Aunt
Cicilly Gilley Is not verry well but the General health Is still verry
Good. Bigheem Is home on Furlow for 30 days. He looks as well as I
ever saw him. I saw A letter from Henry Edwards last Saturday
and he says he Is better all but the Cough he has now. Warren I
must Close with the hope that you will live as becometh your
Profession remember me to all your friends that you think would be
Interested In hearing from us and especially our Brethern. I hope
the rebellion will soon be Crushed and you allowed to return home. I
Commend you to God and the word of his Grace. As Ever yours kind
parents and Brothers & sisters. Signed F Alford Write Soon for I
want to hear from you.

★

[From Wayne and Lafayette to Father:]

February 26th 1862
Bowling green K.Y.
Mr Franklin Alford

Dear Father   I seat myself ... this Morning with a tin plait on my
knee for a Desk to Drop you a few lines to let you know where we
are and what we are Doing. Mothers letter Came to hand this morning. We was verry glad to hear from you all again.   We are Still well
and enjoying ourselves finely since we Started to move.   It is true it is
tolerable hard work but Still by the blessing of heaven we are hearty
and able for the tramp. Besides it looks like we were going to Do
Something. . . . [We are] now at Bowling green as you Can See from
the heading of the letter. [We are] waiting for the Brigade to Cross the
river.   Their is some Difficulty in crossing here as the water is up and
the Rebals Destroyed both the Railroad & turnpike Bridges.   We have a
little Steam boat here crossing the troops.   Our Regiment all got across
this morning but we have to wait untill the Brigade gets across before
we Can march and it is Supposed that we will push right on to
Nashville.   I Suppose that General [Ormsby] Mitchel and General [Don
Carlos] Bewel [Buell] are in nashville now.   At any rait they are near
there it is reported that the Cecesh have Evacuated Nashville.   My
opinion is that all we will have to Do is to walk through for I have
no Idea that we will ever get to fire a gun at the Enemy.   The fortifications at this place beats anything that I ever Saw & they left them
without firing a Single Gun. For this reason I Dont think they will

The Bridge at Bowling Green, Kentucky.   (HPHCW)

Stand to fight us. I Suppose that before your next letter reaches us we will be in Nashville. I have not time to wright much. I would be glad to See you all very well & we think it will Not be long before we will get to come home if the lord Spaires us. May the lord bless us all & grant that we may soon meat around our pleasant fireside is the prair of your affectionate Son. Mother wanted Lafe to get wayed & write how much he wayed. There is no Chance to get wayed now but I think he will way about 195 pounds. [Ed. note: Not sure about the number.] As for his wrist it is not quite as strong as the other one but it Does not pester him at all. You would never notice it if you was to See him at work. I must bring this to a Close. Let this Do for both of us at this time. We remain your affectionate Sons untill Death.

Wayne & Lafayette Alford

[From neighbor Electa Winter to Warren:]

Alfordsville February the 29/62

Mr. Warn Alford

This is to make some inquiries about some boys that are in the first Virginia [Union Army] Regiment company G. These boys names are Benjamin Parsons, John Dunbar, Alvan Hall, Chester Hall, Martial Haney, Henry Johnston. and James Lasure. I wish to know if you have become acquainted with these boys as they are some of my relatives and friends. My respects to Brother Warn A and all the rest of the boys that I am acquainted with.   Electa Winter

[From Warren to his parents:]

Camp Chase Pawpaw Tunnel Va
March the 1st 1862

Dear Parents

Again with Much pleasure I embrace this opertunity to convese with you through the silent Medium of penn and ink which is a great pleasure to me since we cannot have the pleasure of speaking to you face to face. I received your vary kind Letter having date of 23

The Chesapeake and Ohio Canal Tunnel at Paw Paw, Maryland.
(Allegany County, Maryland, Historical Society)

of last Month which found me with all my friends well. B[olivar] Gold had a few days of sickness but is now quite well a gain. The General health of the armey under [General Frederick] Lander [is] Vary good and the 14th Reg is in vary good health never better. Their is hardley a single New case since we came here. Col Kimble [Kimball] is well agane. The Reg was never in beter spirits then at the preas- ant Time. Our Reg belongs to the first Brigad Col Kimble command- ing. We are under orders to hold ous in Readiness to March in a hours warning. Whether we are to move or not I cannot tell. We was Mustered for pay yesterday for the second time since we was paid. I see in the paper that the armey on the Potomac will not be paid till those on the east and those in the west who have bin in the late battles. But as soon as we are paid I shal send you some Money. Money is geting vary scarce among the soldiers. I have some money yet but I believe I am about the onley one in the Com. But I must come to a close soon as I am on guard today. The R Road bridg a Cross paterson [Patterson's] Creek was pracialy [partially] burned the othe night by some Rebel Scouts but did not stop cars but Two days. The bridge is betwixt here and Cumberland [Maryland]. About fif- teen miles from this place. But I must close. Give my best respects to brothers and Cisters, Grand fathers & Mothers and the rest of my conection and friends.

As ever your
Sone in the one hope.
J Warren Alford

N B direct to the 14th Reg Ind Vol, Com C in Care of L Brooks, Virginia and it will follow the reg any where or the name of the Camp.

[From Mary, or Mother to Warren:]

Home March the 2nd 62

Mr J Warren Alford   My son it is with pleasure I seat my self to inform you that we are all well and hope when this comes to hand that you may enjoy the some blessing. We received yours of the 17th. I tell you we was as glad to hear from you. We also received one from wayn and Lafayette having date of 23rd. They was well. They started to march on the 17th and marched till the 19th and only stopped then to repair the road. They are under marching orders and have sent half their baggage on eleven miles. They expect to go on the day they rote. . . . Madison [Alford] and John William [Alford] was left at mumafordsville [Munfordville]. They say the boys are only 15 miles from their. I guess you will wonder at that. I think from what I see in the papers that [General Alexander McD.] McCooks Division started to march towards louisville and turned back [which] accounts [for Madison and John William] being [so close to Wayne and Lafayette]. Madison and john expects to be with them in a few days. I suppose they will follow the retreating tories but I dont know where they will go to. I see that a large force is decending the missis-sippi from st louis. Their destination is not known. Warren it is so dark I cannot follow the time. I could send you meny rumors but I guess you have enough of them. [Confederate] gen [Lloyd] Tilghman and old [Confederate General Simon] buckner are sent to fort warren [prison in Boston after their capture at Fort Donelson, Tennessee]. . . . You rote that [Confederate Generals Gideon] pillow and [John] floyd was captured. That is a mistake. They slipped [off] the night before the surrender. Tom kyle . . . the trifling scamp kep running all sum-mer with A jug but he has got a barrel. It is enough to disgust A per-son to see them old lazy cutthroats laying around dodes store. If he had as mutch spunk as A mule he would kick them out. I heard A letter from peat wininger. They was on their way from St louis to Ft Daldson [Donelson]. The 24th redgment is their at the fort. Charles

Union Brigadier General Frederick West Lander. (USAMHI)

yootee was slightly wounded at Donldson. He was in the railroad Regt. ["The Railroad Regiment" was the name given the 52nd Indiana Infantry; their motto was "Clear the Track."] They was going to play soldier but I guess they mist it. Clem was going with them he said they would have nothing to do but ride on the cars. That woul do for some folks if they could get to do it. Sam has been swindled enough. Bill clark and john was . . . around here a while back but I think they were blowed out. Bill was here when we got the details of the fight at greend brier [Greenbrier, western Virginia]. He heard it red. I said then he was A coward. It is reported that bill perkins, john figgins, and drum gold were taken prisoner at Ft donldson and is sent to indianpolis. I hope it is true.

Warren I have rote A great meny things to you whether it will interest you or not that is for you to say. I allways loved to talk with you and expect to as long as we have. Do not let me carry your mind a way from your saviour remember him at all times. We have had the warmest winter I ever saw. There has bin A great deal of cloudy weather but white river has never bin high nor the ice has never run in it but one time. Their has bin but verry little snow. It commenced snowing here yesterday morning and snowed for a while verry fast last night. It has thundered very heavy all night. It has been raining allmost [ever] since. The ground has not been froze three inches deep this winter and what is more strange it has been as helthy as I ever saw it. Charley is making shugar. Give my love [to] all the boys. Tell them their friens are all well as fair as I now. Cousin James and sissily sent you A letter. They think you did not get it. Your grand parents is well. I close as wain says for the want of soap. Warren Wright often I remain your affectionate Mother until deth.

Mary Alford

★

[From Father to Warren:]

Home March the 2nd 62

Son & Brother

Dear Sir   With much Expection I embrace the present opportunity of penning you a few lines to let you know that we are still mindful of you and that we have pledged ourselves to write to you as often as once A week and If I should neglect It without A reasonable Excuse I would feel my self unworthy of those who are Contending so nobly for the rights that are so dear [to] me which Endears them more to me than any other act of there lives with so noble Exception and there is nothing of Earthly Caracter that I desire more than to meet you all at the Close of this unholy rebellion with A smile upon Each Counteneance by which I may be fully asshured that all my feeble Efforts to Console and Comfort you (both by words and deeds) In your toils and afflictions may have been duely appreciated by you. Warren I feel asshured that If It Is the Lords will that we be so fortunate as to all meet again in the Family Circle with the propper use of our bodys and minds the Joys of that meeting will precisley repay us for all the toils and afflictions born by you and the lonely Hours Experienced by us. Warren It often Causes the Fear of Gratitude to steal from my Eyes almost In Spite of all the fortitude I Can Command when I think of the reply that Col Kimball made to me when In the last Conversation I had with him I told him I had three sons In the service and after answering the numerous questions I asked verry satisfactoryly then he replied by saying that so far as the Honors [for] . . . Crushing [the] rebellion was Concerned my position was preferable to his. I was sorry to hear of the Col being sick and shall feel Concerned about him till I hear of his recorvery.

Good Morning sir   After a quiet Nights rest I believe we are all well so far as I know. Hellen and Green is down at Charleys [their brother-in-law] on a visit and to see them stir of shugar. Barton has had the Measles. He stayes at your grandfathers to sereen his Mother. But about the time he get able to go home your uncle Wayne took them. He has been prety sick but not worse than Is Common. Your Mother has written you A long letter which has so Exhausted our stock of Information that I have nothing left to write but rumors of Army movements and I suppose you have A large amount of that worthless trash on hand at all times. There Is A large portion of It that Is worthless and It is all fifty per cent below par. . . . I will send you the last Thursdays Issue of the Commercial [the Cincinnati *Commercial*], In which . . . you will find Jeffs [Confederate President Jefferson Davis'] Inauguaral address and A speech by Ex Governor but now

Senator Right [Joseph A. Wright] and A protion of [Indiana Governor [Oliver P.] Mortons remarks. . . . Also the same of the most prominent features of the Treasurey note bill as papers by Congress. . . . If you have not saw these things I have no doubt but they will Interest you and many of your friends. The general health Is still very good with the Exception of Measles. I want you to give my love to all the boys but do not stint your self and do not forget Brother Houghton for I have not forgotten him. You may asshure him that he has an Interest In all my Prairs. May the Lord bless you. So . . . write soon.

Franklin Alford

[From Wayne and Lafayette to Father:]

Camp Andy Johnson Tennissee
March 5th 1862

Franklin Alford   Dear Father
I Seat Myself this Eavening to wright you a few lines in answer to your Verry kind Letter which came to hand yesterday and found us well & glad to hear from you again. We are Encamped 4 miles South of Nashville and I learn that general [Ormsby] Mitchels Division is 12 miles in the advance of us. Yet we passed through Nashville on Sunday last and their was a Drenching rain which lasted untill 12 oClock Sunday Night. But enough of this. At the present [we are] well. As for the City of Nashville I think it a real Secesh hole though their is Some union men to be Sure. But Heretofore they Have Not had a Chance to Speak in favor of the union if they were So Disposed to Do So. I have but little time to wright this eavening but thought I would let you know where we are and what we are Doing. We are verry well Situated here with the prospect of the Staying here for a few weeks. It is reported that General [Lovell] Rousseaw [Rousseau] is appointed provincial Governor of Tennissee but as for that I am not Certain. The 42nd [Indiana] Reg is 5 miles [ahead] of us and James kellams stayed with us last night. He is Hearty as a buck and looks better than I ever Saw him. I think if he has luck it will Make a man of him. [James Kellams, Company B, 42nd Indiana was from Spencer County, Indiana, and probably a relative of the Alfords.] Huk Mcmahan was here to day and he is well. We hear that [?] has Shut up and quit business. [?] Sayes he is broke up & that Nob Reitz is also broke. Is it the fact or not you wanted to know who has the Honor of filling his position. There has been none appointed yet but I Suppose Lietenant Solomon will be promoted and a Secont Lieu appointed. Since [Lieutenant Henry S.] Hall resigned [on February 13]

The L & N Railroad Bridge over the Cumberland River. (LC)

we have been marching all the time. I must Close. I will wright to you again in a few Days. I have written in a hurry & Did not take time to hunt up my pen and ink. We would be glad to see you all verry much but we endure all things for the excellency of the hope. Your affectionate Sons in the army.

Wayne & Lafayette Alford

Wright as Soon as you can. I will wright in a few Days.

★

[From Hellen to Warren:]

Alfordsville Ind March the 9th 62
Mr J Warren Alford   Dear sir   I am now seated to drop you A few
lines to let you know that we are all well and my Sincere desire is
that when this few lines comes to hand they will find you well. Now
Warren Aunt Kellams is gon crazy and father brought her here. We
just put her up stairs and made her stay there. Father is . . . going to
send her off tomorrow to Indianapolis. We recieved your letter yesterday baring the date of 1 of this month and we recieved A Letter
from Wayne & Lafayette allso. They wer all well and then wer in
Bolinggreen [Bowling Green] and [were ready] to go rite to Nashville.
He sayed he did not think they would ever get to fir A gun at the
Rebbles. Henry Edwards [Company E, 18th Indiana Infantry] has
came home. He came home yesterday. He has got A discharge on the
way but he will have to go back to St Louis to get it. He sayed he
herd from the Reg the night be fore and they wer in Arkansas about
thirteen miles from the line. Father says the reason that he did not
wright he is so trubbled with Aunt Betsa that he can not wright to
tonight. . . . He will wright in A day or to or at least he will try. It is
A Raining her and I hope you are injoying it very well if it [is]
Raining ther. The Rebbles has Evacuated Columbus [Kentucky] and
never fired a gun.

Hellen Alford

[From Warren to Father and Mother:]

Post at Martinsburg Va.
March the 9th 1862
Father and Mother
    It is once more I embrace the preasant opertunity to drop you a
few lines to tel you . . . my were abouts and all so to let you know
that I am well And that I received you kind favor of the 23 of Feb a
few days ago and was happy to learn that you was All well. We left
Pawpaw . . . on the 5th for this place which is about fifty miles farther down the potomac on the R R. We are now within a few miles
of harpers ferry [Virginia]. Our forces have bin moveing forward
toward Winchester [Virginia]. It was reported yesterday the enemy
was leaving that point and fawling back on Strawsburg [Strasburg,
Virginia] some 15 or 20 miles from Winchester which is this morning
confirmed. [Union Major General Nathaniel] Banks is in hot presuit

of them. He tuck possession of Winchester yesterday. I suppose we will not get to take part in the chase on the account of the death of Gen Lander [Brigadier General Frederick Lander] which I suppose you have no doubt heard of. His death [on March 2 from pneumonia] was vary sudden and unexpected. We were ordered to get ready to march and some of our divisions had gon forward some 15 miles but was ordered back. And we on the 5th started for this

The B & O Railroad Shops at Martinsburg, Virginia.
(B & O Railroad Collection)

place (They had started on the Winchester Rode when ordered back)
Col Kimble [Kimball] was in command of the Division. Gen [James]
Shields is now in command. He is from Illinois. As we came to this
place we passed one of the Old forts erected in the time of the Ware
with the French and Indians by Gen Washington. It was called Fort
Frederick it is built on the north side of the Potomac. It is built of
solid stone. We are quartered in the Germine Reformed Church. We
will get our tents this eavening. This is a nice little town of about 6
thousand inhabitance with 5 or 6 Churches. And it had a vary large
Machien shop but it is now distroid. The boys are all in fine health
and eager for a chance to dicide which is the stronger power. The
boys send there best respects to all their acquintencis. But I must
come to a close for the preaant. Hopeing to hear from you soon. As
ever your in the one hope.

J Warren Alford

PS To them I ow letters I will rite as soon as I can. Post stamps is geting vary scarce with me. I weigh 193 lbs and am as good looking as
ever. Tell My friends.

[From Father to Warren:]

Home March the 10/62

Mr James Warren my Son.
Dear Sir after my love to you I will say to you that I gladly [write
which is] Contrary to my Expectations of last Evening. [Now I]
Embrace the opportunity of scratching you A few hasty [lines to tell
you] that we are all well and much rejoiced with the welcome tidings
of the verry good health and fine spirits Enjoyed [by] you and your
friends to whom I hope to be remembered In love. We have been
Confined to the house for the last three Days and knights with the
Care of your Aunt Kellams. I want to take her to Washington
[Indiana] to Day and make the necessary Arangements to have her
taken to the Lunatic Assylum to be Cared for. For we can do nothing
for her. She is In A very distressed and Distressing Condition and
greatly to be pittied on account of her forlorn Condition. We are willing but only able to administer to her temporal necessities hopeing
that God In his Goodness and mercy may restore her to health again
and that we may be the better able to appreciate the Governings of
God In bestowing upon us health and the proper use of our minds.
Warren I feel In hopes the time Is not far distant when God will

gladen our hearts by permiting us to meet again. Brother Henry
Edwards [Company E of the 18th Indiana Infantry] has got home at
last. He Is or has been very much afflicted but I think he will soon
recover. He thinks he will get A discharge In about thirty days. The
general health Is good. I think England has Cooled off and the war
will soon [be] over. My love to all the boys and Excuse this hasty
scrall. As Ever yours for the one hope. F Alford

[From Dr. Laverty to Franklin:]

Camp Andy Jonston
Medical Department
Tennee March 12th 1862

Mr Franklin Alford
  Dear Friend
    I owe you an appoligy my "old" friend for not answering your
last letter to me and for not writing sooner. I will say this that a
press of duty and excessive hard labour has been the reason. I hope
this will answer as a sufficient excuse for my not replying sooner.
My health is rather poor at this time owing to a attack of Dirreah
assuming a chronic form. I attribute it to a change of Water. We
took posession of a house while at Boldin [Bowling] green formerly
occupied by the rebbels as an Hospitle for our sick and during our
Stay their drank some water out of the Well ajoining the house
which gave me a Dirreah and it seams I cannot controll it with medicine at all. I may eat my supper and in one hour [I have
indigestion]. I beleive the water was poisioned for several that drank
of it is in the same situation. We are now in Tennesee Sourounded
with rebbels on evry hand. But I tell you [we] keep very low and say
"nix." Beautiful Weather heare warm and pleasant . . . for several
days. The season is about one month eariler heare than in Hoosierdom
and as Pretty a country as the eye ever rested upon. But still they
curse the country by being Seshess. But I think it will not be long
until the old Banner shall again float out to the Breases in a
Southern clime when they shall learn the art of seassion no more.
From what I can learn . . . heare from those who I am conversent
with in other Brigades . . . we will be all home by the 4th of July.
God send that happy day when the friends who have been long
[patient] shall meet again. Tell Charles Allen for me that Capt
McCarty sent me a note the other day to call and see him but I was
not able to go over to see him [This probably was Captain Eli McCarty
from Washington, Indiana serving in Company G, 42nd Indiana

Infantry.] Mr Bartell called and saw me. Mr McCarty was well and in fine spirits. . . . Whear their place of destination was is more than I know. I heard tonight to Munfordsville [Munfordville] but it is only a camp Rhumor. The Boys are all well and in fine Spirits. I saw them this evening. My love to family and write soon and I will ever remain your sinceare friend and Wellwisher.

Dr. J. L Laverty

[From the Daviess County Clerk:]

Washington Indiana
March 14th 1862

Mr Franklin Alford
Dear Sir
I have this day received information from the Superintendent of the Insane Isalem that Elizabeth Kellims Can be received immediately. You will therefore Come up at your Earliest Convenience, and Make Such arrangements as will be Necessary for her removal immediately.

Respectfully
John S. Berkshue
[Clerk of Daviess County]

[From Warren to Father and Mother:]

Winchester Va.
March the 17th 62

Father and Mother
I am blessed with an other opertunity to Write to you to let you know that I am still well and I received your letter having date of the second of March yesterday which gave me much pleasure to learn that you was all well and in fine spirits thinking the ware will soon be over. We came in to winchester [Virginia] on the 12th and tuck possession of there works without firing a gunn. Our armey is met every where with Joy [by] a great [many] oppressed in the southern Confederacy. I was to see the 27th Reg Ind vol to day and saw several that I was acquainted with. Among them was Barton Wilson [and] Wm Shively [both of Company B]. They are all well and in fine spirits. They have never saw a fight yet nor do they think they will

The Streets of Winchester, Virginia. (USAMHI)

soon for it seams that they [the Rebels] are not going [to] make a stand this side of Richmond and it will take some time to get their with our provisions. The Old 14th is as good [as] any reg in the service and we have the best Col [Nathan Kimball] in the service. I was talking to him yesterday and give him your respects and he sayed he would write to you but he had no time as he has seven Reg to Command [as brigade commander]. He has got well againe but I must close soon you must not think me neglectful if I do not write a long letter for I have so [many] to write to. So nomore at preasent onley I remain yours in the one hope.   J W Alford

[In the margin:] I am not yet tired of trying to live a Christian [life.]

[In the same envelope:] To Gradmother Winters. I received here note and was glad to hear that she was Well and will comply with her request as soon as I get a chance. The first [western] Virginia Reg is with us some where but I have not saw them for some time but I think it is some where on the rode with in a mile or so of us. I should be vary glad to hear from here againe and much more to see her. But I must close for the preasant. Hopeing to see you all soon but if not in this world in better.   Warren Alford

★

[From Wayne to Father:]

Camp [?]
March 18th 1862

Mr Franklin Alford Dear father It is by axcidnet that I get the opportunity to wright to you but I thought I would try & Let you know how we are getting along in this Land of Cecession. . . . [We started] to march Last Sunday morning and we are now in 7 miles of Columbia Tennisee. Yesterday our Cavalry Chased the retreating Rebals So Close that they just run. . . . And [we] captured 20 of them & a negro as they crossed Duck river. Our men were so Close on them that they threw a Barrel of turpentine on the Bridge and Set it on fire. And [as] our men Came up the Bridge had not Been on fire more than 5 minutes But the turpentine made such a fire that their Horses would not go through. So they Dismounted and run through the fire and Shot at them on the other Side but Did no Harm. I suppose where we are to march to I Cannot tell but I Suppose it will be a

General Buell's Troops Crossing the Duck River at Columbia, Tennessee. (HPHCW)

good peace. I Have No news of interest more than their is a general
move Here but I Dont believe the Rebals will fight us at least they
Dont Show any Sign of fight at present. We Dont get any papers that
is verry new here. But while we are moveing we Can See enough to
Do verry well without papers. We are all well and in fine Spirits and
the regiment is genearaly in better health that they have ben for
some time. Ben [probably Benjamin Gilley] Says that he is Such a
Slow hand to wright that He Cannot wright at present but he is well
and wants you to tell his folks. And he wants them to wright to
Him. You must Direct your letters to Louisville or Nashville to Be for-
warded to the Reg. I Have Nothing more of much importance to
write. Dr Laverty Sends His Compliments to you & all the rest of the
friends. We would be verry Glad to see you all but I think it will not
be long until we can returen Home. Give my respects to the friends
and believe me to Be your affectionate soon untill Death.

Wayne Alford

Wright as soon as you Can. Oblige me.

[From Lafayette and Wayne to Father:]

Columbia Tenn
March 23rd·62

Mr Franklin Alford
Dear Father   It is one time more we have the opertunity of write
ing you to let you kno how we do. We left camp near nash ville on
last Sunday morning. [We] marched two days and then Camped
three days. Then left for the this place but the Cavaldry drove the
sesesh before them. They burnt the bridge across the river at this
place. The river is Called Duck River. This is thirty nine or forty
miles from Nashville. It is A great way into the teritrory that the
Rebels clame so it is not every day we can send letters. But you must
excuse us if we do not write often. We sent our money home it started last monday. You must write and tell us if it came to hand all
rite. You wanted to no who filed the position in lieutenant Halls place
[Lieutenant Henry C. Hall from Washington, Indiana resigned on
February 13, 1862.] Orderly Rodarmel [Oscar Rodarmel] has the position and Wayne filles the position of orderly. There was A slite axi-
dent the other day. Wayne was looking at A pistole one of the boys
had. It was just the sise of the one Wayne hade that he bought of
Alverd when it went off and shot him slitely through the hand. It
went in midel way betwen the thumb and midel finger in the palm
of the hand and it came out between the first and second joint on the

back of the fore finger but it did not inger the bone ore the leader.
The Doctor says it will be well soon. Be sides this we are injoying the
bes of helth. This is A very nice climate. Though it is spiting snow
this evening. Though the sitizens are plowing for the last month with
the expectation of planting. But I must close by saying write often.
We remain ever your affecionte sones.

Lafayette & wayne Alford

★

[From George to Warren:]

Alfordsville Ind
March the 24th 62
Mr James W. Alford

Dear Brother I seat myselfe this morning to drop you a few lines to
inform you of our health and sircumstances. We are all well except
colds and I believe that is tolerable comen [common] here. Father is
going to Washington this morning. Wayne and Lafayette has sent
some money home or rather to Washington and father is going down
to get it. They sent $45 home. They only got pay for 2 months they
are both well and Lafe is so fat that he can hardly sea. Michael
trulove paid Father $40 the other day and he is going to pay it on
that Headric note. He said he would write you the paticulars about it
tomorrow. There has been a hard fight in [Pea Ridge] Arkansas.
[Several local men serving in Company E of the 18th Indiana
Infantry are casualties:] James Murray is killed and Joel S Goldsmith
is severly wounded. The bous thinks that he will git well. And John
Mc mahans boy [George] is killed and to more out of that Company
[were killed: Thomas Wilson and Spinner Lee]. I didnot learen there
names. Alexander Camp run a very narrow risk. Him and 2 more
men was sent after some dead and war surrounded by the Indians
and they killed the other 2 and he got away with the loss of his gun
and hat. The totle killed in that fight was 212, wounded 926, missing
174, total 1812. They are fighting at Island no 10 in the Mississippi. It
will be taken but it will take a long while for they have been fighting there for 5 days. Gen [John] Pope has taken Newmadrid [New
Madrid, Missouri] just belo the island and has crossed over and is giting around them. His guns Command the rivver so that noboddy
can pass up or down. I believe I forgot to tell you where Wayne &
Lafe is at. They are at Camp andy Jonston 3 miles south of Nash V.
Warren the Wheat looks fine. I dont think I ever saw a better

prospect for a crop. Grand Father Gilley was here this morning and he said for me to tell you that him and Grand Mother are well as comen. I was down at Charleys [brother-in-law] last night and they are hardy. I must bring my letter to a close. Write to me as soon as you can. So nomore at present but remains your unworthy brother. Write soon for I want to no how you get along.

George W Alford

[From Dr. Laverty writing for Wayne and Lafayette:]

Camp Stanton Columbia on Duck
River Tennessee March 25th 1862

Dear Father

As we are expecting to March from heare tomorrow or next day and not knowing when I will have an oppertunity again I concluded I would sit down and give you a word or two for the boys. In the first place We are all in [good] health [and particularly when considering the undesireable situation we find ourselves]. The boys are in fine spirits. We received the letters having date of 14th and 21st March. I will explain why I am writing for the boys. We had order [to march] on last friday [and] in the hury and hustle of Starting Wayne axidentely shot himself in the hand. He was fixing it in some way When it went off and shot him in the hand. Now do not get excited about it for I can assure you that he is not dangerously shot but his hand is so that he cannot write. And Lafayette asked me to write for him. I promised obediance and am now at it. Wayne is Shot in the hand the Ball entering about the heal of the hand and comeing out between the thumb and finger But I can assure you that in less then ten day he will be able to handle his gun. This is true. We expect to draw our money soon again and I will have to cary it with me as we have no way of Expressing it home but [if] the opportunity . . . presents its self [we will] express the money home. I was sory to heare of Mother poor health but I hope she will be better soon. We are sory to heare that so many of our friends had the measels but hope that they will soon be better. . . . Tell Charles and [? Minerva] that we are all so busey drilling and marching that if we do not write so often they must not think hard of it. Tell George I will write to him as often as I can but tell him to write often. Wheare our probable destination will be is more than we can tell. Write often and tell the friend to write to us often as we have a poor Chance of writing. Tell us wheare Warren is. We have no word from him for some time. Was he in the Battle of Wincester. I hope not. How long it will be till we get home [I can not tell] but I think about the 4th of July. But I must stop writing as we will have to go to work tomorrow. Farewell. Write soon and often. Your Sons.

Wayne Alford

Laverty   Lafayette Alford

Mr Franklin Alford

Dear Sir

This evening finds me in moderate health. Hope you are well. We march tomorrow but cannot tell Wheare. No more

Your friend as ever

Laverty

John William [Alford] is fatning up again [and] sends his love to all.

[From Warren to the family:]

Strawsburg [Strasburg, Virginia]

Shields Divison

March the 26th 1862

Dear Parents,

We have mad an other Move after a severe battle. We was attacted on the 22nd about 3 Oc AM and had some sharp skirmishing that Eavening. But no general engagement tuck place that day the next day they was skirmishing and cannonading untill about 3 Oc Am [PM] when a general engagement tuck place and lasted till dark. [This engagement is known as the Battle of Kernstown.] The third Brigad was the first to commence the fight. [The] 5th Ohio, 84 Pencylvainia and the 14th came up next. At the time our Reg came up ... the 84th was suffering severley. There Col [Murray] had just bin shot down and there Collors was on the ground. We came up through a Showr of bullets but their was not a man faultered. We went in at a charge bayonett and drove them like a flock of sheep before us. They flue in all directions. We drove them about half Mile when they got reinforced by one brigade and mad an other stand. Our Reg was alone at this [point] but the boys stud up to the work like men at this point amid the hottest Of the fight the 13th Ind Reg came to our relief when we drove them from there Battery and tuck it from them. At this time the [victory] was complete. Them leaving

The Shenandoah Valley Turnpike. (USAMHI)

our men in full possession of the field. Them leaving 200 dead on the field and a number wounded. Our loss not yet known but not over 100 killed and wounded. Our Com[pany] was in the thickest of the fight but we did not get a man kiled. We had two men wounded in our Co but not serious. I will give there names Addam Marks [Private John R. Marx from Martin County] and Edward J Waldrin [Private Waldron also from Martin County]. All the boys that you [know have] made inquiry after you. You can tell their people they are safe. The boys around alfordsville sends particular word to their friends as we have [not] had a chance to right. We have bin following them [the Confederates] up till to day. And material for riting are scarce. The boys thought Green brire [the Battle of Greenbrier River] was tolerable warm but not like going in to them with fixed bayonets. Our Co was on picket when they made the attact. This leaves all well I rec your Letters [of] the 10th [and] one from Wayne. As to them they was . . . well. But I must close. Give my love to all my friends. Ever. J Warren Alford

★

[From Benjamin F. Gilley, Company E, 6th Indiana, Mary Alford's brother:]

Camp Stanton Near Columbia Tennisee
March 29th 1862

Brother F Alford   Dear sir it is with considerable embarisment that I seat my self this morning to drop you a few lines for the purpois of bringing a charg against Bro or rather Elder John Stafford [now in Company C, 14th Indiana, serving with Warren Alford] with regrard to that settlement with he and I. Now Bro F you understand the hole matter and I want you to Bring the matter before the Brethern and if he will yet do what is right I will yet be satisfied. Please wright soon and let me know all about it enough on that subject. My helth is very good again. I was not well a few days ago but hav recovered. The bouys ar all well and in in spirits. We hav sum good news but you will hav it before this comes to hand so I need not say any thing about it. We are now on the north bank of duck river 41 miles from Nash ville and 60 miles from Tennisee River and I dont know whare the nearest rebels is. I sent $20.00 to Mary with the bouys. It will come to your cair per Col J vantrees [Van Tress]. I want her to keep $5.00 of it for her one use. The pay rols is being made out and it wont be long until we ar paid again and I will send more. Now Bro F I must son close. Wright soon and reed this to Mary and tell her to wright in antisipation of shortly returning home to enjoy the pleasures of seeing my friends and brethern. I sub-scribe my self your Brother in the one hope.

B. F. Gilley

PS I am out of post stamps and am under the necesity of sending this without pay as we cant pay without stamps hear.

B. F. G.

[From Father to Warren:]

Home Monday Morning March 31st 62
Mr James Warren Alford

Dear Son   After a lapse of Two or Three Weeks I am seated to [write] you A veary hasty scrall. . . . We hope these lines may Come duely to hand and find you well & also all our Brethren and friends. We received your verry kind and affectionate letter of the 17th Inst and hearts was made glad to hear that you was still In good health. [No] other thing gives me more pleasure than I Can fully Express Is to hear Kyle say he saw A man from the 14th [the] week before last and [he asked] the soldier if he knew the Alfords and he replied he did. He then said he knew you and said there was not A man In the Regt more respected than yourself and that you was always ready to the wants of the oppressed and you ask none but Civil question and gave none but Civil answers. Now you Cannot over Estimate the satisfaction It gives me. We received A letter from Wayne & Lafayette of the 18th Inst & one of the 23rd & one from your uncle B [Benjamin Gilley] & one from J S Laverty & one from James Kellams all last Saturday and they were all well. But Wayne had met with an accident and got A shot throught the hand with one of Allens revolvers but no Bones or Leeders hurt. It went In the palm of the hand half way between the thumb & middle finger & out on the back of the fore finger without Injuring the bone. And he Is now Orderly. They were Forty Miles South of Nashville. Your uncle Eben has got home but has the Rheumatism In the back so that I fear he will not be able to do any thing sone. I have not heard from your Aunt Kellams sinse I left her at the Insane Hospital Wednesday Week. I got Forty Dollars on Edmonds Note A few Days ago and applyed It to Your Note that Hedrick holds on you. Edmund & several other of the Teamsters who went out with Seay has Came back before there time for which they agreed was up and Seay Is sick himself and has got back to washinton. We are about to try to start the Plow to day. I want to sow 20 acres of Oats & put 35 Acres of Corn. And It Is A late spring and [I still have] the wheat to hall off. And you see we will be very busy but you know we generally get through with . . . persiverance. We hear sinse we have been writing [that] Joshua Staffords youngest Child Died last Night and will be Buried at our Grave Yard today. I must Close for It Is about Mail time. I am verry anxious to see a description of the sceans through which you have passed sinse the date of your last [letter]. . . . I have not yet saw an official report of the Causaltys. Your uncle Josephs [and] Waynes, & C Camps have all had the Measles & A Great many others but are all A getting well. Give my love to all my friends and tell them they have an Interest In my Prairs. So nomore but remains you affectionately as Ever In the one hope.

F & M Alford

[From Father to Warren:]

Home April 7th 1862

Mr J Warren Alford

Dear Sir   Another week haveing passed away and this Morning I am again seated as usual to write you A few lines to let you know that we are Still alive and Enjoying Common Health Except Colds. We received your verry kind and affectionate letter of the 26th ult which gave us great Joy In asshuring us that you and all your Comerades of our acquaintenace was well and had passed through another terrible Conflict unhurt and I hope you will give God the Glory. And we hope this may Come to hand in due time and you and your friends [are] quite well. We had A letter [from] Wayne & Lafayette last saturday bearing date of the 28th utl. They [are] well and at Columbia Tenn. 40 miles south of Nashville on duck River on their way to Corinth Mississippi I suppose. Wayne by accident got shot through the hand but not serious. Laverty say he will be able to use his gun In Ten days. He is orderly and it will prevent him from writing for A while the shot was by Allens 7 shooter. I have Just received $115.00 from Wayne & Lafayette and I Expect to get the balance on the Braxton note this week. Well Warren this Morning brings the Commencement of the Twelth Month sinse you bid adieu to the quiet Enjoyment of A quiet Home. The Time has passed slowly and solemnly away but I hope the time Is drawing near when If the Lord spares us we will be reunited In the Enjoyment of Each others society rendered doubly dear to us all on account of the toils and suffering [that] have [been] so manfully born by you. Warren I live to see you all safe home. It will be the proudest day of my life I hope you may be home In time to help us to Save our harvest for I think we will have A fine Crop of wheat and Grass & 10 or 20 Acres of oats but I must Close. Give my love to all the boys and take A portion to your self. I Commend you to God . . . among the sanctifyed. Ever yours.

Franklin Alford

[From Warren to Father and Mother:]

Odenburg Shields Division Va.
April the 10th 62

Dear Father & Mother

This Morning I am Seated to let you know that I am still on the Land and among the Living and blessed with health and streangt. While so many of our friends and fellow Citizens are falling on the right and on the left we are spaired by our heavenly Father for some purposs unknown to us. Since We have gon from home we have saw many that had passed [from] the stage of action. Whether prepaired or unprepaired is not for us to say. But we ar frank to acknouled his goodness and mercy in the highest degree. We have been blessed with healt and with friend where ever we gow. We was vary sorrow to hear of Waynes getting his hand hurt but was thankfull that it was [not] worse. I would be vary glad to see the boys and be with them but we can not as things now are. But we are going to be satisfied with our lot as the same being the rules here that governs them and at his own good time will bring us all safe home. We hope to live in peace the balance of our Days. We have bin Laying in sight of the Enemys pickets for the Last tenn days and nothing on either side that I can see but I supose they are Wating for a move in some othe direction. McClelan [Major General George McClellan, Commander-in-chief of the Union Army] with his force is moving in some direction unknown to us. It was reported in camp yesterday that he was in 25 miles of Richmond. But whether it is so or not is yet to prove. And I suppose Fremont [Major General John Charles Fremont] with his force [the Mountain Department] is Moving on to wards Stanton [Virginia]. And we got a dispatch yesterday bringing us the nuse that our Men had taken possession of Island No tenn [in the Mississippi River] with one Gen and staff and two thousand prisoners. [This was the Battle of Island No. 10.] And that Gen Grant [Major General Ulysses S. Grant, Commander, Army of the Tennessee] had Met and defeated Bureguard [Confederate General P.G.T. Beauregard] at Pitsburg Landing on the Tennessee River. [This was the Battle of Shiloh in which Warren's two brothers took part.] We will get our pay in a few days and I will send you the Money when Virgile comes home if he gets his discharge in time. [Cousin Virgil was discharged on May 3, 1862] And if he does not get it in time I will send it by express to you imediately for I know you stand in need of it to settle up my debts as they have bin due for some time and they are needing the Money. I know these hard times. The weather is vary unsettled for the Last 4 or five days. It has bin sleating most of the time till yester-day when it commenced snowing vary fast. And during the Night the snow fell to the depth of three inches but it is moderating vary fast this Morning. We have bin traveling through some vary pore Cuntry since we left Martinsburg [Virginia] to this place. Winchester [Virginia] is a vary nice town the houses are small but net. The streets are vary Narrow not more than forty feet Wide. John McCord and Virgle [Alford] has not bin well for the last Two days but are boath on the Mend. The rest of the Boys are all well. Addam Marx [Private John A. Marx from Martin County] died [on April 7] from his Wound [received earlier at Kernstown]. It was thought he would have got along well but his leg was taken off three inches below the knee and it proved fatal to him. But I must son come to aclose as I wan to Write to the Chilren on the next page. Boliver [Gold] says he sends you his bes repects and says he is all right. Give my Love to all inquiering friend if any such their be. I am as ever your affection- ate Son. Right soon.

J Warren Alford

[Next page:]

Masters George & Green Alford
I Received your Letters in dew time. One from Geo. about one Week a go but did not have time to answer till this time. I would be glad to see you all but now is the time I am most kneeded here. We have some vary easy times and some vary hard times but upon the hole (as uncle Kelso sayes) we have know rume to grumble. I must ask you to send me some stamps as soon as you get this as I am about out. And When I send a letter I think it is apter to go with a stamp than without. And I cannot get them here for the Money. Hellen I must write you a few lines. I have got several letters from you and would be glad to get several more. Tell Charley and Minerva I want Them to write to me a little oftener and I will write to them when ever I have a chance. I expect them to share all my letters that I send home but I must soon come to a close. Hoping to hear from you oftener and I will write as regular as I can. I am as ever you Brother in the Armey.

J Warren Alford

★

[From Wayne and Lafayette to Father:]

Camp Battle Ground
Near Pittsburg Landing Tenn River
April 12th 1862

Mr Franklin Alford   Dear Parents I feel thankfull this Morning to the giver of all Good for the privilege of writing to you again and of Saying to you that we are as well as could be expected. I am Verry well myself but Lafayette & Benjamin have very Severe Colds owing to the exposure we have been Obliged to undergo recently. I Suppose you heard of my getting my Hand Shot. Well it has got nearly well. Well enough for me to use the pen. ... We were in the battle on Monday Last but Came [to this general area on the previous Sunday night]. We were on the March for this point But we were takeing it Verry Steady. ... About ten Oclock a messenger Came [and ordered] the artillery to hurry up as fast as they possibly Could for they were fighting and our men [at Pittsburg Landing, near the Shiloh Church,]

were [being driven] back from force of [enemy] numbers. We were
then about ten miles from the battle field So we Hurried Down to the
river at Savannah [Tennessee] below the Sene of action. We took a
boat at Savananh a little after Dark and Came up to Pittsburg at
Night. The fireing had all Ceased except 2 gunboats Which fired every
few minute to prevent the enemy from Erecting a breast work
which they were attempting to build. We remained on board the boat
untill Morning. We marched out as Soon as we Could get out.
Lafayette was not able to stand it to march in the ranks. . . . I took
Lafes gun and he went in the rear of the Regiment to take care of
the wounded. I will not attest . . . to the Scene of this as it is impossible. . . . Aaron hunter [from Washington] was Shot Dead by A Six
pound Cannon ball Strikeing him in the side of the head which killed
him instantly. We lay flat on our faces from Six in the morning
untill about 12 Oclock before we were Called into action. Our
Regiment being the reserve but in the eavening we were Called up to
Support a Battery right where the hottest of the fight had been all
Day. The battery played on them untill they Saw that unles they
Could Silence it that the Day was lost. So they made a Charge up on
the battery & General Rousseaw [Rousseau] ordered us to Let Loose on
them. We rose from where we were laying & I thought I never Saw
our regiment advance as firm and Steady in my life. As Soon as the
rebal flag came in Sight we Directed our attention to them untill
they fell & their center gave way & it is Said that Our regiment
Killed General Johnson [referring to Confederate General Albert
Johnston who was killed the previous day and, certainly, not killed
by anyone in the 6th Indiana]. At all events he was killed. . . . He
was found Dead on the Battle field when they gave way in the
Center. The 32nd Ind fell on them & relieved us and they fled from
the field. I will wright to you again Soon but I must Close for the
present. Governor Morton Has Sent a Boat to take all the wounded
Ind Soldiers but I must Close. May the Lord bless and & preserve us
in Days to Come as in Days passed. Your Sons in true Love and affection. Wayne & Lafayette Alford. Dr laverty Send his respects.

[From Warren to Father:]

Woodstock Va
April the 15th 62

Mr Franklin Alford
   Sir you will find Enclosed within $70.00 which you will use as
you see fit for I now it has bin fourth comeing long enough. I

received your Letter this Morning of the 7th ult [Should be "inst,"
meaning "of this month."] wich from which I learned that you had
Rec Mine of the 26th from Strasburg. I will wright to you and sending it by Mall giving you information. . . . Virgle [Alford] Will be at
home in a few days their fore he does not send his Money. . . . The
boys [are] well as ever. Your Son in the Armey. James Warren
Alford

I send you One Hundred and Tenn in place of Seventy if you can
settle the note Charles Allen has Against Me. If you think best but
you can do with it as you think most prudent. I do not know the
seround circumstances. I am your Sone.

J Warren Alford

[From Wayne to Father:]

Battle Ground of Shiloah [Shiloh]
Near Pittsburg Landing Tenn
April 16, 1862

Mr Franklin Alford Dear Father It is with pleasure I Seat myself
to answer your kind letter which Came to hand in Due time. I war
Verry glad to hear from you all again for I am Sure the time Began
to appear Verry long Since we had had any News from you.
Lafayettes health Seamed to get no better and Benjamin [Gilley] Was
also Seck. Since the Battle we lay for a Week on the wet ground
without any tents & it rained Nearly every Day or Night. . . .
Benjamim has [something] Like the yellow Janders & Lafe had
Nothing but Cold & exposure I think. We have Sent them off to a
hospital. They will probably go to Evansville & from their I expect
they will go home. It is at least possible I asked the Doctor where they
were gowing & he Did not know but Supposed they would go home. I
told them to wright & let me know where they had gone to. If they
get a pass from the Hospital to go home they will probably reach
home before you receive this. We have been payed off today and I
have Drew their money for them & their is a man here from
Washington and I Shal Send it all home by him to Col Van Trees. I
Drew $34 & I Shal Send $30 of it home. Lafayette Sold his Revolver
for $14 Dollars & I have Collected it for him. I Send his money all
Home which makes $40.00. I send Benjamins Money all home but
one Dollar and I would have Sent it if I could have mad the change.
I thought that it was Likely they would go Strait home & if they Did

they would get their about as soon as the money would. Dont be
Scared about Lafe for I am Satisfied that if he gets to Some good place
he will recover in a few Days. I Had not heard from Warren for
Several Weeks but thank the lord he has come through another
Battle Safe. But from what I can learn you May put [the Battles of]
Kernstown or Winchester [Virginia] and Peay Ridge [Arkansas] together & they wont Make the Battle of Shiloa [Shiloh]. Dont think I am
exagerating for the Generals Say that it is the Hardest Battle that ever
was Fought on the contineng [continent] & I am of the opinion that it
Was. I have Nothing more of interest to Wright & as I expect to
wright to you again in a few Days believe I will Close. I think from
Signs of the times that we will begin to bring this unhappy Contest to
a Close. May the Lord Speed the time that we may be permitted to
return home to parents and friends. I would Love to See you all
Verry well but I Cannot at this time. Pray for me that I may Be
Spared and Hold out faithfull to the End. I will Give you again the
amount that I Send for Each of us but I will Close for the present.
Your Son untill Death.

Wayne Alford

W Alford $30.00
Lafayette $40.00
B F Gilley $25.00

★

4
BACKGROUND

"the offensives of the North were pressing home."[1]

Father's optimistic interpretation of the War news was justified. Since the New Year, the Union Armies had gained momentum and the setbacks of 1861 were cast out.

On January 19, 1862, Union general George Thomas won a decisive battle in southeast Kentucky. In mid-February, Northern troops, under the command of Ulysses S. Grant, achieved major victories at Forts Henry and Donelson in northwest Tennessee. On February 25, Union forces occupied Nashville, the capital of Tennessee. On the Mississippi River, the Confederates abandoned their fortifications at New Madrid, Missouri. By March 31, Grant's forces were poised at Pittsburg Landing, Tennessee, ready to move across the state line into Mississippi.

In the East, however, it appeared the Army of the Potomac was permanently huddled around Washington, D.C. Nevertheless, there were some bright spots. The Union troops continued to hold western Virginia and, on March 23, a battle was won near Winchester, Virginia. On the south Atlantic coast, Indiana-born General Ambrose Burnside had been victorious on February 8 in a small battle at Roanoke Island, North Carolina. Upon occupying the island, the Union acquired a naval base on the Carolina coast and uncovered a back door to Richmond, Virginia. On March 9, the first duel of ironclads, U.S.S. *Monitor* and C.S.S. *Virginia* (formerly the U.S.S. *Merrimack*), took place near Norfolk, Virginia. Although militarily indecisive, it was a moral victory for the North. They need not fear a southern threat at sea.

West of the Mississippi River, the Union cause was given another boost. On March 8, Union forces in northwest Arkansas, led by General Samuel Curtis, pushed Confederate forces from the battlefield of Elkhorn Tavern or Pea Ridge. Of greater significance, the victory enabled the Union to control all of Missouri. Farther west, on March 28, the Confederates retreated from the New Mexico Territory after losing an engagement at Glorieta Pass.

The events of April 1862 continued to hearten Northern spirits. On April 6 and 7, a major Confederate attempt had failed to drive Grant's Army back to the north. The battle, to be remembered as Shiloh, was the largest and bloodiest to date. In the East, the massive Army of the Potomac moved by boat from Washington to a Virginia peninsula between the York and James Rivers. The men in blue now had a direct path to Richmond. Fort Pulaski on the Georgia coast was taken, isolating Savannah from the ocean. On the Mississippi River, the Union Army successfully fought its way farther down river. At the mouth of the Mississippi, a fleet of ships under the command of Flag Officer David Farragut moved north and fought its way into New Orleans, the largest city in the Confederacy.

The Union's stranglehold on the South was not the result of a coordinated effort or a grand plan, nor could it be sustained. The momentum shifted several times in the next three years. However, in late April 1862, it looked as though the War was nearing the end.

The North Reports the Civil War[2]

When Franklin Alford was eulogized in 1893, many of his achievements were recalled, and exalted. One fondly remembered memory was how Franklin graciously provided his neighbors with the news during the Civil War. Not only was Franklin genial, he was the only person in the Alfordsville area who took a daily newspaper.[3]

Franklin subscribed to the Cincinnati *Commercial*, a seemingly strange choice for someone living in southwestern Indiana. A loyalist paper, the *Telegraph*, was published in nearby Washington, Indiana. There were daily papers in Indianapolis, Louisville and Evansville, so why Cincinnati? Alfordsville was near the Ohio and Mississippi Railroad, an east-west line connecting Cincinnati and St. Louis. The westbound O & M passed through Loogootee and Washington, dropping off newspapers along the way. The Cincinnati *Commercial*, therefore, was the handiest paper available and probably contained the latest dispatches.

The *Commercial* offered an additional edge. Cincinnati was considered a fountainhead of western War news as it was the northern-most terminus for the Louisville and Nashville Railroad. Also, Editor Murat Halstead of the *Commercial* was highly regarded for his journalistic skills. He frequently left his desk to travel into the field to report the activities of the western armies. The *Commercial* not only was highly respected on the home front, but became the most widely read newspaper by the soldiers.[4]

Not all was perfect at the *Commercial*, however. The *Commercial* first published the story, in December 1861, that General William Tecumseh Sherman was insane, or "stark mad." Although false, the story was widely circulated by other papers. After an investigation of its sources, the *Commercial* ran a retraction but the damage had been done.[5]

Large city newspapers of the day exercised political power, including the *Commercial*. In 1861, Halstead sought a private meeting with president-elect Lincoln to seek government jobs for friends. He also touted his choice for a cabinet position.(6) The results of this conduct served to enhance the reputation of the big city editors – with the newspapers' readers, with the Union military officers in the field, and perhaps with the President.

Throughout the Civil War, the *Commercial's* front page was devoted to Civil War news. The latest technology was exploited to catch the reader's eye as column headings exclaimed: "Latest Telegraphic News," "News by Telegraph" and "Yesterday Noon Dispatches." In 1861, the news was being processed faster than ever, although not always at the speed of electricity. By the time of the Antietam Battle, September 17, 1862, newspaper offices were receiving dispatches from the front within hours of the events, and the news was on the street the next day.(7)

Of course, the news was not always accurate. In early September 1861, the *Commercial* ran a story, "Jeff Davis Dead Again."(8) On February 18, 1862, two days after the surrender of Fort Donelson, a column heading announced:

A GLORIOUS UNION VICTORY
[True]

FORT DONELSON SURRENDERED
[True]

GENS. JOHNSTON, BUCKNER AND PILLOW TAKEN
[Only Buckner taken]

15,000 PRISONERS OF WAR
[Perhaps, some put the number as low as 7,000]

10,000 KILLED AND WOUNDED
[Assume Confederate only: 2,000 estimated]

FLOYD RUNS AWAY IN THE NIGHT
[Confederates would call it an escape by General Floyd]

GREAT SLAUGHTER ON BOTH SIDES
[4,600 killed and wounded]

THE REBELS HEAR THE NEWS
[No doubt]

A BATTLE RAGING AT SAVANNAH
[Not true]

REPORTED CAPTURE OF THE CITY(9)
[Not true]

Editorial opinions occasionally were expressed in the larger print; ""Surrender of Harper's Ferry a Cowardly Thing" read a headline on September 19, 1862.(10) Such an indictment deserved further analysis.

For the parents of soldiers, the *Commercial* provided an invaluable service. Most of the front page was consumed with reports from the field. These were entitled "Letters From [a soldier]" or more simply "From [a particular military unit written by a correspondent]."

The Alfords must have been pleased if they read this story:

From Green River
(Special Correspondence Cincinnati Commercial)

The 6th Indiana - The Bridge Over
Green River - The Forward Movement

Camp Wood, Ky., Feb 10, 1862
The 6th Indiana at Green River

Eds Com: - As we have been laying dormant for some time I thought I would again endeavor to write a short letter for the benefit of your many readers. There has nothing of any great importance transpired since my last communication. But tonight the glorious news of a forward move was intimated by Gen. Rousseau to some of the officers of the 6th, and before the noble General got outside of the camp lines a shout from a thousand of Indiana's brave boys made the hills of Kentucky tremble with the ring that came forth from the glad hearts. . . . Green River has been on another high, but at the time of writing is gradually sobering off. The pontoon bridge has been rendered useless by the river spreading so that the bridge was separated leaving a large vacant space in the centre. But fortunately for us our brave commanders had taken the precaution to have the railroad bridge floored so that troops wishing to pass over to the South side of the river could cross over on it with just as much ease as on your street pavement. But of late they have done more. They have so arranged it that wagons and horsemen can pass over it with perfect safety. It is, indeed, a novel idea to see heavy loaded wagons drawn by horses, traveling one hundred and thirty-eight feet above terra firma. Yet such is the ingenuity of man that it has been done. Our brave volunteers are capable of performing almost any task and when such a body of soldiers show such an invincible courage and determination, they can withstand any force that may be brought to bear against them and successfully at that. In speaking of the noble 6th I cannot fail to notice the untiring interest the officers of this regiment take in the welfare of the men under their command, which can easily be told by seeing and hearing the good feeling that exists between officers and men.

Signed   W. (11)

However, not all the news would have been so uplifting. A "Letter from Mumfordsville," dateline December 30, 1861, brought the news of a Christmas celebration:

> Christmas was spent very merrily by most of the soldiers; and much more merrily by the officers. All the officers that could raise a horse were mounted – and to the best of my knowledge and belief, I did not see a sober man on horseback unless it was very early in the day.
> I suspect the sin of drunkenness is not so common in our armies as in those of the rebels – but it is common enough among our officers to disgust those under their command. I have seen an Ohio Colonel drill his battalion when he did not know the right from the left flank, or the front from the rear....

Signed KAPPA (12)

There were similar "Letters from Camp Kimball" and the 14th Indiana. The most heartrending news seemed to come from Cheat Mountain in October 1861. The letters expressed anger over the living conditions. "Miserably neglected by our government" was how one correspondent expressed it. He went on to tell of barefoot soldiers, rain (twenty-four out of thirty days), cold and sickness.(13)

Good or distressing, the news was eagerly awaited and shared in Alfordsville.

the roar of musketry upon each side was terrific, almost beyond conception[14]

In March 1862, Warren Alford became a bit player in a huge military plot. The Union high command in Washington, after months of inactivity, was about to re-implement its "on to Richmond" effort. General-in-Chief George McClellan intended to gather 100,000 men near Washington and transport them in 400 boats to within ninety miles of Richmond. But, it was incumbent upon McClellan to leave an adequate force in the nation's capital to provide a shield against an enemy counter-movement. To carry out this grand strategy required more men than were readily available. Orders were issued to army commands at outlying posts to move closer to the Washington area. Such a call went to Paw Paw, Maryland for General James Shields' division of 16,000 men, which included the 14th Indiana Infantry and Warren Alford.

There were obstacles to McClellan's plan. One was in the form of Thomas Jonathan Jackson – "Stonewall." Jackson and his army of 3,700 had spent much of the winter at Winchester, Virginia. When the Union forces started to move toward Washington, it was detected by Jackson's cavalry scouts. Upon hearing the news, Jackson correctly presumed this was the beginning of

Union Brigadier General James Shields.
(Louis A. Warren Lincoln Library and Museum)

the Union Army Spring offensive and another "on to Richmond" maneuver. (15)

As the Union forces consolidated in the lower (northern) Shenandoah Valley, they eventually outnumbered Jackson's forces by ten to one. On March 11, Shields' division moved into Martinsburg, Virginia. That same day, twenty-five miles south, there occurred the first clash of rival skirmishers. Beaten back, Jackson summoned his subordinates to a council of war to discuss the situation. A joint decision was reached to evacuate Winchester and move southward.(16)

The huge Union army under Major General Nathaniel Banks moved toward the Blue Ridge and Washington. Shields' division was assigned the trailing position. By March 22, all of Banks' divisions had cleared Winchester except Shields'. Shields' men had been sparring with Jackson's cavalry as they provided a cover for Banks' main body.(17) Late on the 22nd, Jackson's cavalry commander, Turner Ashby, attacked Shields' outposts south of Winchester. The Union boys were pushed northward to Kernstown, three miles south of Winchester. Shields was wounded in the melee and Nathan Kimball, the firebrand from Loogootee, assumed command of the three-brigade division. In the early morn-

*Confederate Major General Thomas Jonathan
"Stonewall" Jackson.* (Miller's)

ing of the 23rd, Kimball moved his old (First) brigade, which included his old
regiment (the 14th Indiana), to a commanding hill where they observed
Jackson's approaching army.(18)

   With a two-brigade front, artillery, and the high ground, the blueclad soldiers successfully held back a Jackson assault. The 14th Indiana was in the center
of the line, facing south, with its left resting on the Valley Turnpike (now Route
11). At 4 p.m., the situation changed drastically. Jackson found higher ground

Union Major General Nathaniel
Prentiss Banks. (Miller's)

Confederate Brigadier
General Turner Ashby. (LC)

on the Union right flank. Now the Confederates looked down on the Union infantry and artillery. Kimball dispatched the Third Brigade, which had been in reserve, to meet the Confederate threat head on. He also swung his two, previously engaged, brigades to the right. Warren and the 14th were part of this movement.(19)

Lieutenant Colonel William Harrow, commanding the 14th, remembered how his Hoosiers moved toward the Confederates, under fire and a double-quick, "cheering at the top of their voices." For two hours, the boys attacked and fell back, again and again, all under murderous fire from the enemy's cannons and rifles. Their position was opposite the now-famous stone fencing at the point where it connected with the heavy timber.(20) When a section of Jackson's forces ran out of ammunition and pulled back, the entire butternut line started to fold. The Union forces increased the pressure and the Confederate troops withdrew, leaving the Northern army in full possession of the field.(21)

Warren's account, written March 26, provides a vivid description of his involvement. His pride was not containable as he related how the boys went "in to them with fixed bayonets" and "stud up to the work like men . . . amid the hottest of the fight." For Warren, victory came when the 14th overwhelmed an enemy battery. Like most soldiers, he was unaware of the overall situation and

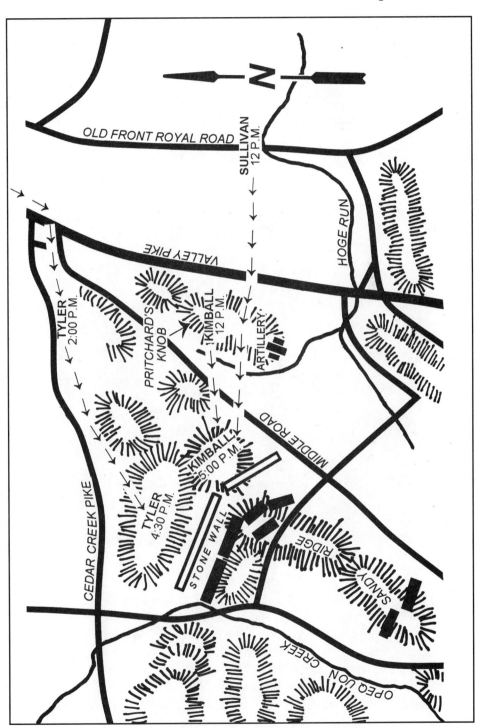

Battle of Kernstown, March 23, 1862.

254 □ *The Alford Brothers*

Union Brigadier General William Harrow.
(*Indiana at Antietam*)

had an exaggerated understanding of the outcome. Warren reported "our loss . . . not over 100 killed and wounded" and "them leaving over 200 dead on the field. . . ." Officially, the Union dead and wounded totalled 568, and the Confederate dead totalled 80.(22) Kimball's men pursued the Confederates until it was deemed imprudent by Major General Banks. He wanted to await reenforcements.(23) The engagement at Kernstown was over. Nathan Kimball would be remembered as the only Union general to defeat "Stonewall" Jackson in the Civil War. Of far greater significance, Banks' army of 16,000 never made it all the way to Washington to support McClellan (and McClellan never made it all

A Portion of the Stone Wall at the Battle of Kernstown.
Photograph Taken in 1939. (Morningside Bookshop)

the way to Richmond). The Battle of Kernstown was the first phase of Jackson's "Shenandoah Campaign of 1862," a brilliantly executed strategic diversion. Although defeated at Kernstown and outnumbered four to one, "Stonewall" Jackson controlled the Shenandoah Valley for the next twelve weeks. The movements of his relatively small army, indirectly dictated the movements of the Union forces, including the 14th Indiana for the next two months.

The situation could scarcely have been worse....[24]

On April 6, 1862, sixteen days after the Kernstown, Virginia battle and 700 miles to the southwest, 44,000 Confederates smashed into 40,000 surprised Union troops at Pittsburg Landing, Tennessee. Union Major General Ulysses S. Grant, the recent hero of Forts Henry and Donelson, was nine miles downstream unaware of what was happening to his Army. The previous day he had sent a message to Washington with the smug observation that the enemy was twenty miles away at Corinth, Mississippi – no problem.(25)

Grant (belatedly) made it to the battlefield on April 6, but it made little difference. The fighting was well under way. His Army of the Tennessee was being

Union Lieutenant General Ulysses S. Grant. (LC)

pushed back. Grant urged his generals to hold but it was too late. There was hope, however. If he could hang on, Lew Wallace's division (6,000 men) and Don Carlos Buell's Army of the Ohio (18,000 men) soon would be available to turn back the Southern tide. Throughout the day, the Confederates pushed forward, and Grant anxiously awaited the reinforcements. By day's end, help came but thousands of men had breathed their last and many thousands more lay wounded, uncertain about their future.(26)

Grant had been beaten badly. The Confederates had successfully pushed the Union Army into a precarious box. Union men were surrounded by a river, flooded streams and confident Confederates. Nevertheless, Grant was in control of the field. The Confederate drive, in effect, had packed the Northern troops

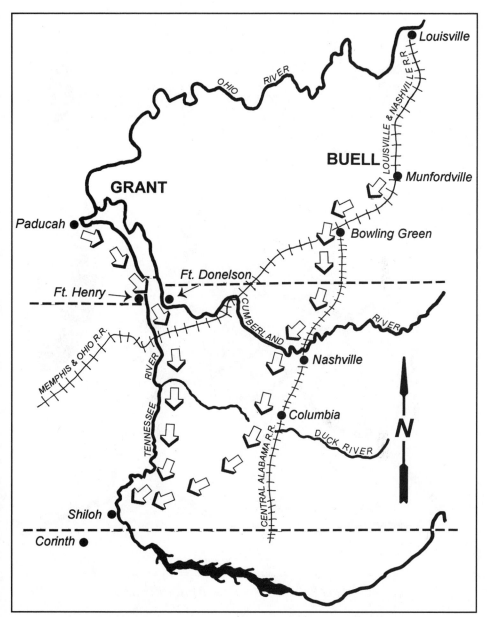

Generals Ulysses S. Grant and Don Carlos Buell Move Their Armies South.

en masse' on the high ground. With the arrival of fresh troops, a bold Grant pronounced, "I propose to attack at daylight and whip them."(27)

Wayne and Lafayette Alford were elements of Grant's new-found strength. The 6th Indiana was one of thirty-four infantry regiments in Buell's (arriving) Army of the Ohio. Unknown to the Alford brothers, they had been moving toward a rendezvous with Grant's Army of the Tennessee since March 15. The

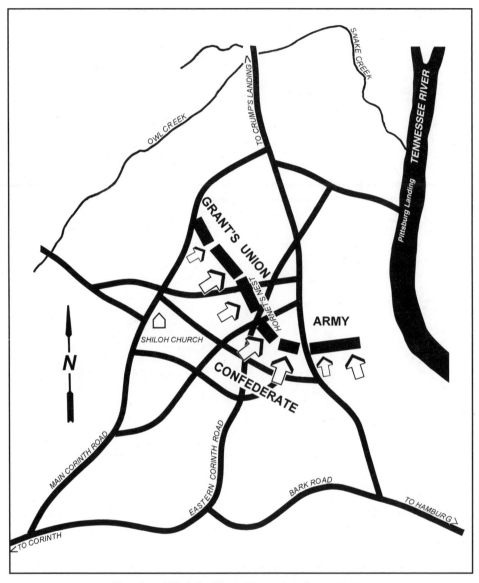

Battle of Shiloh, First Day, April 6, 1862.

intention was for the two armies to join and advance on the Confederates at Corinth, Mississippi. The Confederates shattered that plan when they took the initiative and attacked Grant at Pittsburg Landing, before the arrival of Buell. As luck would have it, the Army of the Ohio had been slowed by flooded streams, burned bridges and waterlogged roads.(28)

Whatever the daily problems, Wayne expressed the limited perception of a foot soldier when he wrote Father on March 18, "where we march to I cannot tell" and later, "I dont believe the Rebals will fight us. . . . " Activities took on a

Union Major General Lew Wallace. *(The Soldier of Indiana)*

precise purpose on Sunday, April 6. The men in the Army of the Ohio hurriedly marched toward the sound of the cannon. The 6th Indiana, within Alexander McCook's division, struggled forward (perhaps for twenty-five miles) reaching Savannah, Tennessee at 8 p.m. Three hours later, they were loaded on steamers for the nine-mile trip to Pittsburg Landing. The 6th Indiana's historian reminded the boys years later of the "worst night of our entire three year service."(29)

Sergeant C.C. Briant explained the misery of the night, shared by all members of the 6th Indiana at Pittsburg Landing:

Union Major General Don Carlos Buell. (LC)

My clothes were wet to the skin, my feet and ankles were blis-
tered, and my legs pained me so badly that to sleep would have
been impossible, even had there been a chance for it; but none
but the dead could sleep. Standing in the open air in mud, ankle
deep, and the rain simply coming down in torrents, and, to make
matters worse, it turned cold; the rapid heavy marching through
the day had warmed us to a copious sweat, and in cooling off we
passed to the other extreme . . . and to add to this condition, there

Pittsburg Landing, Tennessee. (HPHCW)

The Shiloh Meeting House. (HPHCW)

was a hospital within thirty steps of us, where the doctors were busy dressing the wounded, extracting balls, and amputating shattered limbs. The groans and shrieks of the wounded and dying drowned every noise except the pelting rain.

Daylight finally came and Briant remembered, "there was confusion and disorder everywhere, and a worse looking set of men would be hard to find than the old Sixth."(30)

When the orders came at 7 a.m. to move forward, Wayne wrote that Lafayette could not make it; he had a "Severe [Cold] owing to the exposure we

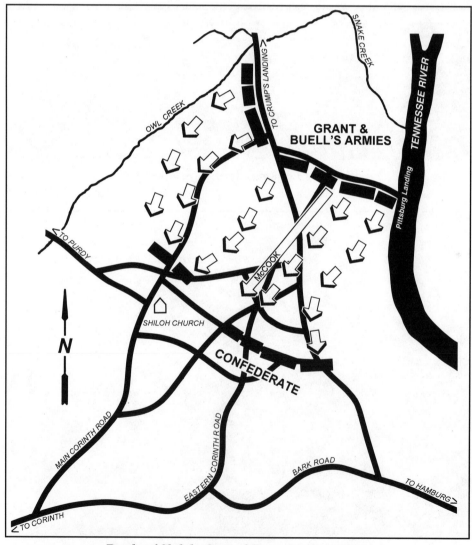

Battle of Shiloh, Second Day, April 7, 1862

have been Obliged to undergo recently." Lafayette would stay behind and help the wounded, while Wayne, still recovering from the accidental gun shot wound in the hand, moved forward with the regiment.

The armies of Grant and Buell stepped off on a one-mile front, 45,000 strong. Only about 25,000 Confederates stood in their path. The 6th Indiana, commanded by Thomas T. Crittenden, was part of Lovell Rousseau's Brigade of Alexander McCook's Division. Rousseau's orders were to move down the main Corinth Road (now Confederate Avenue). The 6th Indiana proceeded from the north and to the east of the road.(31)

Colonel Crittenden reported that shortly after the 6th Indiana deployed, a Confederate battery found their mark – a baptism for the 6th. For much of the day, Wayne and his comrades hugged the ground, firing occasionally from the prone position. When they advanced, they passed near the timber where General W.H.L. Wallace had been mortally wounded the previous day. They crossed the Sunken Lane and Duncan Field, all the while under Confederate battery fire. The heaviest fighting of the day occurred when the Confederates countercharged a Union battery the 6th was supporting. Crittenden remembered how the boys stood and fired twenty rounds each, stopping the Confederate assault.(32) Wayne wrote his Father we "Let Loose on them."

By 2 p.m., McCook's division had recaptured General Sherman's camps of the previous morning. Within hours, the Confederates fell back to Corinth and the Union army rested on the old camp ground. But much had changed. Sergeant Briant of the 6th Indiana remembered the second day as a terrible shock to the system. He wrote, "Roll Call on the evening of the 7th of April, 1862 found the Sixth Regiment thirteen short of only a few hours before, with seven of this number cold in death, lying here and there over the battle field, half buried in mud and water, while the other six, pierced by the enemy's bullets, had been carried to the rear to suffer, and perhaps, die of their wounds."(33) Wayne was disconcerted, too. He wrote of the "impossible scene" and how a comrade had been struck in the head and killed by a six-pound cannon ball.

After Shiloh, the Civil War would never be the same. For the first time, the inhumanity of the American Civil War was fully realized. People at home saw the casualty lists. It was inconceivable. North and South, there were 23,750 casualties in two days, one of every five men present for duty.(34)

In spite of the losses and the horrors, the two sides became more determined to keep fighting. Too much blood had been spilled at Shiloh to ever forget.(35)

Few men who go to the hospital are ever fit for duty.(36)

After the battle of Shiloh, the dead were buried near where they fell. The wounded Union soldiers, about 12,000, were moved north. There remained on the battlefield, however, another killer.

C.C. Briant, the 6th Indiana's historian, summarized the situation:

We changed camps several times in order to get clear of the filth and mud, for it rained constantly for two weeks; nearly the whole of April was put in here on this battlefield floundering around in the mud and rain; quite a number of men took down sick and had to be sent to the rear, and the wonder is nearly every man of the regiment, and in fact the entire army did not get down sick, yet where should we get water to drink and to cook with except the drainings of this battlefield, which was covered with the decomposing bodies of both men and horses, as well as the accumulation of filth of both armies.(37)

Briant's assumptions (written in 1891) as to why there was so much illness were correct: rain, putrid water and filthy camp sites. Also contributing, but not mentioned, were unclean personal habits, insects, rodents and monotonous diets. The greatest single contributor, however, was yet-to-be-discovered microscopic viruses.(38)

Seely Jayne of B Company, 6th Indiana, wrote to "My Dear little woman" on April 24, 1862 from Camp Shiloh. He stated he was well with the "acception of a diaree which I have had for Some two weeks." Two comrades, also from Jennings County, had been sick for two weeks, but were getting better: "Stephen

Pittsburg Landing after the Battle. (USAMHI)

has had a bad cold Settled on his lungs . . . and John has had the glanders."(39) Glanders generally is considered a contagious animal disease (horses and mules). The human symptoms are swollen glands under the jaw accompanied by the excretion of mucous.

The sickness at Shiloh did not start with the aftermath of the battle. As in the case of Lafayette Alford and others, the illness came with them to the battle-field. Those who had arrived earlier and camped on the banks of the Tennessee, were infected while "benefiting" from the proximity of the river.

Surgeons had suspicions as to the causes of disease, but no facts. No tests were available to determine specific diseases. Many sick soldiers manifested symptoms of several diseases, each masking the other. The surgeons, therefore, guessed at appropriate treatments.(40)

Fortunately, medical information was collected which now provides a large sample of data. For instance, data are available for two-thirds of the troops who were camped on the field after the battle. The most common illnesses were diarrhea and dysentery. If a soldier's only disorder was a "little diarrhea," he was considered fortunate. Many soldiers were suffering a "little." One surgeon, after Shiloh, came to the (erroneous) conclusion that sulfate magnesia was beneficial for treating diarrhea. He ordered 150 barrels for his division.(41)

Malaria, in its various forms, was the second most prevalent disease. This illness, thought of as one of the "fevers," flourished in the transitional Spring and Fall months. Acute respiratory disease was the next most common. Typhoid, another "fever," followed in the ranking of occurrences, and was the most deadly of the diseases.

The distinguishable childhood diseases, measles, mumps and smallpox were starting to die out in the warmer months. Other diseases confronting the Shiloh veterans were consumption (tuberculosis), jaundice, syphilis, gonorrhea, rheumatism and scurvy.(42)

The seriousness of these illnesses is highlighted when examining data from the Official Records dated May 31, 1862. Three Union armies (the Mississippi, the Tennessee and the Ohio) were in northern Mississippi, moving toward Corinth. The field returns indicate a total "strength" of 201,559, of which only 59.8 percent are available for combat. The balance consists of those on leave (the majority of whom were sick), or those moving with the army but unfit to carry a rifle.(43)

Data from the rolls of General Sherman's division on May 12th offers further insight into the impact of disease in the western armies. Sherman had 5,289 present for duty, 2,557 absent sick, 855 absent wounded and 600 sick in camp. More significantly, but less determinative, is the knowledge that many of the 2,557 absent sick had "gone home to die."(44)

Acquiring a disease (or a wound) may have been the cause of a mortality, but there were other contributing factors. Doctors, referred to as Surgeons, were rarely trained (or licensed). If "educated," a physician had learned all there was to know in twelve months – or possibly, weeks. Field hospitals usually were

Union Major General William Tecumseh Sherman. (Miller's)

filthy. The nurse cadre was made up of shirkers and misfits. Hospitals were inadequate, nothing more than houses, mills, churches and tents. Medical equipment was primitive; thermometers and stethoscopes were yet to reach acceptance. A 1966 study of medical care in the Civil War suggests that the death rate would have been lower had there *not* been surgeons and medicine.(45)

Not surprisingly, approximately two-thirds of all Union deaths occurring in the Civil War were related to disease. The chances of a Union soldier dying of a disease were one out of thirteen or fourteen, compared to one out of sixty-five who were killed in action or one out of fifty-six who died of wounds.(46)

Endnotes

(1) Long, *ibid.*, p. 205. This entire section was gleaned from that source.

(2) From the title of J. Cutler Andrews' *The North Reports the Civil War* (Pittsburgh, 1955).

(3) Houghton, "Memoriam" for Franklin Alford, *ibid.*

(4) Andrews, *ibid.*, pp. 27, 28.

(5) *Ibid.* p. 116.

(6) Emmet Crozier, *Yankee Reporters 1861-65* (New York, 1956) pp. 25, 26.

(7) Andrews, *ibid.*, pp. 281-283.

(8) *Cincinnati Commercial*, September 5, 1861.

(9) *Ibid.*, February 18, 1862.

(10) *Ibid.*, September 19, 1862. This was a follow up on previously reported news.

(11) *Ibid.*, February 14, 1862.

(12) *Ibid.*, January 3, 1862,

(13) *Ibid.*, October 8, 1861.

(14) Phrase from Lieutenant Colonel William Harrow's report; O.R., v. XII, part I, p. 367.

(15) Robert Tanner, *Stonewall in the Valley* (Garden City, 1976) pp. 106, 107.

(16) *Ibid.*, p. 108. Jackson regretted the decision and this would be not only his first council of war, but also his last.

(17) Nathan Kimball, "Fighting Jackson at Kernstown," *Battles and Leaders* (New York, 1884-1887) v. II, p. 303.

(18) *Ibid.*, p. 304 and William Allen, *History of the Campaign of Gen. T. J. (Stonewall) Jackson in the Shenandoah Valley of Virginia* (Reprint; Dayton, 1987) p. 44.

(19) O.R.s, ibid., pp. 360, 361. Kimball's official report.

(20) *Ibid.*, p. 367. Harrow's official report.

(21) Allen, *ibid.*, pp. 51-53.

(22) O.R.s, ibid., pp. 347, 384. For the Union, total casualties were reported as 118 dead, 450 wounded and 22 missing. Totals for the Confederates were reported as 80 killed, 375 wounded and 263 missing.

(23) Kimball, *ibid.*, p. 308. Some question as to whether this was Banks' or Shields' decision. Regardless, Jackson moved on unmolested.

(24) Quote from J.F.C. Fuller's *Grant and Lee* (Bloomington, 1957) p. 203. The rest of the phrase is: "consequently Grant was at his best." This was a generic comment about Grant's personality but it is appropriate for Grant's demeanor on the night of April 6, 1862, at the time Wayne and Lafayette arrived on the Shiloh battlefield.

(25) Wiley Sword, *Shiloh: Bloody April* (New York, 1974) p. 131. One of two modern, published, studies of Shiloh. The other is James Lee McDonough, *Shiloh – In Hell before Night* (Knoxville, 1977). Also, an unpublished doctoral dissertation: Edward O. Cunningham, "Shiloh and the Western Campaign of 1862," Louisiana State University, 1962.

(26) Sword, *ibid.*, passim.

(27) McDonough, *ibid.*, p. 182.

(28) Don Carlos Buell, "Shiloh Reviewed," *Battles and Leaders*, v. I, pp. 490-493. Buell contended that the battle did not turn because Grant was "at his best," but rather because he (Buell) showed up with more men. He was making the point that battles are won by the side with the greater number of guns.

(29) Briant, *ibid.*, p. 102.

(30) *Ibid.*, p. 103.

(31) O.R.s, v. X, pp 309, 3 10. Rousseau's official report. Also, refer to D.W. Reed's "Map of Shiloh Battlefield" (Second Day) 1900.

(32) *Ibid.*, pp. 311, 312. Crittenden's official report.

(33) Briant, *ibid.*, p. 123. This is a major discrepancy with the O.R.s which lists the 6th's casualties as four killed, thirty-six wounded and two missing. The IAG suggests that both reports are understated.

(34) Sword, *ibid.*, pp. 460, 461.

(35) George A. Reaves and Joseph Allan Frank, *"Seeing the Elephant" Raw Recruits at the Battle of Shiloh* (New York, 1989) pp. 180, 181. The authors provide an analysis of the fighting men at Shiloh: their motivation, behavior and reactions when "seeing the elephant" (a euphemism for seeing the first shots fired in anger).

(36) Howe, *ibid.*, p. 141. A diary entry for January 31, 1863. Howe stated "that there is a great aversion to hospitals and many will not go until there is no other choice."

(37) Briant, *ibid.*, pp. 127, 128.

(38) Paul E. Steiner, *Disease in the Civil War* (Springfield, 1968) p. 179. For a non-technical overview of disease in the Civil War, see James I. Robertson, Jr., *Soldiers Blue and Gray* (Columbia, 1988) Chapter 8, "The Grimmest Reaper."

(39) Seely Jayne Civil War Letters, Indiana State Library; letter dated April 24, 1862. Jayne was killed at the Battle of Stones River; Murfreesboro, Tennessee; December 31, 1862.

(40) Steiner, *ibid.*, p. 172.

(41) *Ibid.*, p. 168.

(42) *Ibid.*, pp. 172, 173. Steiner's data (appropriately for these purposes) pertains to the first Union campaign for Corinth, Mississippi, April-May 1862.

(43) O.R.s, v. X, part II, p. 235. Steiner also used this data (differently) to highlight the point; *ibid.*, p. 171.

(44) Steiner, *ibid.*, p. 171.

(45) Stewart Brooks, *Civil War Medicine* (Springfield, 1966) Chapters I-IV, passim.

(46) Long, *ibid.*, p. 713.

CHAPTER

5

General Hospital No.

Evansville, Ind., *April 18th* 1862

Lafayette Alford a *Corporal* of *Captain Chas R Vantrice* Company E Regiment *6th Ind Vol* having applied to me for a Certificate on which to ground an application for Furlough. I do hereby certify that I have carefully examined said *Alford* and find him suffering from *General Dibility Diarhea* which in my opinion unfits him for duty.

The U.S. Marine Hospital in Evansville, Indiana. (Miller's)

I further certify that said   *Alford*   will not be fit for duty in
less period than   30   days

Approved:

Samuel [?]   Surgeon

★

[A government document:]

TO WHOM IT MAY CONCERN:

The bearer hereof Lafayette Alford   a Corporal   of Captain   Van
Tree's Company E   6th   Regiment of Indiana Volunteers aged
Eighteen   years, five feet 9   inches high, light complexion,   blue
eyes, dark hair, and by profession a   farmer   born in the   County
of Daviess, State of Indiana   and enlisted at   Washington, Daviess
County in the State of Indiana on the   14th day of October eigh-
teen hundred and sixty-one to serve for the period   During the War
is hereby permitted to go to his home (Washington) in the County of
Daviess   State of Indiana   he having received a Furlough from the
19th   day of   April   to the 19th day of May   1862 at which period he well rejoin his Company or Regiment at Pittsburg Landing,
Tenn   or wherever it may be, or be considered a Deserter.
Subsistence has been issued to said Alford   to the 19th   day of
April 1862 and pay to the   day of   given under my hand at
Evansville this 19th   day of   April   1862

Signature of the Officer Giving the Furlough

J.J.Huntington
Surg Genl Hospital

★

[From Warren to his parents:]

Edenburg Va Shields Division
April the 18th

Dear Parents
    With Much pleasure I take the preasant opertunity to Write you a
few Lines to let you know that I am well at this time and hope this

may reach you in dew time and find you all well. I Received your
vary kind Letter having date of the 7th of April which came to hand
in dew time and was gleaned with much interest to me. It will soon
be one year since I bid Adiew to home and friends but I have never
thought that I went without a cause. Their fore I can put my trust
in God with full asurance that he will eaver be with me in the hour
of peril and if it be his will that I should suffer for our Country I
will bare it with patience and think I am doing only my dewty as
an American Citizen and when the Nation fully repents he will
bring peace to our land. We Received our Money the 14th of April
and I experessed to Loogootee $110.00 to you Marked Franklin Alford
Loogootee Indiana With my name On the back. Their was a Ageant
sent here by Gov Morton to take the Money home for the Ind Regts
that was here and I sent it by him to be expressed. Bolivar [Gold] sent
his to James Gold. You can tell him if he does not get a Letter from
him. Stepen [Stephen H. Collins] sent his to sam Collins. Also the boys
are all well. The Weather is Vary fine. I must come to a close as I
want to write a few Lines to Hannah an Send it in your Letter.
Give My Love to all inquireing friends and ever remember your Son
in the Armey.

J Warren Alford

Write to me as soon as you Rec my Money if you can.

[From Wayne to Father and family:]

Battle field of Shiloah
April 20th 1862

Mr Franklin Alford & family
    Dear parents Brothers & Sisters It is with pleasure I embrace the
present opportunity to answer your Very kind Letter which came to
hand in Due time and found me well as Common & as ever glad to
hear from you again. I rote to you in my last letter that Lafayette
and Benjamin [Gilley] Had gone to the Hospital or gone Home I Did
not know which. I have not heared any thing from them yet
though I told Lafayette to wright to me as Soon as he got a Chance &
learned where they were gowing. We are all well Here and in good
Spirits. Day before yesterday our General [Richard W.] Johnsons
Brigades mad a Reconaisance in force. We went Down Almost to the
Enemies Outposts & in fact Drove in some of thier pickets. Our men
fired after them as they run but I Suppose Did no harm. They [are
not] so anxious to fight now as they were Before the Battle here.
After we made all the Discoveries we Could we came back and went

on picket and I think their was Some of the Most horid Sights that ever I witnessed. I Did not go Down myself for the Sight from the post where I was Stationed Satisfied me. They were men that had been Killed During the Battle Still laying unberried (about 2 Weeks) and the Creapers had almost Eaten all the flesh from there Bones. But the men Seame perfectly Hardened to any thing. But believe me the Sight of a Battle field is truly Horrible or it would be to you. But Soldiers get Hardened So that they Care but little for it. Dont understand me to Say that we become perfect Heathens or Cannibals but you Dont get a Chance to take a Sober Second though[t] from the fact that we are pushed on without waiting for any thing at a Sober thought. The Sight is just as Horrible to me as it ever was.

Union Brevet Major General Richard W. Johnson. (LSU)

This morning I remarked that it was the third Sunday if I had not forgotten (our labor is just as hard on Sunday as any other & if we Dont keep count we Cant tell when Sunday Comes) & that I would like verry much to be at home at meating today. But as I could not I felt assured that their would be a great many Suplications Sent up today for us poor Soldiers who are Deprived of the privaledge of meeting with their friends at the House of God and there worship is in according to His word & no Dare to hinder or make afraid. But notwith Standing we look forward to a better Day when we in Common with all who have Served there Country faithfully Can again meet at the House of God & there worship him according to his mood with the assurance that we have at least Done our Duty. But I must close. I hope Lafayette has got home or if not at Some good place where he can recruit his health. I think from the Signs of the times that this rebellion is about played out. I rote you in the last letter that I Sent My Money with all of Benjamins & Lafayettes & I think it is all most home by this time. Hopeing to hear from you Soon. I remain your Soon untill Death.

Wayne Alford

As for Johns Health See the top of page.

[top of page:] When Bartle Saw John He Looked tolerable bad but at this time he looks as well as he Did the Day he left home & as for his looking like a Shaddow their is nothing of it. – Wayne

[From Wayne to Father and family:]

Field of Shiloh
April 20th 1862

Mr Franklin Alford & family
Your Verry kind letter which you rote me at Evensville Came to hand this Eavening & found me with the rest of the Boys Well & glad to Hear from you again & to learn that you had Sucess in getting Lafayettes furlow. [Brother] George rote me that you had gone after him & as you Did not get him Saturday Eavening they Did not look for you untill Monday. I rote George a letter las night & there has nothing transpiered today only we received orders to Cook one Days rations & prepare to move at a moments notice. I Dont know what the intention of this is probably . . . a move on Corinth but it is all conjecture with me as I Dont hear anything about Such things. Today we received News of the takeing of New orleans by our men and I hear all the regiments Cheering & I Suppose that is what it is about & you Can Scacely imagine how it Makes a Soldiers Heart Leap for Joy to hear of Some great victory on our Side. . . . We Consider that Every Victory of our men is Drawing this unhapy rebellion that much nearer to a Close. We received the News from General Rousseau. He told Col Crittenden he told us. If we move Soon it is probable that I Cannot wright untill we Stop again but it is my opinion that we will stay her for a Day or two yet. But it you Dont hear from me regular it will be because we are moveing or my letters fail to reach you. I am of the opinion that if Mclellen [Union General George McClellan, now in Virginia] whips them at Yorktown and we whip them here (that is if they Stand) that this rebellion will be about Played out. If we get into another fight I Shal try & put my trust in him that is able to Save & to Destroy & therefore I think I will come out all right. I Desire [an] interest in your prairs. I would like to See you all again & Enjoy the pleasure in the family Circle that we have [had]. . . . But By the help of God I hope we Can Soon meat again. But it is getting two Dark to wright So I must Close. Hopeing to hear from you Soon. I remain your affectionate Son.

Wayne Alford

PS Tell Charley that a line from them would be Verry acceptable & I believe I rote last.

[Stationery with the letterhead:]

INDIANA HOSPITAL FOR THE INSANE

Indianapolis, Ind., April 21st 1862

Franklin Alford Esq

Dear Sir:
    I am in receipt of yours of the 17th inst. and in reply have to say
that Mrs Kellams mental condition remains about the same as when
she was admitted into this hospital. I hope that time and judicious
treatment will restore her to reason. Her physical health is tolerably
good. Rest assured that we will do all that we can to make her comfortable, and to restore her to mental and bodily health.
                                        Respectfully Yours
                                        James H. Woodburn
                                        Superintendent

★

[From Wayne to brother George:]

Field of Shiloah
April 25th 1862

Mr George W Alford   Dear Brother   This is in answer to your letter
which came to hand in Due time and fond me well & glad to hear
from you all Again & to learn that you were all well. I had A letter
from Warren the other Day And He is well I Suppose you have
heared from Him. He Said their pickets & the rebels were in gun
Shot of Each other One mile from where he was writing But Did not
know whether it would bring on a general engagement or not. The
troops Still Continue to Come in here as if they were never gowing to
Stop. Their is no news here of interest only Yesterday our men went
Down to where there was a Brigade of Rebals encamped and fell on
them and Some of the Cavalry told us as they Came Back that they
Just Set fire to there tents & threw Down there guns and run run
for life. One thing. We were marched Down that way to Support
them if Necessary but met them Coming back with Some Dozen prisoners and a lot of guns and camp Equipage. They Said they left

them Running So we Just about faced & marched back to Camp. I
have nothing more of interest. I have not heard from Lafayette &
Benjamin [Gilley] Since they left. I am very anxious to hear from
them not that I am uneasy but I want to Know where they are. In
Some of your letters you wanted to know which Hand it was that I
Had Shot. Well it was my right hand. I never thought to tell you
that it was my right hand from the fact that I could not wright.
Well it is got well Enough for my Duty and has been Since the Battle.
Wright to me if the Money I Sent last Came to hand. All wright
[and] tell me all about how the things are Doing and how you are get-
ting along with your work. I would be Verry Happy to See you all
but you know it is impossible at this time but I think the time Not
Verry far Distant when the Lord will [arrange that] we Can meat at
home again. This leaves us well and in fine Spirits. Some think the
Rebels will fight us again at Corinth but as for Myself I Dont know.
I Sometimes think that it is Doutfull if they do. I have Confidence so
believe we Can whip them and that will end the thing. But I must
Close for the present. I will wright Father a letter Soon. I have
writen three or four letters Since the fight. Wright as often as you
can & all wright. I remain as ever your Brother untill Death.

Wayne Alford

[From Wayne to brothers George, Greene and sister Hellen:]

Field of Shiloah
April 27th 1862

George, Green & Hellen
    Dear Brothers and Sister
Your letter Came to hand this Eavening & found me well & Glad to
hear from home Again. I have no news of interest to wright but as I
have to Set up untill Eight Oclock Roll Call I thought I had just as
well be wrighting to you as Doing nothing. Was Verry anxious to
hear from Lafayette & Benjamin [Gilley] for I had had No new from
them Since they left until I received your letter tonight. I am in
hopes that father will Succed in getting a Permit to take Lafayette
home untill he gets well. I was very glad to hear from Warren as
your letter is the latest News I have had from him. I rote to him the
other Day but have not Had time to get an answer. I want you to let
me know whenever you get a letter from him for you know that I
am anxious to hear from him as often as possible. You must all
wright as you Can & Be Sure & let me know How Lafayette is getting
along. You must let me know any thing that you think I would like

to know. I Do not know whether we will have a fight at Corinth or not but if we Do I think we are able to whip them but I must close for the present. Wanting to hear from you Soon. I remain your affectionate Brother until Death.

Wayne Alford

[In same envelope:]

Dear Mother

I must wright a few lines to you before I close though I have Never writen a letter Specialy to you. I have intended all the letters that I have written Home for all. Mother I am getting along verry Well. George wanted to know if I was scared to go into Batle. Well as for that I was as composed as if I was gowing to Breakfast. I was fully aware that I might get Killed but Still I put my trust in Him that is able to Save & Destroy & I was well aware that he could pro-tect me as well on a Battle field as any where Else. I Come out here to try & do my Duty as a Christian & a Soldier & if I fall on the Battle field I will willingly resign my Spirit into his hands that Doeth all things well. Although I often feel like I would love to be at home, Yet I never regret the Day that I enlisted in the Service of my coun-try. I Did not Come here but to Serve my Country & thus can [?] these words. First my God then my country & then my friends at Home. But if the lord will[ing] I hope Soon to be able to return to the enjoyment of home & friends. But it is getting late & I must Close. Wright as oftern as you can. I remain your affectionate Son.

Wayne Alford
This leaves me
Well.

[From Warren to the family:]

Near Harrisonburg [Virginia]
Shields Division
May the 1st 1862

Dear Parents & Brothers & Sisters

With much pleasure I take the pen and opertunity to inform you that I am Well at this time. I Received your vary kind letter Written from Evansville baring date of the 19th of April Bringing me the Inteligence of Lafayettes Illness but I Was much gratified to Learn that he was going to get to go with you home where he can be under your imediate care [and] where he will no doubt be better cared for

than he posibley could have bin at the Hospittal. . . . I hope by this time he is much better if not intirely. Well your Letter brought me the first nuse of the safety of the Boys that was in the Great Battle of Shilo[h] or Pitsburg Landing in which so many of our brave Soldiers now sleep in death. . . . We saw in the papers that the 6th Reg was their but could not hear of the Casualtys of the Reg. We saw in the papers that Gen Bewell [Union General Don Carlos Buell's] men was spoken of in highest termes in Regard to their fine disiplin and drill and especialy General McCooks division and Gen Reausaus [Rousseau's] brigade in that division. We are now about 32 Miles from Stanton [Staunton, Virginia] going up the Shanada [Shenandoah] Valley. Our Brigad is comanded by Col Masom [John Mason] of the fourth Ohio. Gen Kimble [Nathan Kimball] is commanding Shieldses [General James Shields'] division since Shields was wounded. But I think he will soon be able to command in the field but whether Kimble will comand our brigad then or not I cannot tell. I supose you have got the Money I sent home before this time. The boys are All well excep Boliver [Gold] he has bin unwell for a few dayes. I think he is better to day. I should be vary glad to be at home and see you all as it has bin Allmost one Year since [I] left home but I am still determined to live so that I will not be shamed to come home when I get the chance. I must close.
. . . J Warren Alford

[From Wayne to Father:]

Camp 9 miles from Cornith
May 4th 1862

Mr Franklin Alford   Dear Father   I Seat myself to answer your kind Letter which you Sent by Georg M Wheeler. I Was Verry glat to hear from you Again for I was Verry anxious to hear from Lafayette again. Wheeler Reached our Camp this Morning he Says he feels better Now than when he Left home. [George Wheeler, from Washington, will die of wounds at Chattanooga in December 1863.] Well I Suppose we are on the Eave of A Great Battle & Ere this Reaches you the Decisive blow may be Struck which in my opinion will be the Downfall of Rebellion in this part of Country for the Enforcement of the Laws. Dont understand me to Say that this will End the war but it will in a manne Decide the Contest. I have No fears of our undertaking the Job for I know that our forces are Superior to theres in number & our cannons [are] both larger and better maned than there. This morning there was a Battery of large Siege guns passed along Enrout for Corinth. Lafayette they are them large guns that

lay at the landing During the last fight. Lafayette you know Capt
Cotter was mustered out of the Service Well he has been ordered back
to his battery & Just reached here last Eavening & you had better
believe his boys Jumped when he Came up. The Secretary of war
Ordered him Back & the President Signed the order. You nead not be
uneasy about us in the Comeing fight for I feel that I Can put my
trust in him that is able to Save & to Destroy & I Shal try to Repose
entire Confidence in his word. But it is time to Close for the mail is
ready to start out. Remember me at a throne of grace. This leaves
me well. I remain as ever your affectionate Son. Untill Death.

Wayne Alford

Wright as often as you Can & I will Do the Same.

★

[Lafayette Alford died on May 7.]

★

[From Warren to his parents:]

May the 8th 1862
Camp near
Newmarket

Dear Parents
    Brothers & Sisters
This Morning I am seated to drop you a few lines to inform you of
my Good health. I am in as good health as I ever was in my Life. It
is now one year since I Left home to help defend the Rights garanteed
to us by the Constitution of our Union. We have had some scurmish-
ing in the last few days. It is reported this Morning that their was
about one Hundred of the 13th Ind taken prisoners yesterday [while
on reconnoisance near Summerville, Virginia. The casualties were
four wounded and twenty-four captured]. We heard of the evacuation of York Town [Virginia] and ... that Little Mack [General
McClellan] over tuck them at or near Williamsburg and routed them
with severe lossess. We did not hear the particulars as yet. Cap
Brooks got here about the 1st [and] brought your Letters and envelops
& paper you sent me. Cap is going to resign on account of his ill
health. [Which he did on May 8th, but reenlisted as a Lieutenant
Colonel in the 80th Indiana on September 4, 1862.] Virgle [Alford]
started home the 3rd ... And that is why I did not Write soner as he
[can] answer all your questions. I have bin Looking for a letter from

you for some days. The Last Letter I got from Alfordsville was dated the 27th of Apr it stated that Lafayette was some better. I would love to get a letter from you a gane. The health of the Reg is very good at this time. Boliver gold is about well a gane. He has bin about [the same] for some time All the boys are well at this time. All send their respects and best wishes to you. I hope you have got the Money I sent to you as it has bin time enough for it to get home. You will write as soon as you get it and let me know for I would Love to hear from it. I want you to write as soon as you can a gain. I am very Anxious to hear from Lafayette. I am still trying to live so that if we neaver meat on earth we will meet you all in a better world where their will be no more fighting nor no more dying nor sorrowing. I would Love to be at home with youall where we could enjoy all the plea- sures of home. I am as ever your Affectionate sone. Give my love to all and except a protion for your self.

J Warren Alford

★

[From Warren to the family:]

Front Roil [Royal] Va Shields Division
May the 15th 1862
Home

Again I take the preasent opertunity to write home to let you know that I am still well. I Receved your letter dated the 2nd which came to hand in dew time. We are all well but not vary well pleased with the way Brooks acted with us when he Resigned. It would have sooted the company vary well if he had never come back to the com- pany . . . He [should have] acted more of the gentleman with the Co. When he Resigned he was going to give us a chance to Elect our offi- cers till he found out the one he wanted was not going to be elected. When he found that out then he went and recomended the one that sooted him. An that was the last of electing officers and if that is the way a Gentleman act we do not care whether their is any more such gentleman in our Co. It is said in the comp that the recomendation could have bin bought for tenn Dollars. Every dog has his days. That is all. We are on a march for some unknown place. I have now Idea where. John McCord got a letter from home this morning dated the 5th stating that he [? Lafayette] is not well yet. I got a Letter from Wayne the other day he Was well. The boys are all well but Boliver [Gold] is not with us as he was not able to March With the Reg. But I must come to a close for [now] and hoping this will find you all well boath in body and mind. So no more at preasent.

Scene of the Battle at Front Royal, Virginia. (HPHCW)

Hoping to see you soon.

J Warren Alford

Direct as before only put Shields Division Va.
Give my respects to all enquireing friends. Tell Grandfather I
have traveled neerly all over Va and their is some vary fine Cenerys
here but Ind is the Land for me.

Good by.
J Warren Alford

[This is an extensively edited version of a letter Wayne wrote to
his parents. The original was not located.]

Camp near Corinth, May 18, 1862

Mr. Franklin Alford and Family:
Dear Parents, Brothers and Sisters:
I received your letter of the 11th, this morning, which bore the sad
intelligence to me that my Dear Brother is no more. This is sad news

for me; this leaves me apparently alone here; this is something that I have been almost afraid of, since you delayed writing so long. I was afraid that you had no good news or you would have written. This is a heavy blow upon me, here, and I have no words adequate to express the grief that was at once heaped upon me. From the time he left the regiment, I have been afraid that he was going to be bad sick; and, as often as I could, I have been in the habit of strolling away from the noise and bustle of camp to some lonely tree and there implore God; and I have an assurance (a living hope) that by a faithful continuance in well doing that when we are called to pass through the valley and shadow of death that it may be well with us; and, in the Glorious Resurrection Morn, we will meet our brother who has gone before and be permitted to strike the immortal hand on the banks of sweet Canaan where parting will be no more; where there is no roaring of cannon or rattle of small arms to disturb our peace; but where we can enjoy all that is meant by Heaven and happiness to worlds without end. This stroke seems more hard to me, since the hardship of the last seven months has strengthened the ties of affection and caused him to appear nearer to me, if possible, than before; but I feel Christians ought to submit quietly and without murmuring to the dispensation of Divine Providence; and, although it seems hard, we will try and submit quietly and without a murmur. During his stay in the army, I never saw anything but a manifestation of a true Christian spirit.

Mother, I would say to you that, notwithstanding the shock is great, it is my desire that you will bear these afflictions and, if possible, not let them overcome you; this is all I am afraid of now. Notwithstanding it falls heavily upon us, we should put our trust in the Lord, that we will meet again in the sunlit regions of endless happiness; this is my earnest prayer.

But I must close for the present, as my space is about full and it is very hard for me to write at all this evening under surrounding circumstances. When I become a little settled, I shall write again, if I have a chance. I would not have written, this evening, but we have been under marching orders for two days and I did not know whether I would have a chance again. They have a skirmish with the enemy almost every day; there has been considerably cannonading today in the direction of the enemy. Lieutenant Soloman [Alanson Solomon from Washington, Indiana] is dead; he went home and died there.

I want you all to write to me often as you can; I desire an interest in your prayers. I remain,

Your affectionate son until death,

WAYNE ALFORD

[From Warren to Father and Mother:]

Catlet Station Shields Division
May the 20th 1862

Father & Mother

I take the preasant opertunity after a long March of 7 days we reached this place about 85 miles from New Market. We are now about 40 miles from Washington City on the Orange and Alexandra Railrode. We are now in Eastern Virginia about 40 miles west of the blueridge [mountains and] 3 miles from Warington [Warrenton] junction & 10 miles from Warington. We was ordered to report at this place and I suppose we will go on in a day or two. The Troops are all in good health. The Reg never was in better fix for service. Their is a Brigade of troops here that never saw a wild cecesh. They are most-

Catlett Station, Virginia. (USAMHI)

ly from new york and they had to draw crackers to day and thought they could not stand it and their officers told them if they would not make a fuss about it they should have soft bread half the time. One of them asked me how a man would feal on going in to a fight. He alowed we had got use to it so that we did not care. I want you to Write to me whether any one of Uncle Harmons boys is in the armey or not. Bolivar gold is not with us on this March. The Dr thought he had better not go on the March though he was as well as ever though not so stout. All the Rest of the Boys are well. Simon tracy [Private Simeon Tracy from Martin County] got back to the Co a bout two Weaks ago. He went to the Hospital from North Branch Bridge. I must come to a close soon as I have now nuse to rite you. I only thought I would write to let you know where I was. I want you all to Remember me at a throne of grace for with out asistance from our heavenly Father we can do nothing. Give my love to all my friends and reserve a portion for your selves.
I am your Affectionate Son.

J Warren Alford

This Leave me well And I hope it will come to hand in Dew time and find you All Well. Write to me soon.

★

[From Dr. Laverty to Franklin:]

Camp in front of Corinth Miss
Medical Department
June 1st 1862

My Friend Franklin
    You may think it strange to know that I am writing to you this morning but heare [is] the reason and then my friend you can arrive at your own conclusions. It is done by request from Wayne. He is now laying in our hospitle, with Typhoid feavr of a long lingering type. He has been unwell for some time before comeing to the hospitle but did not consider, neither did we think, that it would result in any thing of such character. He received two letters from you this morning [and] requested me to read them. I did so and found from the tenor of them that you were desirous of knowing how he was getting along. So we have but to give you what we consieder Waynes situation to be. That he is taking Campr Typhice is sure Franklin and you will have to use your own discussion relative to him. He is receiving all the attention from us that is possible for him to have heare under the presant circumstances. "But it is no

Corinth, Mississippi – The Tishomingo Hotel. *(USAMHI)*

home." In your [letter] to him You said if it "wer possible you" would
do all in your power for him. . . . It is True that [there] may [be
many] a long mile . . . between us But as Wayne says do whatever
you think for the best. I have in the last day or two written some
letters to Alfordsville and to some of the friends [and] told them that
I was fearful [that] Wayne was going to be bad. But [he] told me
that he would rather I would not let his parents know any thing
about it owing to their recent afflictions. Now my friend Franklin I
have tryed to give you Waynes case as neare as I can. I consider him
[and] John [William Alford to be] in a critical condition. Now I will
give you some information relative to your getting them home should
you come to the conclusion to come to see your boy. Their has been
an order isued lately that no cases of Typoid feaver should be taken
on board an Hospitle Boat or transportation granted to any such cases
from Camp. As it is considered to be or prove unfortuanate for cases
of Typhoid feaver. So you will see Franklin that in case you should
come out heare, glad as we would all be to see you, you could not
even get to take him home. Corinth is now evacuated by the rebbels
and of Course their will be some disposition made of our Sick heare.
But in their presant situation (I mean John William & Wayne) are
to low and week to have transportation to the [Tennessee] river. In
even in moving them to the river in an ambulance I do not think

they could possibly . . . be moved, especially John William. They are
too weak for the journey. I suppose that in Case the regiment should
move that I will be left in Charge of our Sick untill they will be able
to go home. I will endevour to do my duty to them so far as layes in
my power. Not only for their comfort heare but of attending to their
evry want And I will [take] the first oppurtunity that presents its
self and [if] I think they will have transportation, I will send them to
Evinsville. Should Death end their sufferings I will still be [as good]
to them that I have been during our acquaintenance. But I hope for
better things.   Now Franklin I will have to write to Wayne Reve for
John. I am going to send this letter to be mailed in Indiana by a
friend of mine from Seymore [Seymour] and I thought that you
would be more sirtin to get them. If we should succeade in getting
the boys to Evinsville I will write immediatly and make you
acquainted with the facts in the case. So now I will bid you farewell
from your friend as ever.

Dr. J.L. Laverty

★

[From Franklin to the family:]

Evansville
Tuesday Morning June the 10th/62

Dear Wife and Children   I take the present opportunity of dropping
you a line to let you know that we arrived at this place yesterday
about 4 P.M. and have Examined all the Hospital In the place but A
Convelesecent one and found but one mans name belonging to the
6th [Indiana] and we Expect to leave at 9 P.M. to day for Pudduca
[Paducah, Kentucky] where we will be better able to get A Boat for
Shilo[h]. I Cannot tell when we will be able to be home. I want you
to do the best you Can and Expect us at home as soon as we Can
accomplish our Mission. You may Expect to hear from us again the
first opportunity after A fine nights rest. We are In good health [and
we are] at the Browns desk. He and Family Is well and A gentleman.
I think we will get along with out difficulty. I have no nuse but the
Capture of Memphis by our fleet so I will Close by subscribing my
self. Your Affectionately.

F Alford

★

[From Warren to one of his brothers at home:]

Luray [Virginia] Shields Division
June the 13th 1862

Dear Brother

Once more I am seated to drop you a few Lines to let you know that I received your Letter in dew time but have not had time to answer it till now. Since I received your Letter I received the painful nuse of the death of our beloved brother [Lafayette]. But we sorrow not as those that have no hope but we sorrow as one traveling to a Cuntry where their in no mor sorrowing nor sying. But as it is impossible for us to compos one unbroken family on Earth Let us Live so that we will all meet in Heaven where parting will be nor more but one Continualy stream of happyness for eaver & eaver. In the last Month we have Marched and countermarched in all about 400 miles but I shal not attemp to give you an account of it at this time. Suffise it to say we have had a vary hard time of it. . . . [Part] of our division had a vary severe skirmish [Referring to a battle at Port Republic, Virginia.] Their Loss was vary severe. Their was only two brigades in the fight. The third and fourth brigades Commanded by Carol [General Samuel Carroll] and Tyler [General Erastus Tyler]. The first and second brigades was not in the fight. It is rumored in Camp that McLelen [Union General George McClellan] was repulsed at Richmond. Whether is so or not I cannot tell but if it is so I hope they will put some one in command that will go a head and do something. It is reported Allso that part of the forces that was at Corinth have gon to Richmond. All the boys are well. I am well as ever [If] you saw me. I should be vary glad to be with you but I suppose you cannot be [expected] to get her. Wm Houghton is now our Capain. I want you to write to me soon and let me know all about how you are geting along. Give my Love to all the boys and Reserve a double portion for you self. As ever your brother. Warren Alford

[In the margin:] Excuse me for not Writing sooner.

[From Warren to his parents:]

Luray Shields Division
June the 14th 1862

Dear Parents

This Morning I am seated [to] drop you A few Lines to let you know that I am still on the land and among the Living. And still blessed with health and I hope when this come to hand it will find you with all the friends well. We have bin on the March for some time and I have not had a chance to write to you as often as I would wish and have not wrote to many that have written to me. But I hope you will pardon me and ask others to do the same. We have bin in camp three days since we cam to this place. This is a vary nice little town with three or four Churches in it. Their is a Christian Church here of about 150 Members but I have not had a chance to talk to a one of them. Alexandear Camel was through hear preaching last spring one year ago. All of the boy of your acquaintence are well John McCord and Stephen Collins and bolivar [Gold] and [Richard] Conolly are vary well. Thair is more change in [John] McCord than any boy i ever saw. I do not think I could be with better boys than I am. [What is interest to one, is of interest to all] and we have now [no] trouble about geting along to geather. I hope [this will not change] when we can all come home and be with our friends. We would be vary glad to be with you [and have the] privolidge of going to hear John Mathy or Uncle preach to us on Christianity. That is a privolidge that I regret more than all others. But we will do the best we can under the circumstances and thank our Heavenly father it is no worse. I must close by saying he that continueth faithful to the end shal not be ashamed. As Ever you Son. Warren Alford

★

[Handwritten note:]

Washington, Ind Jun 22, 62

Alfordsville
    Sir you will inform the relatives of Wayne Alford that George Bradford of Com E arived home this eavening from Corinth Miss.
    [He] Request me to Saye to them that Mr Wain Alford departed this life the 14th [of June] at Corinth Miss Sad inteligence. You will Convey the information immediately if you please.

Yours
Rept

S. S. Rodermel

★

[From Warren to Mother:]

Camp Bristo[e] station
June the 27th 1862

Dear Mother
    I received your vary kind Letter & the one father rote the Week
before on the 25th of the Month. I was vary sorry to hear of Waynes
being unwell but I hope it will not be long before he will be well
again. We are on the plains of Manassas about 30 Miles sout of
Alexandria. The hole Cuntry from here 20 Miles toward Alexandria
and for miles around was one continual seen of Rebel camps all last
summer. Every thing was laid in ruins. We have a vary nice
Camping ground And I think this is one of the healtheyar countreys
in the world. Their is now [no] sickness in the Armey of any
Consequence and I think our Co has bin wonderfulueley favored
ever since we have bin out for which I am vary thankful and hope
we may still be blessed with the same blessing. Give my best respects
to Mother force and tell her I would love to be [there] and take dinner with her. Barney berrey [Berry, a sergeant from Martin County,]
sends the same word to her. Give my love to all enquireing friends.

Master Green. I received you Letter the other day and was much
pleased with it. You must be a little man and write soon Again.
George I want you and Hellen to write to me often and never spend
your time in idleing and never be Caught in bad Company. But with
such as will be an honor to yourself and to your Brothers so fare
from home. And I hope that none of us will ever do any thing that
will bring reproche on our name. I must soon Come to A close. All
the friends are well excep one of Lem Kelleys boys [William] and he is
much better this morning. . . . I am vary well myself And when this
comes to hand I hope it may find you All well time is passing swiftly
by. It is all most 14 months sinse I left home and to look back it is
onley a short time but oh the changes in one short year who can tell.
But I am as ever.

Yours in the one Hope.
J Warren Alford to his Mother.

[From Warren to Mr. Hillery Houghton:]

Camp Near Manassas
June the 27th 62

Mr Houghten [forwarded to Mt. Pleasant, Martin County, Indiana]
    Sir   After the Receip of your Letter some days [ago and] not hav-

Warrenton, Virginia. *(USAMHI)*

ing A favorable opertunty till now I take the preasant opertunity to
answer your vary kind and Apropriate Letter on the death of our
much beloved Brother [Lafayette]. The nuse of which was sorrowful
to me but we sorrow not as those having now hope as we Mourn we
remember that he had taken upon him self the obligations of a Holy
Life and we learn from those who was with him in the campaign
that he never disgraced his profession and with this consolation we
Look forward with joy to the day when we will all meat in a better
world than this where their will be now more hurting. We are
Camped on the plains of Manassas About 30 miles from Alexandra.
Our Company is in good health and is the best Company in the Reg.
We have had some vary hard Marching but we are the boys that is
able to stand the hardships. It [is] thought their will be a change in
the commander of this Division as Shields is Rejected as major Gen . . .
It is thought he will resign if has not allready done so. But I must
soon come to a close as I have now Nuse. Writing this leaves all well.
Give my respects to all enquiring friends and reserve a portion for
your self. I am as Ever yours in The Hope.

Jas Warren Alford

★

[From Warren to the family:]

Camp Turkey bend
July the 9th 1862

Dear Father & Family
This morning finds me time enough to answer your letter which
came to hand on the 6th which bore the sad nuse of the death of my
much beloved Brother [Wayne]. . . . I had heard of it be fore I received
your Letter. The shock was vary heavy since he was left alone and
fair from home and friends. But know [no] dout he was cared for in
the best way posibly. As their is now [no] hope of Meating them on
this Earth we must strive the more earnestly to Meat them on the
Sunney banks of far deliverance where their will be now more parting. Nothing but one continualy stream of bliss through the ceceless
ages of ever ending Eternity. Now I would say we are brought to see
the powerful hand of god on our family. But I hope we will bair the
Trials as best we can for we know that if this Earthly house of [ours]
is desolved [and] if we have [obeyed] our heavenly fathers [we] will
house highest in the Heavens . . . to dwell for eaver and Ever. We
know while we was at home they was trying to live in the discharge
of their deuty as Christain soldiers and from what [I] see of their
writing that they have bin trying to discharge their deuty [with] god
being their helper. And we know that he is only one in [trust] for
salvation. . . . This morning I fell more determined to press forward to
the end when eternal Life will be ours [for]ever. . . . I hope you will
never Allow our dificuleys to over come us and ever bair in mind
that it is God that givet and god that taketh away. Blessed be the
name of the Lord. Now I desire . . . the prairs of all the people of god
and especialy of my Christan Acquaintances. And I know I will
have the prairs of those who are neer to me by the Ties of nature for
my safe return home. . . . Allso those that left with me who are all
most as near to me as my brother. While we pray for our selves and
now I know you will truly . . . perfrom your deuty and if you put
your trust [in] god you will never fall. I want you to Write to me all
the particulars about his sickness as soon as [you] get them as I am
anctious to hear the full account of his sickness and Death. We
Landed at this place [Harrison's Landing, Virginia] the 2nd of July
and was marched immediately to the front [on] the third. We had a
right smart skirmish and our Co got Two men Wounded. One of
them was Fred Sholtzs son [Private George W. Sholts, to be discharged
in November for a disability]. The other was Levi Dunlap [Sergeant
Dunlap later was promoted to 2nd Lieutenant]. We had an other
skirmish the 4th. Thomas Noland was wounded [and will die on
July 4, 1862.]. . . . Those were all that was hert in our Co. Their was

two more wounded in our Reg but I will not say any thing more onley we are trying to mak this place safe. The boys are all well. I am well my self. Give my love to all inqurieing friends and reserve a double portion for your selves. Write to me often and tell others to rite to me when convenient. But I must close by saying again for you to remember me at a throne of Grace as often as you pray for your selves and I will do the same. I am your son till death.

J Warren Alford

[From Warren to the family:]

Harrisons Landing
Virginia July the
13th 1862

Dear Father & Family

    With much Respect I am seated to write you a [few] lines in answer to the Letters I received from you and the Children last Night for I asure you it a great pleasure to me to get a letter from home.

Camp at Harrison's Landing, Virginia, in July 1862. (B&L)

And that letter you sent me of Waynes I think was one of the nicest things I ever saw and worthy of our solem meditation and of our patronage through Life that we may be like him when we come to dye. Ready and willing to go to that Rest that a waits the Christian. We now belong to Mclellen's [General George McClellan s] armey And I suppose you have heared before this time of the driveing back of Mclellens armey [in the Seven Days Battle] and of the results of same. Their for I will not attemp to give them to you in detail as my knowledg of it is vary limited. Never the less they do not try to keep it a secret but think Mclellan done well to save his Armey under the circumstances from total anihilation. And now I think the President [Linclon] has acted wisely in Calling for more Volunteers. And I am confident they will be fourth comeing immediately and especialy from the good old Hoosier state. And I think the people will respond to the call at once and fill the Eleven [regiments] called for from Ind.

And now father I would say if some good man will try they can get a Company at Alfordsville. Say John Chandler and Joh Harris and if you can get [such a] thing on foot in courage it all you Can. And if the company can be got and they would like to have me go along with them and would get me a position in th Co I will do all I can for them. Not that I am tired with the Co I am in but I mite do more in an other Co than in this as the [comrades] have all bin in the service as long as I have and are as apt scollars as my self. . . . And if they would give me a position worth being tranferred from this Company And I am sur their will be no difficulty in geting A Recommendation from my officers if you Write to them stating the facts in the case now. I want you to write if you think the prospect is good. As soon as you have time to fell [feel] around a little and see what the chance is. But I mist soon come to a close. This Leaves all well so far as you are acquainted. I hope the time will soon come when we can all worship around the same alter and Live to gether in peace while we live on the earth. This is my prair. I am ever yours in the one hope.   J Warren Alford

[From Warren to the family:]

Harrisons Landing Va
July the 20th 1862

Dear Parents and family
    With much Respect I take the preasant opertunity to Drop you a few lines to let you know that I received your letter on friday after you started it dated the 13th. We have the most direct rout from here

home we have ever had since we came to the state. But I suppose you do not get my letters as soon after they are rote as I do yours on the acount of their being so much mail to one place and it all has to be Mailed at Washington Citty. But I hope you have Recieved my letter before this and have atended to it before this. And since I rote I heared some one was trying to make a Company at Alfordsville but I did not hear who it was. But I hope you will do all you can for me if their is any chance to get a company their. And I hope you will be successfull in the attempt. If you can get sixty men to go in to a Co and you Can get me in do it and let me no at once as seventy men will hold the company in an organization if you can get it organized with that maney. The health of Company still continues to be good. Lem Kelley [Kelly, from Martin County] is not well now. Has not bin for some time though I think he will get along. He is [up and] about some every day. The rest of the boys are well. You wanted to know what to do about going after Waynes boddy. I would like vary much for it to be brought home and Laid in our own Church yard if you can do it. If you think it can be done.... If you can find the place where he was laid it is my wish that it be should be done if you think it proper to do so. You as the head of the family can do as you think best in reguard to the matter.... I must close for the preasant. Hoping god will Spair us all to meat and may he hasten the time of the our Meeting and Comfort us with the ... his Blessing.
Warren Alford

[From Captain William Houghton to Franklin Alford:]

Harrisons Landing on James River Va.
July 25th 1862

Eld Franklin Alford
Dear Sir
    You will doubtless be surprised at the reception of this letter from me but "queer people have strange ways." I write to know your opin- ion on the subject of the new enlistments and the prospect of the men in our ranks who have labored months in the servive till they understand the drill perfectly – are acquainted with all the details of the service – rules and regulations for the government – of the army in the garrison and field – and are qualified in every practice to take charge of new recruits ... [and] in a few weeks – drilled & disciplined men. I would not like to loose any men from my company nor any in fact but there are a dozen men in this Company who are ten

times more capable of governing men than any you can select among those remaining at home. I cant give them [a better] position [here because] there are to many. But I am liberal enough to want to see every [good] man raise and [I] am willing (though it will weaken me and take the best men away) to do all I am able to do to get them positions which they deserve. I would not write to you but I heard that you are getting up a company in your town again and I was asked by J.W. [James Warren] & Jno M [John McCord] what I thought about their making a strike for the postitions. I promised to help them all I could and take this opportunity to write you to know what the prospect was. I can only do this. I recommend them to your citizens there and if they receive them and elect them I have influence enough with "the powers that be" to get them a recomendation to Gov [Oliver] Morton who will commission them. You may feel some delicacy in this advocating the claims of Warren he being your son but I think it not more than right. These new positions must & will be filled and why not place these in command [of men] who we know are competent rather than try others who have all to learn. I would recomend Warren to the volunteers as a man worthy of promotion. I offer no comment on his character. They all Knew him and as he was so he is now – unchanged – save he is more manly and shows the marks of a terrible campaign of 15 months. I recomend John McCord as one who is eminently fitted to command or act in any position of trust and authority that a company can give him. I can certify that his character is unexceptionable – his behavior that of the Soldier & the man – and his courage (tried in many a field) is of the order of those that know not fear. If you can get them these positions you will not only do justice to manly worth but will render an efficeint aid to the serice. I would rather you would not give any publicity of my name concerning this affair as it might injure me in some respects. I do this from the respect & esteem I cherish for the men – and will aid them all I can but would rather that my connection would not be publicly Known. Speak to Joe McCord. [If] there is a prospect of success . . . I believe he will take interest enough to act upon it. I have not other suggestions to offer till I hear from you. It may be that these things will all be Settled before you get this and it may that there are men who will deserve the places before them and if so - of course the affair is settled.

You are doubtless posted as to our doing here and any thing I could offer would only be rehearsel of what you already Know. We are lying inactive here and waiting till Some reinforcements come or some movements from another quarter makes it necessary for us to move.

The weather is awful hot during the day and close & sultry at night. We drill twice each day which with Guard Mount & dress parade form the principle part of our exercise.

Health is not so good as formerly on account of the Malaria aris-
ing from the swamps around and the . . . many camps.

Boys from your neighborhood are all well. There is nothing further of interest that I know of. I would like to hear from you on the
subject soon. Please consider this as private & Confidential

My respect to all the friends especially yourself. I remain as ever
Your Obt Servt.
   Wm Houghton Capt
   Ind Comp C 14th Reg

[From Warren to Father:]

Harrison Landing
July the 26th 1862 Va

Dear Father

Sur I embrase the preasant opertunity to write you to let you
know that I am still well And that I receive you vary kind letter of
the 21st Just last eavening. But was some what surprise to find that
you had not received anyting later from me than the 19th. For I
have Writen to you eavry week since the first. But I hope their will
be more regularity in the male in time to come letters come from
home more [quickly] than they ever have since we have bin in Va. I
am vary anxious to get an answer to the Letter I wrote next to the
one you just recieved before you rote your last letter to me. I was
sorry to hear of you not being well but was glad it was know worse
and hope you will soon be well again with all the rest of the family.
I want you to tell Charley and Minerva this letter is for them as well
as the rest of the family and give them a scolding for not writing
oftener for I write to all as oftern as once a week if posible and as
much oftener as I can. (That is I write one a week to father and
Mother to be shaired with all and to my brothers and sisters as much
often as I can) and look to them for the same. I hope by the time this
comes to hand you will be through with your work and get a little
rest for I am sure you will try to do more than you [should] as you
are surrounded with a large farm and on it their is always plenty of
work to do you must not work to hard. I want you to let me know
how money matters are with you. Do not fail to keep me posted in
reguard to such matters as I can send you a little occosionaly if you
stand in need of it. But I thought I would not send you any more
mone before about Christmas as I mite need it fore some unknown
purpose to me at this time. But I will not spend it without I have

need to do so but if you kneed it before that time do not fail to let me
know [and] do not be embarassed with any thing I can possibly
relieve you of. For I feel my self under [?] obligations to you to help
you in the persuits of life and am sure you will help me in every
case you can as it is our duty to help one another in our Christian
life so we are in daily avocations of life. Father as I have mentioned
in two my letters about your trying to get A company at Alfordsville
And get me in to it if their is a company made in Daviess Co and you
can be influential in geting me aplace in the Co as Lieutenant. I do
not want you to let the opertunity pass as Lost but I would be glad to
see a company made at Alfordsville. It would please me the best of
any thing I could see. And if you can get sixty men to organize on
go ahead and if you can get 40 hold them to gether till you can get
more. And I think if the right kind of men will take hold of it they
will not fail to get a company as their is many that will volunteer in
the bend of the River and on the Black [?] ridge. And a good many
in our ow noborhood that is patriatic enough to go fourth in defense
of their Cundry Against all their enemey. Col [Capt.] Houghton say he
will give me a recommendation and he is sure Col Harrow [recently
appointed commanding officer of the 14th] will sign any recomendation he will give. And Harrows influence with the governer is as
good as any man in the first district. Col [Capt.] Houghten say he will
write to John Chandler for me soon giving you and him all the
instruction. He [knows] how to manage the thing to the best advantage in organizing the Company. You must work on the sympathy of
all and do not give your influence to any man making a company
any where without you can acomplish the proper end unless you
find their is know chance to do any thing for me. I would seek higher than Lieutenant with a good man over me other wise use the judg-
memt of the Co for I do not wan to go in to a company unless I am
their choice. I want you to answer this promptly. Ceep me posted
with matters going on at home. All the boys are well and in fine spirits. Ever remember me. . . .

[From Warren to Father:]

Harrisons Landing Va
August the 11th 1862

Dear Franklin Alford
    Sir this eavening I thought I would write you a few lines to let
you know I am well. James Tracy had bin here about two weaks

and is going to start home in the Morning. And I can send it direct
to you. We are under Marchng orders and I do not know where.
You will here from me nex but I will continue to write as usual and
expect the same from you. Tracy says he will go down and spend a
day with you. He would be a good hand to assist you with your Co
[if] you should nead help when he gets home. I have gathered nothing as yet to write to you. Houghten [Houghton] thinks the Best
thing you can do is to do what you can. He is going to under take
[my cause] for me but do not let that stop you if their is any Chance. .
. . Uncle John will be as good councelor as you can get. See what he
thinks is best to do. All the Boys are well but I must close as it is geting dark. Good by to All. Hoping to see you soon. I am your
Affectionate son.

J Warren Alford

[Note on outside of envelope:] I send this by Male as he has not started home yet.

[From William Houghton to Franklin:]

New Port News August 25th 1862

Eld Franklin Alford
Dear Sir
    I take the opportuinity of addressing a few lines to you again, hop-
ing that you wll not consider me tiresome. I wrote you some time ago
concerning Warren and you answered it through a letter to him.
Soon after we started on our long march from the Landing via
Williamsburg & Yorktown to this place where we arrived yesterday.
Previous however to leaving Harrisons Landing I framed a very
strong recommendation to Gov [Oliver] Morton and getting it properly
endorsed sent it about the 12th of the present Month. I can not tell
how it will succeed. There are so many at home to press their own
claims to the Governor in person that mere recommendations from
here avail but little unless supported by strong influences at home. I
have a strong desire to see him rise and would like to have an effort
made in your section. You can enlist some such man as Delmiler [?]
who will make the effort a success. . . . You might get another recommendation signed by a few men Known at the Capital and there
would be many assurances of success. This is all I have to advise on
the subject. I am fettered and can do nothing more than give my
ascent to any measure. I believe I am doing right in thus recom-
mending and as acting on the belief.

There a few items that would interest and doubtless you hear more than I can write. Our march from Harrisons Landing to this place occupied seven days of suffocating dust and extreme heat. We did however much better than I expected and are now lying on the beach of Hampton Rhodes [Roads] and waiting for transports to bear us [elsewhere].

The general impression is that we will Join Pope [General John Pope and his Army of Virginia] – though some of us will doubtless be sent southward and may see New Orleans.

The weather here is warm but made very pleasant by the Constant breeze that comes from the broad Atlantic. We have splendid facilities for bathing in salt water and the oyster & clam beds give the boys plenty of employment as well as enjoyment in diving after them.

Health is unusually good considering the hard march just gone through. All the Alfordsville Boys are in good health & consequent good spitits. The war spirit is as high with the Boys as ever and all are as anxious for a vigorous prossecution of the war as ever. Our new levies will certainly give us an army with which we can crush the Rebellion and defy the world.

I am anxious for the affair to end. It is taking all our men from home and next years crops will fall far below the standard of other times. Indiana will go disunion at the next election while her Loyal sons are in the field but they have let the election go and give themselves to save the country. God bless them.

Let our legislature [?]. And if they refuse to vote any supplies we will play Cromwell on them and hang them as a warning.

Ive written more than well interest you. There is an inspection this evening and I must prepare.

Remember me kindly to all who may inquire for me. Accept my regards & think of me as your friend.

> Will H.
> Capt Co C 14th Ind

[Handwritten statement:]

State of Indiana
Daviess County

Franklin Alford being duly sworn upon his oath says that his name is Franklin Alford, that his age is forty seven years, that he resides in Daviess County, and that he is the Father of Wayne Alford, that the said Wayne Alford died on the 15th day of June 1862, that at the time of his deathe the said Wayne Alford was a Sergent in Company "C" 6th Regiment of Indiana Volunteers, that at the time of his deathe the said Wayne Alford was unmarried and without descen-dants.

And that Franklin Alford as the father of the said Wayne Alford claims the arrears of pay and Bounty due for the services of the said Wayne Alford decd.

Franklin Alford

Subscribed and sworn to before me this 5th day of September 1862.
State of Indiana
    Daviess County

James L. Laverty and Joseph A. McCord being duly sworn upon their oaths say that they are personally acquainted with Franklin Alford and know him to be the father of Wayne Alford decd and the said Wayne Alford died unmarried and without descendance and that they are disinterested in the claim of Franklin Alford for the arrears of Pay and Bounty due for the services of Wayne decd.

James L. Laverty
Joseph A. McCord

Subscribed and sworn to before me this 5th day of September 1862 and I also certify that the above witnesses are good and creditable witnesses.

Thomas H. Kyle
Justice of the Peace

[From Warren to his parents:]

Summers Corps Kimbles [Kimball s] Brigade
District of Columbia Sept
the 6th 62

Dear Parents

This morning I take the true pleasure of writing you a few lines to let you know I am well and in vary good Spirits. I have not writen to you since I left harrisons Landing about the 15 of last Month except a few lines Col Houghten [Houghton] wrote for me at New portnuse [Newport News, Virginia] in answer [to] your letter which I Received their. That was the 23 of Aug. I have not had a let-ter from home sinse. Donaldson [Charley Donaldson, his brother-in-law

Government Wharves at Alexandria, Virginia. (USAMHI)

who, on August 30, 1862, enlisted in Company K of the 14th Indiana Infantry] has not got to the Reg yet but I here he is in Washington City and will likely be here to day. I got a letter that Minerva wrote the 8th and as I had not had a letter for so long I had to opened it and was vary glad to hear from you All again but was sorry to hear of Greens being sick. But the letter stated he was better. We have bin on the tramp since the 15th but have not bin in any skirmis since the one at harrisons landing. The Boys are all well except John McCord. He had a light chill last night but is about this morning and I think it will wair off as he has a resolution that will not give way under small things. But I will come to a Close soon and I will write soon a gain. We will get our old male to day. Excuse me for not writing sooner as I have not had a chance to write. I still live in hope of seeing you. If not in this world in a better [one]. Remember me at a throne of grace. Your onley Son in the armey. I am ever yours in the one hope.

J Warren Alford

★

[From Franklin to Warren:]

Alfordsville
Sept 21st 1862

Dear Warren Two week have passed away sinse I have had A
favorable opportunity of addressing you A line but I am now seated
after so long A silence under a sense of duty. And with that respect
that we have Ever Cherished and [is now] more Deeply seated In our
affections by our late bereavements which no doubt press heavyly on
you. Also to Inform you that we are still blessed with Common
health and we Earnestly desire that these few thoughts may Come to
hand In due time and find you . . . well. We received Charleses
[Donaldson] letter of the 9th Inst yesterday which was A source of
unbounded gratitude to us all and doubly gratifying on account of
the Inteligence of his arrival In the [14th Indiana] Regt and that you
were well. In my imagination I Can see the Tear of affection Stealing
down your care worn yet manly Cheeks while you grasp Each others
hands after being sepearated from home and kind friends for almost
Seventeen Months. We can but faintly picture In our Imagination
the Joys that was Experienced on that occasion. Warren the nuse we
get from the seat of war relative to the Army under [General George]
McClellan Is verry Cheering. But the Carnage Consequent [and neces-
sary] to . . . put an End to the rebellion In that vicinity has Caused us
Considerable Anxiety to hear from you again. But I hope to hear
from you soon.

It is now just after dinner and I am again seated to add A few more
lines to what I had writen this forenoon. Well perhaps you wish to
know how we are getting along In regards to our dificulties In
Church. . . . After removeing Father Gillock and myself from the pos-
tion we occupied In the Church your uncle took staford back Into the
Church again. And brother Chandler says he does not Consider he
made any acknowledgement and he Is so disgusted that he has
applied for A letter of standing. And also Father Gillock and your
Grandmother Gilley. Your uncle told me that Stafford was turned
out [previously] without any Evidence of his guilt that deserved any
Credence. Now think for one moment of the Caracter of the men
who Investigated his Case and see If you Can think for one moment
that they would pass sentence against him In the absence of substan-
tial Evidence of his guilt. But I hope you will not let these things dis-
courarge you for all the brethren such as Mathes, Hays, Hickson,
Berry, Riley, Rout, Alverd, Trimble, Houghton and A host of others
that I might mention think It Is all to save stafford. I refer you to
Clem and Charles. Monday Morning. I am now about to bring my
letter to A Close. Well I have heard from the Agent of revision society
and I think I will [pay] on your arrears this week which I believe is

six dollars. I have Collected the balance of the note you held on Trulove and I have paid the borrowed money which I had from the Treasury. I have paid Chester fifteen dollars on the payment of what I agreed to pay him for the dowry on your Land and I Expect to get the Deed as soon as I have time to attend to It. I have had to borrow some Money of Minerva but I have plenty Comeing to me to replace It. So you need not Cause yourself any uneasiness In that direction. I have some notion of selling your mare and Charleses If I Can get A price to suit me. Charley I should have Written more Especially to you had not Minerva been Writing but I want you to share with Each other In the Enjoyment of those few lines and we will do the same with yours. Warren I talked with Vantrees [Captain Charles R. Van Trees of the 6th Indiana] some time ago about pressing your Claims and he told me that the Secretary had hedged up the way so that there Could be nothing done for you by the Governor. Now I have the Clover field nearly broke up and I want to begin to sow this morning and I must Close. We are all well this morning. Elizabeth Sutton Stayed with us last night and Is In good health. Dr Laverty sends you his respects. Give my love to all my friends and believe me as Ever your affectionate father. Until death may God Bless and save you Is the prair of your affectionate Father.

Franklin Alford

★

5
BACKGROUND

"The Big Battles is not as Bad as the fever."[1]

ON APRIL 12TH, WAYNE WROTE HIS parents that "I am Verry well" and mentioned that younger brother Lafayette had a "severe cold." Sixty-four days later, Wayne and Lafayette were dead. They had died of disease. Lafayette went first on May 7, 1862; Wayne followed on June 15.

How it happened so quickly is speculative. Wayne reported Lafayette was sent to a hospital in mid-April with "Nothing but Cold & exposure." Wayne was offering comfort to his parents, although he possibly sensed something more serious. He predicted (correctly) that Lafayette would be sent to Evansville and then, home.

The first documented, professional, diagnosis of Lafayette's illness indicated he had "General Dibility Diarhea." This report was made by an Evansville Surgeon. Upon his death, Lafayette's muster roll records attributed the cause as "hemorage of the bowels."(2) As time passed, the Alford family ascribed Lafayette's death to typhoid.(3) Given only these small bits of information, typhoid fever appears to be the most likely cause of death.

Lafayette's "severe cold" and "Diarhea" accompany the early symptoms of a typhoid infection. The signs occur approximately one to two weeks following infection, then the germ spreads quickly. Stomach ulceration and "hemorage of the bowels" are advanced phases; then the deadly bacteria may enter the blood stream or the bone marrow. The fact that Lafayette did not recover also suggests typhoid fever. The mortality rate for the reported typhoid cases in the Union Army was thirty-seven percent.(4)

Typhoid bacteria thrives in the conditions that prevailed at Shiloh after the battle: dead bodies, open latrines and insects. The bacteria finds its way into the soil and then seeps into the water supply. Once the water supply is contaminated, the typhoid bacillus is transmitted quickly in the drinking water and food. The disease also is highly communicable, or contagious. Adding to the pervasive nature of the organism, humans, although not infected themselves, may "carry" the germ and infect others.

Hospital Tents. (USAMHI)

Hospital Scene. (USAMHI)

Not surprisingly, diseases were rampant after the Shiloh battle. By May, 11,000 sick Union soldiers had been evacuated from the field and transported north. Lafayette Alford was one of this number. As Wayne and the Union armies moved farther south, the problem became larger. Three hospitals were set up to accommodate 15,000 soldiers.(5) Available statistics reflect an overall hospital mortality rate of 9.76 percent. A modern pathologist and author studied the findings and concluded that, "This high rate probably resulted chiefly from typhoid fever, the most lethal of the prevalent diseases."(6)

Lafayette, seemingly fortunate, escaped the disease-ravaged campgrounds in mid-April and was transported to Evansville, probably on a river boat. The early "hospital" boats actually were freighters, otherwise returning empty, or perhaps they were the fanciest of passenger steamers.(7) The first official, single-purpose,

U.S.S. Red Rover. (USAMHI)

Union Army hospital boat was formerly a Confederate troop ship. That side-wheeler was captured during the battle of Island No. 10, in early April 1862, and designated the USS *Red Rover*.(8) It is improbable Lafayette was transported on the *Red Rover*. More likely, he was taken to Evansville on one of the steam boats contracted by the State of Indiana and Governor Morton specifically for that purpose.(9)

Upon reaching Evansville, Lafayette was taken to the Marine Hospital. Built by the United States government in 1856 during a time when there were few hospitals, this building was imposing: three stories, 110 by 90 feet, all brick and sandstone. The 100-bed facility occupied a city block near the river front.(10) Both Union and Confederate soldiers were treated in Evansville, and as the demand for beds increased, nineteen temporary wooden structures were built surrounding the stately brick hospital.(11)

The course of events encompassing Lafayette's evacuation to Indiana are sketchy. Wayne wrote on April 16 that Lafayette had been taken to a field hospital, probably earlier that day. On April 18, Lafayette is in Evansville and on Saturday the 19th he is granted a thirty-day furlough. George Alford wrote Wayne with the news that Father had gone to get Lafayette and they expected their arrival in Alfordsville on Monday, April 21. The next documented incident is Lafayette's death on May 7, sixteen days after arriving home.

The reference to Lafayette's burial in "our" cemetery is proper in two respects. First, the cemetery was on property owned by Franklin Alford. In the larger sense, the cemetery was intended for use by the members of the Alfordsville Christian Church.

Brother Wayne's death on June 15 took a different course. On May 18, he wrote to "Dear Parents, Brothers and Sisters" and acknowledged the receipt of the news that Lafayette "is no more." Although personally distressed, Wayne offered words of strength and compassion for his grieving family. He also reaffirmed his faith that they will be reunited with Lafayette on resurrection morn. This consoling correspondence was cherished by the Alford family as "Wayne's Last Letter."(12)

In the same May 18 letter, Wayne, apparently healthy, wrote of being prepared for an anticipated march. Surprisingly two weeks later, on June 1, Dr. Laverty wrote to Franklin Alford with the news that Wayne was near death – dying of typhoid fever. Laverty explained that Wayne was too weak to be moved, even if Franklin should come to take him home.

Franklin, nevertheless, did try to find Wayne. On June 10 he was in Evansville expecting to leave by boat at 9 p.m. When Wayne died five days later, Franklin was within twelve miles of reaching his side.(13)

Wayne's military records indicate his cause of death as "erysipelas." Erysipelas is a microorganism that may infect the skin through a cut or wound. Wayne, with a bullet wound in the hand, would have been a candidate for erysipelas. However, there are tell-tale effects of erysipelas which would have been noticeable, the most obvious being redness and swelling near the wound. Rather, in Dr. Laverty's letter, the fact emerges that Wayne is in a hospital, presumably being observed by several Surgeons, and was being cared for as a typhoid fever patient.

A letter to the editor of the *Indianapolis Daily Journal* from "General Hospital, Buell's Army, Near Corinth, June 27, 1862" brought the news of the Indiana soldiers' deaths at the hospital during June. The list of twenty Hoosiers included "Wayne Alford." The correspondent sent along some advice, "You will probably save much anxiety to their friends by saying that these men are all [with one exception] buried at Sawyer's House, near Nicholas's Ford, four miles northeast of Corinth, and a plat of the burial place taken. Yours truly, L[uther] D. Waterman, Surgeon 39th Ind."(14) The mystery remains as to what transpired at Corinth. It is assumed that, given the opportunity, Franklin would have returned to Alfordsville with Wayne's body. What is known, however, is that Wayne's remains were moved to a national cemetery in Corinth which opened in 1866. He is among the "Unknown." It is curious, but not unusual, that Wayne's body was unidentifiable. Today, in the Corinth National Cemetery, there are the remains of 5,719 Union dead, 3,937 are unknown.(15)

The terrors of the battle were beyond the imagination.[16]

The 6th Indiana Infantry had been a part of the Union Army's Corinth Campaign. The campaign ended successfully on May 30 when the Confederates abandoned the northern Mississippi rail center. The Union's western armies pushed farther into the south throughout the summer of 1862. The Mississippi River, critical to both sides, was slowly becoming a Union path through the Confederacy, although Vicksburg, Mississippi remained in southern hands. In late August, however, Confederate forces under the command of General Braxton Bragg broke away from Chattanooga, Tennessee and headed north. The rebels scored a crucial victory on August 30 at Richmond, Kentucky. Cincinnati and Louisville appeared to be Bragg's targets.(17)

In the East, during the summer of 1862, the Union Army had fared badly. First, General T.J. "Stonewall" Jackson's Shenandoah Valley Campaign was an overwhelming success for the Confederacy. Jackson marched his men 650 miles in forty-eight days, won five battles, inflicted twice as many casualties as received and "paralyzed" 60,000 to 70,000 Union troops. The effect this effort had on the Union troops is exemplified in Warren Alford's letter of June 13. He tells of having "a very hard time of it" as they had "Marched and counter-marched in all about 400 miles." The 14th Indiana had been as far south and west as Harrisonburg, Virginia, and as far east as "40 miles west of Washington City." All of this was in reaction to "Stonewall" Jackson's elusive maneuvering. The 14th Indiana took a minor role in the battle of Front Royal, Virginia, on May 23, one of Jackson's victories. Otherwise, they marched and counter-marched.

Jackson's strategy was intended to prevent the Union troops in northwest Virginia from joining with General George McClellan's Army of the Potomac in

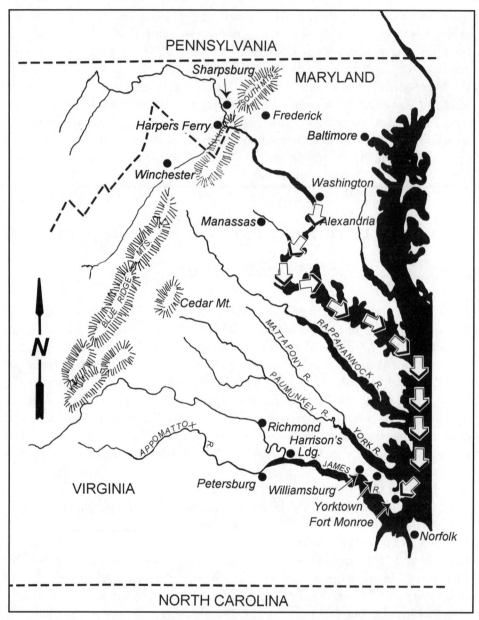

General George B. McClellan Moves His Army South, March 17, 1862.

southeast Virginia. McClellan had set out to capture Richmond, Virginia, by moving up a peninsula formed by the York and the James Rivers. Jackson's strategy was successful although McClellan did move to within eyesight of Richmond. On June 25, a series of battles to be known as "The Seven Days" began. Five battles (and seven days) later, McClellan's Army of the Potomac

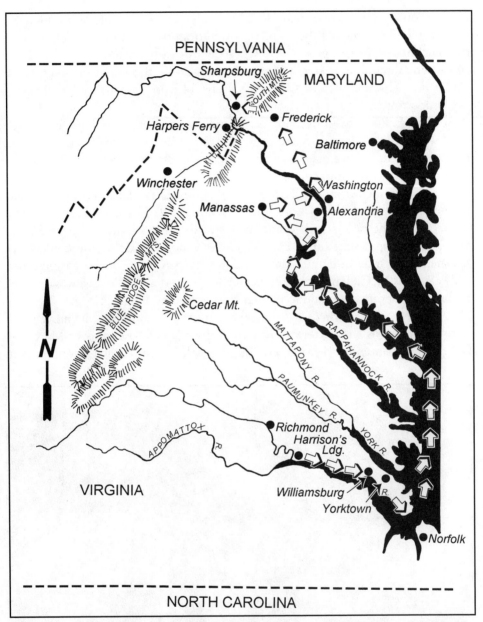

Warren Alford's and the Army of the Potomac's Move to Sharpsburg, Maryland.

retreated to Harrison's Landing, an area south and east of Richmond on the James River. The 14th Indiana and its parent division reinforced the Union army on July 2, too late. McClellan's grand plan had been thwarted.

The 14th camped at Harrison's Landing until August 15 when it was moved to Alexandria, Virginia. McClellan's troops were being dispatched northward to stop a Confederate thrust near Washington. Cleverly, Confederate General Robert E. Lee had moved the scene of action from the outskirts of Richmond to the outskirts of Washington. The Confederates won a major battle at Cedar Mountain, Virginia, on August 9. On August 29-30, the Battle of Second Bull Run was fought, and lost, by the Union. The 14th Indiana assisted in covering the Union retreat.(18)

Robert E. Lee moved his men into Maryland on September 4 and continued northward. McClellan, who had been relieved of his command by Lincoln and then reinstated, followed Lee on a parallel course. On September 13, McClellan was presented with a miraculous opportunity to destroy Lee's Army of Northern Virginia. Two men from the 27th Indiana found Lee's orders. This is the now-famous incident of "Lee's Lost Order Number 191" or the "Lost Order of Antietam." The orders spelled out, exactly, the various routes of Lee's divided army, including a schedule. Had McClellan moved quickly, he could have smashed Lee's army in detail. But it did not happen; instead, the characteristically cautious McClellan moved characteristically. Meanwhile, Lee was apprised of the lost order incident and took steps to counteract McClellan.

As the Northern army (eventually) began its pursuit of Lee, its movements were contested as they attempted to cross the South Mountains of Maryland. On Sunday, September 14, fiercely fought battles occurred at three mountain

The Streets of Sharpsburg, Maryland. (LC)

passes. Involved were 28,000 Union troops and 18,000 Confederate soldiers; there were at least 5,000 casualties. The 14th Indiana Infantry and its division (French's) was held in reserve.(19) On September 15, the outflanked Confederates fell back toward Antietam Creek, near Sharpsburg, Maryland, and the scene was set for the bloodiest day of the American Civil War.

By September 17, Lee had positioned his army of 35,000 on a strong north-south defensive line to the east of Sharpsburg. McClellan, after due consideration, intended to use his 80,000-man army to attack both of Lee's flanks simulta-

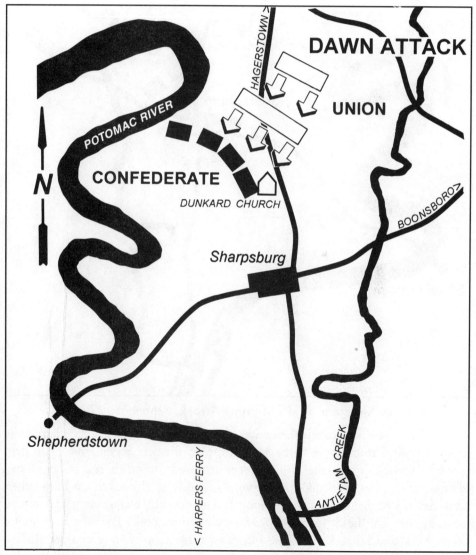

Battle of Antietam, The Dawn Attack, September 17, 1862.

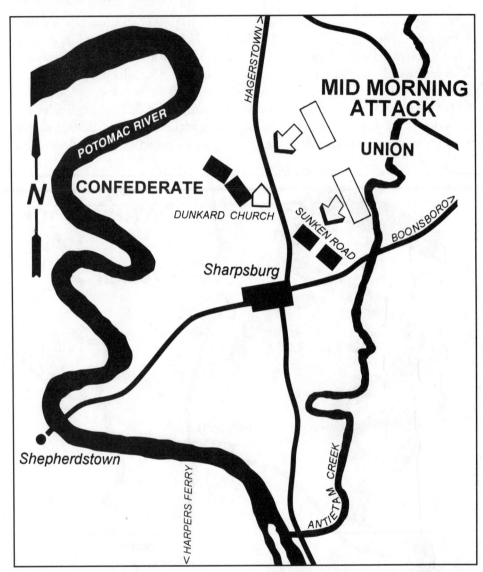

Battle of Antietam, Mid - Morning Attack, September 17, 1862.

neously, then punch through the center. As the day unfolded, McClellan's plan went awry and there were three separate, piecemeal engagements. The first phase began at dawn as the Union forces attacked the north end of Lee's line. (The attack that was to take place simultaneously to the south on Lee's other flank did not occur until mid-afternoon.) The opening engagement was fought furiously in a cornfield, in woods and over open ground. For four horrendous hours, back and forth, three Union attacks, three Confederate counterattacks; men were cut down by sheets of rifle fire and bursts of artillery missiles. The

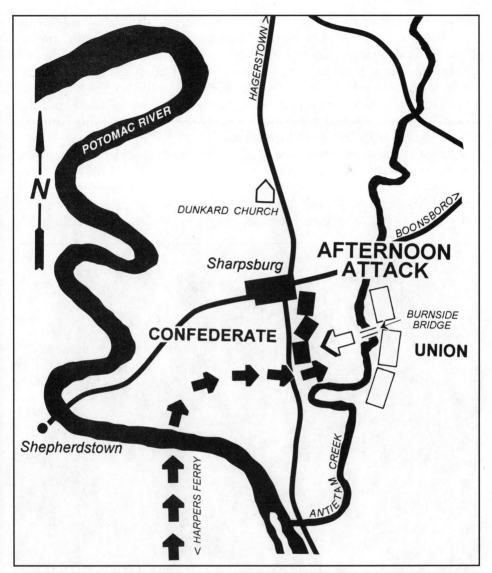

Battle of Antietam, Afternoon Attack, September 17, 1862.

results were devastating for both sides: the dead and wounded totalled 12,000.(20)

At mid-morning, the fighting shifted to the center of the Confederate line and Warren Alford became a participant. The 14th Indiana Infantry was one of four regiments in Nathan Kimball's brigade which was one of three brigades in General William H. French's division of about 5,700 men.(21)

French's division had been at rest until about 7:30 a.m. when it was given orders to support a unit badly "cut up" in the early morning fight. As it forded Antietam Creek and proceeded to the west over the rolling farm land, the division encountered menacing Confederate skirmishers on their left flank. French immediately ordered his three brigade commanders to turn their units and face to the left in three lines. Kimball's brigade was in the third line. As the division scurried around the Roulette barn, they came under heavy Confederate fire from the front and on the right flank. French ordered Kimball's brigade to the front. The Confederates were in a superb defensive position, a recessed farm road that divided the Roulette and Piper farms. In a matter of minutes, this farm road became the Civil War's famous "Bloody Lane."(22)

After the battle, French praised Kimball, writing that he charged toward the sunken road with "unsurpassed ardor," "sweeping over all obstacles" and "brought his veterans into action" where he fought with "desperate courage." To perform these heroics, Kimball first marched his brigade to the crown of a small hill, which overlooked the sunken road. The 14th was on the far right of the

The Sunken Road at the Turn of the Century. (National Park Service)

Union line, its right flank unprotected. To the left, in line, marched Kimball's other regiments, the 8th Ohio, the 132nd Pennsylvania and the 7th West Virginia. As the 14th crowned the hill, they became silhouetted against the sky. Parallel to their line and fifty yards to the front was the sunken road. The fire from the natural entrenchment was murderous. Kimball's men advanced shoulder to shoulder, leaned forward as if facing a driving rain, and began to fall. A private in the 8th Ohio remembered how Kimball rode his horse along the line shouting "God save my poor boys!"(23)

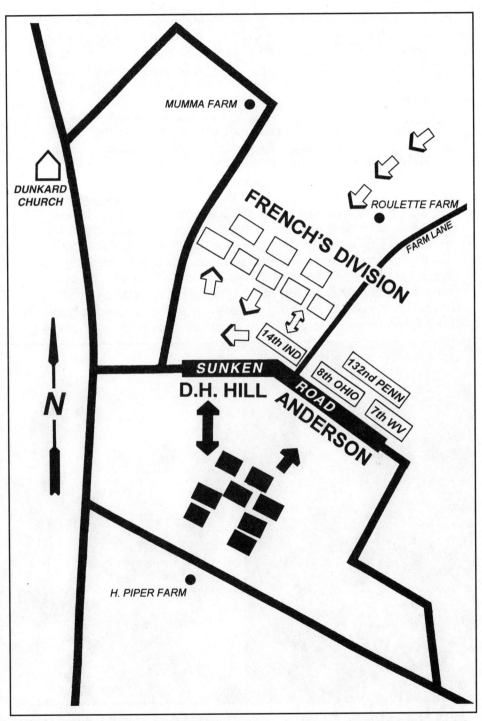

Battle of Antietam, September 17, 1862, 14th Indiana at the Sunken Road.

French concluded his official report with a glowing tribute to Kimball and his men, "to whom the division is indebted for a brilliant display of courage never surpassed."(24) French's superior, Major General Edwin Sumner, at some point, referred to Kimball's unit as the "Gibraltar Brigade." (25)

The brigade's behavior on the battlefield justified the accolade. Kimball's official report told the story:

> Directly on my front, in a narrow road running parallel with my line, and, being washed by water, forming a natural rifle pit between my line and a large corn-field, I found the enemy in great force, as also in the corn-field in rear of the ditch. As my line advanced to the crest of the hill, a murderous fire was opened upon it from the entire force in my front. My advance farther was checked and for three hours and thirty minutes the battle raged incessantly, without either party giving way. The enemy, having been re-enforced, made an attempt to turn my left flank by throwing three regiments forward . . . which I met and repulsed. Being foiled in this he [the Confederates] made a heavy charge on my center, thinking to break my line, but was met by my command and repulsed with great slaughter. I then, in turn, ordered

Union Major General Edwin Vose Sumner. (LC)   Union Major General William Henry French. (LSU)

a charge, which . . . resulted in driving the enemy entirely from the ditches, &c, and some distance into the [Piper farm] corn-field beyond. In this charge my command captured 300 prisoners. . . .

[The enemy attempted to turn the 14th Indiana's right flank,] and by that gain my rear, and succeeded in gaining a corn-field directly on my right. To repulse them, a change of front was made by the Fourteenth Indiana and Eighth Ohio Volunteers, which resulted in driving the enemy from the right, and restored my line. . . . For four hours and a half my command was under most galling fire, and not a man faltered or left the ranks until the field was left by the rebels in our possession, those who were sent to the rear with the wounded quickly returning to their place in line. For three and a half hours of this time we . . . maintained our position without any support whatever. My men having exhausted all their ammunition, the fight was maintained for some time with the supplies stripped from the bodies of their dead and wounded comrades.

Every man of my command behaved in the most exemplary manner, and as men who had determined to save their country. The Fourteenth Indiana and Eighth Ohio, in the change of front which saved our right, executed as veterans and as only brave men could. . . . The loss in my command is a lasting testimony of the sanguinary nature of the conflict, and a glance at the position held by the rebels tells how terrible was the punishment inflicted on them. The corn-fields on the front are strewn with their dead and wounded, and the ditch first occupied by them the bodies are so numerous that they seem to have fallen dead in line of battle, for there is a battalion of dead rebels. We maintained our line and drove the enemy from his.(26)

Confederate Colonel John B. Gordon commanded the 6th Alabama Infantry, a regiment in the sunken road opposing Kimball's on-coming brigade. Gordon never forgot what he saw on September 17, 1862; he wrote in his memoirs:

The day was clear and beautiful, with scarcely a cloud in the sky. . . . The brave Union commander, superbly mounted, placed himself in front, while his band in rear cheered them with martial music. It was a thrilling spectacle. . . . Their gleaming bayonets flashed like burnished silver in the sunlight. With the precision of step and perfect alignment of a holiday parade, this magnificent array moved to the charge, every step keeping time to the tap of the deep-sounding drum. As we stood looking upon that brilliant pageant, I thought, if I did not say, "What a pity to spoil with bullets such a scene of martial beauty!"(27)

Later in Gordon's narrative, he described graphically his recollection of one of the Union assaults. Although likely, it is not known with certainty that Gordon is recounting the actions of Nathan Kimball and the 14th Indiana:

Confederate Major General John Brown Gordon. (NA)

> The stillness was literally oppres-
> sive, as in close order, with the
> commander still riding in front,
> this column of Union infantry
> moved majestically in the
> charge. In a few minutes they
> were within easy range of our
> rifles, and some of my impatient
> men asked permission to fire.
> "Not yet," I replied. "Wait for the
> order." Soon they were so close
> that we might have seen the
> eagles on their buttons; but my
> brave and eager boys still wait-
> ed for the order. Now the front
> rank was within a few rods of where I stood. It would not do to
> wait another second, and with all my lung power I shouted "Fire!"
>   My rifles flamed and roared in the Federals' faces like a
> blinding blaze of lightning accompanied by the quick and deadly
> thunderbolt. The effect was appalling.(28)

General Kimball quantified the effect: brigade casualties were 121 killed, 510 wounded and eight missing.(29) Colonel William Harrow, who commanded the 14th Indiana regiment on that terrible day, reported, "We went into the fight with 320 men and lost in killed and wounded 181."(30) Corporal Warren Alford was one of the wounded. At some point in the battle, Warren had been struck in the lungs with a bullet.

  In the immediate aftermath of battle, the survivors recalled their experi-ences. Augustus "Gus" Van Dyke, a Knox County attorney, confided in a letter to his friend Angie:

> No less than eight stands of colors were . . . seen in our front.
> Heroically did our little band stand up against these odds and . . .
> found us masters of the position having killed and wounded or
> captured nearly the whole of two brigades opposed to us. Our

Augustus M. Van Dyke, First Lieutenant, Company G, 14th Indiana Infantry. (IHS,M42,C6334)

men had fired near a hundred rounds of ammunition and had but few left when a large force of the enemy was seen approaching us upon our right. I'll confess I was a little alarmed, but the brave boys [were undaunted] by the new danger [and] changed front toward the enemy and taking cartridges from their dead and wounded comrades waited until the rebels were within one hundred yards of us when they poured such rapid and well directed volleys into their ranks of the two brigades of the enemy. I do not think that more than fifty escaped unharmed. . . .

The terrors of the battle were beyond the imagination. Death from the bullet is ghastly, but to see a man's brains dashed out at your side by a grape shot and another's body severed by a screeching cannon ball is truly appalling. May I never again see such horrors as I saw that day. . . . (31)

On September 19, Captain David Beem of H Company wrote his wife in Spencer, Indiana. He reported the condition of those she knew: Lieutenant Porter Lundy was killed instantly, Jess Harrold struck in four places, Hugh Barnes broken leg below the knee, Henry Woodsmall was shot twice through the leg. And there was some good news, two acquaintances were not in the battle, three others had been detailed to the ambulance wagons. Beem closed the letter:

Oh! the rush and roar of the battle! I wonder if the dreadful sounds will ever get out of my ears! Of the thirty seven of my company present, three were killed instantly, three I fear will die and fifteen others are more or less seriously wounded.(32)

On the 20th, Beem wrote his wife again, his third outpouring since the battle:

I have today visited the wounded boys. Poor fellows, many of them are badly hurt, some of them will doubtless die, and they are suffering much. But all that can be done by us to render them comfortable has been done, and we will continue to do our best.

Yesterday evening I took a walk over the battlefield. It was a hard battle, but our victory was complete. The ground presents a scene of horror that cannot be well imagined. Our own dead have all been buried, but the enemy's dead still lie in thousands on the bloody ground. All the remains of the desperate conflict are scattered thick in every direction – hundreds of dead horses strew the fields in every direction. Where our Brigade met the enemy, the rebels are scattered in great profusion, laying even in piles all about. . . .

When I reflect what a terrible ordeal we have passed through, and how many have fallen around me, I feel thankful that I have been so remarkably preserved. I presume that at least a half dozen men were killed within six yards of me, and some of them fell at my feet.

Today I have to perform a sad duty in writing to the wife of Lt. Lundy. Poor woman, I scarcely know what terms to convey the dreadful news to her and her two little children. . . . (33)

Confederate Dead in the Bloody Lane. The 14th Indiana Infantry Assaulted this Position from the Left. (LC)

North Carolinians in the Bloody Lane. (USAMHI)

A Battlefield Place of Business. (USAMHI)

In Beem's letter of notification and condolence to Mrs. Lundy, he explained the burial situation at the battle site:

> I am filled with regret at our inability to send his corpse to you
> at present. The great numbers killed and the want of facilities
> for embalming have rendered it absolutely impossible. Myself, Col.
> Harrow and Gen. Kimball did all we could to have it done, but
> found we could not. It may be a satisfaction to you, however, to
> know that we buried him decently in a country cemetery under
> a beautiful tree, and have placed a suitable head board at his
> grave, so that his resting place can be identified in after years.(34)

A Burial Party at Antietam. (USAMHI)

Captain William Houghton, the Alfordsville Christian Church member and Warren Alford's company commander, had taken a bullet in the elbow. Disregarding the wound as "tis but a scratch," he carried the extracted bullet in his pocket. In a letter to his mother, he wrote:

> I saw my brave boys [in Company C] fall like sheep led to the
> slaughter. Bryant was shot through the brain. McCord was shot
> near the heart, and while blood was gushing from the wound, he
> sat up and with an almost heavenly smile playing upon his fea-

The Roulette Farmhouse. (USAMHI)

The Field Hospital at Dr. O.J. Smith's Farm, Upper Bridge, near the
Antietam Battlefield. Photograph Taken about September 20, 1862. (LC)

tures he told us he was dying but to mind him not, he was happy and we must go and avenge his death. "Farewell boys, farewell Captain," he exclaimed as I reached him and he fell forward to the earth.(35)

"McCord" was John McCord, Warren's cousin from Alfordsville and tent mate. John and Warren also shared an ambition to be officers. Among the others wounded was Warren's brother-in-law, recently-recruited Charles Donaldson.

The wounded from French's division were first taken back to the nearby farms, the Roulette's being the closest. Amputations were performed in the barns, and the surrounding area was covered with wounded and dying men.(36) Dr. Anson Hurd, the 14th Indiana's surgeon, had accompanied the regiment to the Bloody Lane area and set up a field hospital, probably near the Roulette farm. As the number of injuries multiplied, Dr. Hurd moved his patients about one mile and a quarter north, nearer Boonsboro. This was a larger, better-equipped, division hospital which had been set up on the O.J. Smith farm before the battle.(37) It is probable that Warren Alford was moved to the Smith farm.

Dr. Anson Hurd, Surgeon for the 14th Indiana Infantry, Attending to the Wounded at the Smith Farm. (USAMHI - MOLLUS COLLECTION)

William Houghton, Captain, Company C,
14th Indiana Infantry. (IHS,M42,C6332)

On September 20, Captain Houghton wrote his mother from Boonsboro: "It was an awful fight Mother & death reigned like an avenging angel." Then, he reported on the casualties from (his) Company C:

I can't give you a perfect list at present but will give the most important.

Sergt R. Bryant	Killed
Corpl Jno McCord	do [ditto]
Private Jas B Padgett	do
" Ed S Trainer	do
Sergt Levi N. Dunlap	Wounded slightly

328 □ *The Alford Brothers*

Corp Levi Reed	do do
" Isaac N. Craim	" arm broken
Sergt Hugh Hopkins	" very slight
Private Ike Hutton	" both ankles
" Geo Boner	Knee flesh wound
" Chas Donaldson	Shoulder slight
Corpl Jas W Alford	very severly – lung
Private Ed Hall	arm broken
" Levi Lansdall	ankle broken
Willis Lemmons	Abdomen not fatal
Arch Gilskin	back slight
Jas McCoy	Shoulder Slightly
Lew Berry	Hip not dangerous
Wm R Inman	thigh flesh wound
Chas Conkright	ankle slight
Elias Lloyd	Shin very slight
Wm Davis	Shoulder slight
Mat Stafford	bruised by a spent grape
Wm Lloyd	Missing supposed Killed
Steph Collins	" " "
Wm Harris	Wounded slightly in head

and two others may be hit but not serious. It is a fearful list.(38)

Shortly after the battle, Captain Houghton took leave in Indiana and then returned to the east in late October. The dutiful son wrote his father on October 29, 1862 (39):

Fountain House
Baltimore

Dear Father
    I take the opportunity while here to send you a line to let you know where I am.
    I arrived here last night and will stay till morning. Our Regt is Still at Harpers Ferry unless it moved yesterday evening or this morning. I left [?] at Cincinnati all right. Did not reach there till 5 oclock A. M. Found George waiting at the Depot. Went with Him & Staid all night. Left for Pittsburgh at 10 oclock & traveled with out stopping till reached here. I wished to get a few articles and Mr. Alford had to get a coffin. . . .

Endnotes

(1) Brooks, *ibid.*, p. 6.

(2) Lafayette Alford's service records, National Archives, File nos. 26404354 and 26404442.

(3) Franklin Alford's "Declaration for Dependent Father's Pension," dated July 16, 1891, National Archives.

   Also, Houghton, "Memoriam" for Franklin Alford, *ibid.*

(4) Steiner, *ibid.*, p. 24. Much of Steiner's data was found in the *Medical and Surgical History of the War of the Rebellion*, v. I, part I.

   Stated in different numerical terms, 30,000 Union soldiers died in the Civil War of typhoid fever; see Brooks, *ibid.*, p. 118. Also, it is noteworthy that Lafayette's death may not have been recorded as typhoid fever. If so, this suggests that more than 30,000 died of typhoid and the cause was recorded in some other category.

(5) *Ibid.*, p. 167. The 11,000 were in addition to the 12,000 Union wounded who had been shipped north.

(6) *Ibid.*, p. 170.

(7) Francis Trevelyan Miller, Editor, *The Photographic History of the Civil War* (New York, 1912) v. VII, p. 316.

(8) William C. Davis, Editor, *Fighting for Time* in The Image of War series (New York, 1983) v. IV, p. 253.

(9) *Ibid.* p. 240. This is from a chapter entitled "Caring for the Men," written by George W. Adams.

(10) Joseph P. Elliott, *A History of Evansville and Vanderburgh County, Indiana* (Evansville, 1897) p. 223.

   After the Civil War, the hospital was sold by the Federal government, renamed St. Mary's, and was operated by the Daughters of Charity. Later the hospital became one of the largest tenements in Evansville. Refer to Emma Lou Thornbrough, *ibid.*, p. 582 and Mary Boewe, "Annie & Albion: Reformers of Riverville," *Traces*, a publication of the Indiana Historical Society, (Indianapolis, 1995) Winter issue, v. 7, no. 1, p. 10.

(11) Kenneth P. McCutchan, editor, *Dearest Lizzie* (Evansville, 1988) p. 157.

(12) Wayne's letter was edited, typeset, printed and distributed to family memebers.

(13) Houghton, *ibid.*, "Memoriam" for Franklin Alford.

(14) "Military Deaths," abstracted by Ruth Dorrel, *The Hoosier Genealogist,* published by the Indiana Historical Society, Indianapolis, December 1993, v. 33, n. 4, p. 231.

(15) Dyer, *ibid.*, p. 19.

(16) Van Dyke, *ibid*, from a letter to Angie, dated September 21, 1862.

(17) Long, *ibid.* Again the best source for sweeping summaries of Civil War activities.

(18) IAG, *ibid.*, v. II, p. 121.

(19) *Ibid.*

(20) James V. Murfin, *The Gleam of Bayonets* (New York, 1965) p. 241. This is one of three modern (and excellent) Antietam Battle accounts. The other two are Stephen W. Sears, *Landscape Turned Red* (New Haven, 1983) and John M. Priest, *Antietam: The Soldiers' Battle* (Shippensburg, 1989). For a shorter account, and one with a local history flavor, refer to John W. Schildt, *September Echoes* (Shippensburg, 1980) and *Drums Along the Antietam* (Parsons, 1972).

(21) Sears, *ibid.*, p. 236.

(22) *Ibid.*, pp. 235-237.

(23) Priest, *ibid.*, pp. 156, 157. The quote is attributed to Thomas Francis Gawley in his *The Valiant Hours* (Harrisburg, 1961) p. 42. Gawley fought with the 8th Ohio, the regiment to the left of the 14th Indiana.

(24) ORs, v. XIX, part 1, p. 324.

(25) Priest, *ibid.*, p. 209. The "Gibraltar Brigade" sobriquet was remembered with great pride among Kimball's men.

(26) ORs. *ibid.*, pp. 326-328.

(27) John B. Gordon, *Reminiscences of the Civil War* (New York, 1903) pp. 84, 85.

(28) *Ibid.*, pp. 86, 87.

(29) ORs, *ibid.*, p. 326.

(30) ORs, *ibid.*, p. 329. Harrow's official report.

(31) Van Dyke, *ibid.*, Letter to Angie, dated September 21, 1862. George Washington Lambertson recorded that as the Confederates approached on the right flank, a nervous Colonel Harrow shouted "Shoot G_d D_m you then!" Lambertson, *ibid.*, journal entry for September 17, 1862.

(32) David Beem papers, Indiana Historical Society. One- page letter of September 19, 1862.

(33) *Ibid.* Three-page letter to his wife, September 20, 1862.

(34) *Ibid.* Three-page letter to Mrs. Emaline Lundy, September 20, 1862. For more on the burials and cemeteries near the battlefield, refer to Steven R. Stotelmyer, *The Bivouacs of the Dead, The Story of Those Who Died at Antietam and South Mountain* (Baltimore, 1992).

(35) William Houghton papers, Indiana Historical Society, letter to his mother, dated September 20, 1862.

(36) Franklin Sawyer, *A Military History of the 8th Regiment Ohio Infantry* (Reprint, Huntington, 1994) p. 81.

(37) William Frassanito, *Antietam The Photographic Legacy of America's Bloodiest Day* (New York, 1978) p. 221. Sawyer, *ibid.*, p. 81, tells of the wounded being removed to Boonsborough [sic]. The division hospital actually was located two miles northeast of Sharpsburg, and one mile west of Keedysville, not quite to Boonsboro. For a fascinating historical "look" at the Bloody Lane, the Roulette house and the hospital areas where French's wounded men were taken, see Frassanito's Chapter 9, "Bloody Lane." Frassanito established the location of the division hospital and Dr. Hurd's activities. Until Frassanito's research, this information was unknown, or imprecise.

(38) Houghton, *ibid.*, letter dated September 20, 1862.

(39) Houghton, *ibid.*, letter dated October 29, 1862.

EPILOGUE

"We spend our years as a tale that is told."

FRANKLIN ALFORD RETURNED TO INDIANA with Warren's remains. The body was laid to rest in the same small cemetery where Lafayette had been buried three months before. The body of the third son given to the cause was never interred with his brothers; his remains were buried in Mississippi, evidently unidentifiable.

At the Alfordsville cemetery the road makes a bend. Perhaps that is symbolic because after the deaths of three sons, something wonderful happened to the Alford family. It started in 1866 when they moved to Bloomington, Indiana.(1)

Before the Civil War, Franklin Alford had planned, someday, to divide the farm among his children, not upon his death, but at a time when the land could provide each child with the means for a good start in life. After the deaths of Warren, Wayne and Lafayette, the surviving unmarried children persuaded their father to change his plans. They would give up the land, if he would fund their education. He agreed, and, with the exception of Minerva, they all moved near Indiana University.(2)

In 1869, twenty-four-year-old George Washington Alford was awarded two degrees, bachelor of science and doctor of laws. Two years later in a graduating class of twenty, there were two more Alfords, Helen and nineteen-year-old Thomas Greene.(3) (Hellen, it seems, became Helen.)

Once the children were educated, Franklin and Mary moved to Loogootee where they became significant land owners. They also owned lots in Bloomington and 200 acres of the old Alfordsville farm. In the 1880s, Franklin became co-owner of a grain elevator near Wheatland in Knox County. He also owned a heavy-duty scales operation in Loogootee, a community landmark. For a time, he carried mail between Loogootee and Jasper, Indiana. Mary Gilley Alford died March 23, 1890 at the age of seventy-one after an eight-week illness and was buried in the Goodwill Cemetery at Loogootee.(4) Franklin stayed in Loogootee until June 1892, when he moved with Helen and her family to Elwood, Indiana.

Helen, after graduation from Indiana University, married C. Jules Berry and lived the life of a teacher and mortician's wife. The Berrys were the parents of two daughters and a son: Clara, Una and Omar, respectively. Jules died in 1898 and Helen moved to West Lafayette where she lived until her death in 1933. She was buried next to Jules in Elwood.(5)

*A Memorial to the Alford Brothers Who Died
in the Civil War, Alfordsville Cemetery.*

After the Civil War, Minerva Alford Donaldson and husband Charles continued to live in Alfordsville where another son was born in 1873 or 1874. The
son was named Franklin. By 1893, the Donaldson family was living one mile
south of Loogootee.

When the family patriarch, seventy-seven-year-old Franklin, died on
February 23, 1893 in Elwood, his body was brought back to Loogootee where it
lay in state at the Donaldsons'. Funeral services were conducted in the
Loogootee Christian Church at 10:30 Sunday morning, February 26. The body
was interred next to Mary, his wife of fifty-four years. The services were conducted by Pastor (and Professor) Walter R. Houghton. Houghton had lived with
the Alfords in Bloomington when he attended Indiana University – and graduated with Helen and Thomas Greene in the class of 1871.(6)

All four surviving Alford children attended the services. Franklin Alford's
legacy included a small trunk-like case containing the Civil War letters and
other family documents.

In 1897, Charles Donaldson died. He had been at Antietam in 1862 and was one of the last to see Warren Alford alive. Minerva Alford Donaldson, sixty-seven, passed on in 1904. The Donaldsons also were buried in the Goodwill Cemetery.

George Washington Alford, while a student at Indiana University in 1868, had married Florence Sluss of Bloomington. When George graduated in 1869 (with two degrees), he already was the father of a daughter. George practiced law, served as postmaster in Loogootee, published the Loogootee *Tribune*, served in the Indiana State Senate, and sat as a city court judge in Elwood. It was about 1890 that he and Florence were ordained ministers in the Christian Church.

The Reverend George Alford was a pastor in Washington, Worthington and Elwood before moving west after the turn of the century. In Hutchinson, Kansas, George ministered, practiced law, and operated a manufacturing company. The Alfords lived in five communities in Kansas and one in Arkansas before returning to Hutchinson, their final resting place. Along the way, George and Florence Alford gave life to six daughters and two sons: Eula Belle, Grace, Cora, Zella, Ida, Ruby, Forest and Asher, respectively. George Washington Alford died in 1927, and when Florence died in 1929, there were thirteen grandchildren and three great-grandchildren.(7)

The Alfordsville Christian Church.

Thomas Greene Alford.

Thomas Greene also lived a noteworthy life. After receiving his bachelor of arts degree at age nineteen, Thomas returned to Daviess County and taught school for three years, one year as the (second) superintendent at Washington High School. In 1874, he entered Indiana State Normal School (now Indiana State University), where he earned additional administrative credentials. Thomas Greene moved to Vevay where he became the superintendent of the high school. In 1881 he married Effie Wilson, and a daughter, Muriel Joy, was born in 1882. Six years later, Thomas was awarded a master of arts degree from Indiana University and was appointed superintendent of an Indianapolis-area high school.

In 1892, Thomas Alford was hired by Purdue University as chairman of the mathematics department. His wife, Effie, died in 1899 and was buried in Grand View Cemetery in West Lafayette. Professor Alford continued his dedication to serve the Purdue students. Among his accomplishments, he sought and achieved acceptance for a Phi Kappa Psi fraternity on the campus. He also devoted much of his time to the management of the University-sponsored Young Men's Christian Association. In 1917, Thomas was appointed executive secretary of the Purdue Union, a job that entailed the raising of money for a Student Union Building. Professor Alford, or "Daddy" as the students called him, did not live to see the results of his fund-raising efforts.(8)

Thomas Greene Alford died March 25, 1919, one day short of his sixty-seventh birthday. Due to a lingering illness, he had been living with daughter Muriel Joy and her husband, John Walter Dietz in LaGrange, Illinois. Professor Alford's body was brought back to West Lafayette and funeral services were held on the campus in Fowler Hall prior to the burial in Grand View Cemetery.(9) On November 25, 1922, the cornerstone was laid for the Purdue Student Union Building. And today, Thomas Greene Alford's portrait hangs in a faculty lounge.

Muriel Joy Alford and her husband, John Dietz, are of particular significance to "The Alford Brothers." Married in 1907, the Dietzs' had three children, one of whom, Dorothy Louise married Richard Andrew Lobban in 1933.(10)

Dorothy Louise and Richard Lobban created three children: Jean Alford, Sarah Louise and Richard Andrew, Jr. In 1993, Dr. Richard A. Lobban, Jr. made available the Alford family's Civil War letters for publication. One year later, Jean Alford Thompson and Richard Lobban, Jr. donated the small trunk containing the personal papers of Franklin Alford to the Indiana Historical Society. Thankfully, the documents, which include more than the Civil War letters, are accessible to the public.

In closing, there is one inescapable thought: The mysterious way the tragic deaths of three young brothers touched the lives of the Alford family and their descendants – and perhaps those who read the story.

Endnotes

(1) Walter R. Houghton, *ibid.*, "In Memoriam," the eulogy for Franklin Alford. Houghton also gave the eulogy for Mary Gilley Alford. Walter Houghton was the younger brother of William Houghton, Warren's company commander during the Civil War.

(2) *Ibid.* The Alfords moved to Lot 38, Seminary Street which suggests they lived near the original school, or the Seminary as it was called.

(3) Theophilus A. Wylie, *Indiana University Its History from 1820, When Founded, to 1890* (Indianapolis, 1890) pp. 244, 249, 250. Helen was among the first eight women to graduate from Indiana University. The first occurred in 1869, none in 1870, and seven in 1871.

(4) Walter Houghton, "In Memoriam," the eulogy for Mary Alford, *The Martin County Tribune*, n.d. The tribute was given on March 25, 1890 at the Christian Church in Loogootee. "Wayne's Last Lettter" was read at the services for Mary.

(5) Genealogical notes provided by Richard A. Lobban, Jr., Cranston, Rhode Island, great-grandson of Thomas Greene Alford; and phone conversation with Alice Berry Anderson, granddaughter of Helen Alford Berry. The *Lafayette Journal*, on October 23, 1933, headlined Helen's obituary with reference to her seventy-one-year church service and the kindness she extended to Purdue students.

(6) Houghton, the eulogy for Franklin.

(7) Alford family genealogical notes.

(8) Obituary, "Professor Alford Succumbs to Illness," *The Purdue Exponent*, March 26, 1919. The family referred to Thomas Greene as "T.G."

(9) *Ibid.*

(10) Walter Dietz, *Walter Dietz Speaking*, self-published, (Summit, New Jersey, 1972); appendix material entitled "Dietz Family." Deitz met Professor Alford's daughter, Muriel Joy, while attending Purdue where he graduated in 1902 with a bachelor of science degree in electrical engineering. He, no doubt, admired and respected Professor Alford. Young Dietz had been the first president of Phi Kappa Psi, the president of the Young Men's Christian Association and his class president.
Dietz became a distinguished personnel manager for Western Electric Company. Early in World War II, he was the Associate Director for the Training Within Industry program as part of the national Manpower Mobilization effort. He returned to West Lafayette in 1944 where he received an honorary doctorate degree from Purdue University.

ACKNOWLEDGMENTS

WARREN, WAYNE AND LAFAYETTE ALFORD continue to do good deeds. Their letters have brought friends closer together and made friends out of strangers.

The Alford Brothers had its genesis in 1993 when my third grade classmate, Dr. Helen Jean McClelland Nugent, now a professor at Franklin College, Indiana, struck up a conversation with a total stranger, Dr. Richard A. Lobban, Jr., from Rhode Island College. Lobban was seeking someone who might be interested in the letters of Civil War soldiers from Daviess County, Indiana. Nugent suggested my name and a congenial, long-distance, cross-examination followed. It was not long before Richard Lobban was sending me copies of the Alford family letters and, as time passed, our friendship grew and he began to close his letters with "Peace and Love." Now, I do the same.

This exceptional friendship developed to a point where he and his sister Jean Alford Lobban Thompson flew to Indiana for a visit. Understandably, we shared many precious moments, such as standing together at the graves of Alford family members. There was another special occurrence when a phone call was made to Mrs. Dorothy Lobban, granddaughter of Thomas Greene Alford and mother of Richard Lobban and Jean Thompson. It became evident that Mrs. Lobban was carrying on the remarkable characteristics of the Alfords.

Certainly, there would not have been any Alford family letters to be published if it were not for the survivors. For 130 years, several generations of Alford descendants have preserved the letters and passed them on. Specifically, the Alford documents passed from Franklin to Thomas Greene Alford to his daughter, Muriel Joy Dietz, then to her daughter, Dorothy Louise Lobban, then to her son, Richard Lobban. Now, not only have the Civil War letters been made available for publication, but the family also graciously gave all the Franklin Alford family documents to the Indiana Historical Society. These "Alford Family Papers," which cover the period 1856-1889, are now available for further reading and research.

Two old Civil War buddies provided extraordinary technical support. Eric Losey, from Scottsburg, scrutinized the manuscript, made corrections, and offered helpful style suggestions. Larry Ligget, from Terre Haute, drew the maps, suggested the page layouts, and provided excellent advice. Their work is a big part of this book. Hereafter, I will treat these guys with professional respect.

Terry and Pat McCarter at Greencastle Offset Printing continued to be gracious and patient. A special thanks to the gang downstairs and in the press room. And to Darrin Dillman and Rex Franklin at Franklin's Bindery in Spencer. They were helpful, as always.

Many paths were crossed in the course of publishing this book; one occurrence will not be forgotten. Through a series of inquiries in Washington, Indiana, my wife and I were referred to Howard and Enid Gabhart. It was said Howard "knew all about Alfordsville" and had an old picture of the town. All this was true. It seems the Gabharts, at one time, lived in Alfordsville and sent their thirteen children through the Alfordsville schools. For one Saturday afternoon we heard delightful stories, drank coffee and ate homemade pie. Such are the many rewards.

The good people at the William Henry Smith Memorial Library, Indiana Historical Society, cheerfully continue to provide valuable assistance. There were other Indiana repositories of pertinent information: Madison-Jefferson County Public Library; Martin County Public Library; Daviess County Public Library; Tippecanoe County Library; Vigo County Library; Howard Steamboat Museum and the Indiana State Library. A photographic print was obtained at the Jefferson County (Indiana) Historical Society. Also, images were obtained in Louisville at the Filson Club Historical Society and the University of Louisville Archives. The Cincinnati Public Library was a key source for Civil War newspaper research.

Many individuals contributed information and guidance: Steve Remmel at the Alfordsville Christian Church, Mrs. Clifford Bingham at the Daviess County Historical Museum; Rex Myers in Washington, Indiana; Rick Potts in Cannelburg, Indiana. In Greencastle, Indiana, some relevant unpublished material was shared by John and Emma Walton, and Bob and Mariam Breese. Also, in Greencastle, Marilyn Clearwaters provided a needed education in plat map reading. In Louisville, assistance was received from Mary Jean Kinsman, Charles Castner and Bob Moore. And much appreciation goes to the authors enumerated in the endnotes and to the keepers of the photographic archives – those contributions are obvious.

Now the biggest thanks of all. My wife, Wilda, has endured all the less-desirable aspects of editing a book. No one has read the Alford letters and background material more often than Wilda. She grappled with continuous streams of paper, finding the errors the spellchecker is incapable of finding. Her suggestions on the conceptual aspects were equally valued. She is my "in-house" expert, my most respected advisor, and my best friend.

BIBLIOGRAPHY

GENERAL BOOKS

Ade, John. *Newton County*, Indianapolis, 1911.

Allen, William. *History of the Campaign of Gen. T. J. (Stonewall) Jackson in the Shenandoah Valley of Virginia*, reprint, Dayton, 1987.

Andrews, J. Cutler. *The North Reports the Civil War*, Pittsburgh, 1955.

Baxter, Nancy Niblack. *Gallant Fourteenth: The Story of an Indiana Civil War Regiment*, Traverse City, 1980.

Briant, Charles C. *History of the Sixth Regiment Indiana Volunteer Infantry*, Indianapolis, 1891.

Brooks, Stewart. *Civil War Medicine*, Springfield, 1966.

Brown, E.R. *The Twenty-Seventh Indiana Volunteer Infantry*, Monticello, 1899.

Burgess, Joe H. *Hamilton County in the Civil War*, np., nd.

Cohen, Stan. *The Civil War in West Virginia*, Charleston, 1985.

_____. *Pictorial Guide to West Virginia's Civil War Sites*, Charleston, 1990.

Coons, John W., compiler. *Indiana at Shiloh*, Indianapolis, 1904.

Crozier, Emmet. *Yankee Reporters 1861-65*, New York, 1956.

Current, Richard Nelson. *Lincoln's Loyalists, Union Soldiers from the Confederacy*, Boston, 1992.

Curry, Leonard P. *Blueprint for Modern America: Non Military Legislation of the First Civil War Congress*, Nashville, 1968.

Daviess County, Indiana, Atlas of, Philadelphia, 1888.

Davis, William C., editor. *Fighting for Time* (The Image of War series), New York, 1983.

Dietz, Walter. *Walter Dietz Speaking*, Summit, New Jersey, 1972.

Doll, William. *History of the Sixth Regiment Indiana Volunteer Infantry*, Columbus, 1903.

Elliott, Joseph P. *A History of Evansville and Vanderburgh County, Indiana*, Evansville, 1897.

Esarey, Logan. *A History of Indiana from its Exploration to 1850, third edition*, Fort Wayne, 1924.

Fehrenbacher, Don E., editor. *Abraham Lincoln: Speeches and Writings 1859-1865*, New York, 1989.

Foote, Shelby. *The Civil War A Narrative*, Garden City, 1958.

Foster, John W. *War Stories for My Grandchildren*, Washington, 1918.

Frassanito, William. *Antietam The Photographic Legacy of America's Bloodiest Day*, New York, 1978.

Fulkerson, A.O. *History of Daviess County Indiana*, Indianapolis, 1915.

Fuller, J.F.C. *Grant and Lee*, Bloomington, 1957.

Funk, Arville. *The Morgan Raid in Indiana and Ohio (1863)*, Corydon, 1971.

Gawley, Thomas Francis. *The Valiant Hours*, Harrisburg, 1961.

Gordon, John B. *Reminiscences of the Civil War*, New York, 1903.

Gresham, Matilda. *Life of Walter Quintin Gresham*, Chicago, 1919.

Harrison, Lowell. *The Civil War in Kentucky*, Lexington, 1975.

History of Greene and Sullivan Counties, State of Indiana, reprint, Evansville, 1975.

History of Knox and Daviess County, the editors of Goodspeed Publishing Company, Evansville 1886.

Holliday, John Hampden. *Indianapolis and the Civil War*, Indianapolis, 1972.

Holt, Harry Q. *History of Martin County Indiana*, Paoli, 1953.

Howe, Daniel Wait. *Civil War Times*, Indianapolis, 1902.

Katcher, Phillip. *The Civil War Source Book*, New York, 1992.

Klement, Franklin L. *The Copperheads in the Middle West*, Chicago, 1960.

_____. *Dark Lanterns*, Baton Rouge, 1984.

Lord, Francis A. *They Fought for the Union*, New York, 1960.

Madison, James H. *The Indiana Way*, Indianapolis, 1986.

McCutchan, Kenneth P., editor, *Dearest Lizzie*, Evansville, 1988.

McDonough, James Lee. *Shiloh – In Hell before Night*, Knoxville, 1977.

McKinney, Tim. *Robert E. Lee and the 35th Star*, Charleston, 1993.

McLean, William E. *The Forty-Third Regiment of Indiana Volunteers: An Historic Sketch of its Career and Services*. Terre Haute, 1903.

McPherson, James M. *Battle Cry of Freedom: The Civil War Era*, New York, 1988.

Merrill and Company, editors. *The Soldier of Indiana*, Indianapolis, 1866.

Miller, Francis Trevelyan, editor. *The Photographic History of the Civil War*, New York, 1912.

Mitchell, Reid. *The Vacant Chair, The Northern Soldier Leaves Home*, New York and Oxford, 1993.

Moehring, Eugene P. and Keylin, Arleen, editors. *The Civil War Extra*, New York, 1975.

Murfin, James V. *The Gleam of Bayonets*, New York, 1965.

Myers, L. Rex. *Daviess County Indiana History*, Paducah, 1988.

Nelson, Jacquelyn S. *Indiana Quakers Confront the Civil War*, Indianapolis, 1991.

Pickerill, W.N., compiler. *Indiana at Antietam*, Indianapolis, 1911.

Priest, John M. *Antietam: The Soldiers' Battle*, Shippensburg, 1989.

Reaves, George A. and Frank, Joseph Allen. *"Seeing the Elephant" Raw Recruits at the Battle of Shiloh*, New York, 1989.

Robertson, James I., Jr. *Soldiers Blue and Gray*, Columbia, South Carolina, 1988.

_____. *Tenting Tonight*, Alexandria, 1984.

Roll, Charles. *Colonel Dick Thompson: The Persistent Whig*, Indianapolis, 1948.

Sawyer, Franklin. *A Military History of the 8th Regiment Ohio Infantry*, reprint, Huntington, 1994.

Schildt, John W. *September Echoes*, Shippensburg, 1980.

_____. *Drums Along the Antietam*, Parsons, 1972.

Sears, Stephen W. *Landscape Turned Red*, New Haven, 1983.

Skidmore, Richard S., editor. *The Civil War Journal of Billy Davis*, Greencastle, 1989.

Smith, John Martin. *History of DeKalb County*, Indiana, Auburn, 1992.

Stampp, Kenneth M. *Indiana Politics During the Civil War*, Bloomington, 1978.

Steiner, Paul E. *Disease in the Civil War*, Springfield, 1968.

Stevenson, David. *Indiana's Roll of Honor*, Indianapolis, 1864.

Stotelmyer, Steven R. *The Bivouacs of the Dead*, Baltimore, 1992.

Stutler, Boyd B. *West Virginia in the Civil War*, Charleston, 1966.

Sword, Wiley. *Shiloh: Bloody April*, New York, 1974.

Tanner, Robert. *Stonewall in the Valley*, Garden City, 1976.

Thornbrough, Emma Lou. *Indiana in the Civil War Era 1850-1880*, Indianapolis, 1965.

_____. *Since Emancipation A Short History of Negroes*, *1863-1963*, Indianapolis, n.d.

Tredway, G.R. *Democratic Opposition to the Lincoln Administration*, Indianapolis, 1973.

Walker, Charles. *Sketch of the Life, Character, and Public Services of Oliver P. Morton*, Indianapolis, 1878.

Wallace, Lew. *Lew Wallace An Autobiography*, New York, 1906.

Wiley, Bell I. *The Life of Johnny Reb*, Indianapolis, 1943.

_____. *The Life of Billy Yank*, Indianapolis, 1951.

Winslow, Hattie Lou and Moore, Joseph R.H. *Camp Morton 1861-1865: Indianapolis Prison Camp*, Indianapolis, 1940.

Wylie, Theophilus A. *Indiana University Its History from 1820, When Founded, to 1890*, Indianapolis, 1890.

Zinn, Jack. *The Battle of Rich Mountain*, Parsons, West Virginia. 1971.

_____. *R.E. Lee's Cheat Mountain Campaign*, Parsons, West Virginia, 1974.

REFERENCE WORKS

Boatner, Mark M., III. *The Civil War Dictionary*, New York, 1973.

Dyer, Frederick H. *A Compendium of the War of the Rebellion*, reprint, Dayton, 1979.

Hunt, Roger and Brown, Jack. *Brevet Brigadier Generals in Blue*, Gaithersburg, 1990.

Livermore, Thomas L. *Numbers and Losses in the Civil War in America*, reprint, Dayton, 1986.

Long, E.B. *The Civil War Day by Day: An Almanac, 1861-1865*, New York, 1971.

McCormick, David I. *Indiana Battle Flag Commission: Battle Flags and Organizations*, Indianapolis, 1929.

Official Records of the War of the Rebellion, 128 volumes, Washington, 1880-1901.

Reed, D.W. "Map of Shiloh Battlefield" (Second Day) 1900.

Terrell, W.H.H. *Report of the Adjutant General of the State of Indiana*, eight volumes, Indianapolis, 1866.

United States Census Records. 1850, 1860, 1870.

Warner, Ezra. *Generals in Blue*, Baton Rouge, 1977 printing.

_____. *Generals in Gray*, Baton Rouge, 1978 printing.

Welcher, Frank J. *The Union Army 1861-1865*, two volumes, Bloomington 1993.

NEWSPAPERS

Cincinnati, Ohio. *Cincinnati Commercial*, September 5, 1861.

_____. October 8, 1861.

_____. January 3, 1862,

_____. February 14, 1862.

_____. February 18, 1862.

_____. September 19, 1862.

Lafayette, Indiana. *Lafayette Journal*, October 23, 1933.

Loogootee, Indiana, *The Martin County Tribune*, March 3, 1893.

Terre Haute, Indiana, *Terre Haute Express*, August 9, 1885.

Terre Haute, Indiana, *Terre Haute Tribune*, November 27, 1962.

West Lafayette, Indiana. *The Purdue Exponent*, March 26, 1919.

ARTICLES, PAMPHLETS AND PERIODICALS

"The Civil War Letters of Amory K. Allen," editors, *Indiana Magazine of History*, Volume XXXI, Number 4, Indianapolis, December 1935.

Barnhart, John D. "The Impact of the Civil War on Indiana," *Indiana Magazine of History*, Volume LVII, Number 3, Indianapolis, September 1961.

Buell, Don Carlos. "Shiloh Reviewed," *Battles and Leaders*, four volumes, New York, 1884-1887.

Dorrel, Ruth, "Military Deaths," *The Hoosier Genealogist*, (Published by the Indiana Historical Society), Volume 33, Number 4, Indianapolis, December 1993.

Fetcher, William B. "The Civil War Journal of William Fletcher," *Indiana of Magazine History*, Volume LVII, Number 1, Indianapolis, March 1961.

Kimball, Nathan. "Fighting Jackson at Kernstown," *Battles and Leaders*, four volumes. New York, 1884-1887.

Landon, William (using the pseudonym "Prock). "The Fourteenth Indiana Regiment on Cheat Mountain," *Indiana Magazine of History*, Volume XXIX, Number 4, Indianapolis, December 1933.

_____. "The Fourteenth Indiana Regiment in the Valley of Virginia," *Indiana Magazine of History*, Volume XXX, Number 3, Indianapolis, September 1934.

Lynch, William O. "A Glance at Indiana History," *Indiana Magazine of History*, Volume XXXIII, Number 1, Indianapolis, March 1937.

Parsons, Joseph A. Jr. "Indiana and the Call for Volunteers, April 1861," *Indiana Magazine of History* Volume LIV, Number 1, Indianapolis, March 1958.

Stampp, Kenneth M. "The Impact of the Civil War upon Hoosier Society," *Indiana Magazine of History*, Volume XXXVIII, Number 2, Indianapolis, March 1942.

Steinson, Barbara J. "Rural Life in Indiana, 1800-1950," *Indiana Magazine of History*, Volume XC, Number 3, Indianapolis, September 1994.

UNPUBLISHED MATERIALS

Alfordsville Christian Church Record Book.

Alley, William A. Civil War soldier's journal, John and Emma Walton Collection.

Beem, David Enoch. Papers (M 15), Indiana Historical Society.

Boehm, Richard Blair, "The Civil War in Western Virginia: The Decisive Battle of 1861," Doctoral Dissertation, Ohio State University, 1957.

Brown, Francis M. *The Brown Family History*, privately printed, 1976.

Cunningham, Edward O. "Shiloh and the Western Campaign of 1862," Doctoral Dissertation, Louisiana State University, 1962.

Gilley, Lou & Wayne. Letters in Alfordsville Christian Church historical records.

Houghton, William. Papers (M 147), Indiana Historical Society.

Jayne, Seely. Civil War Letters (S 176), Indiana State Library.

Kuppenheimer, Judson. Diary entries, unpublished typescript, Vigo County Library Archives.

Lambert, George Washington. Papers (M 178), Indiana Historical Society.

Military Records for James Warren, Wayne and Lafayette Alford. National Archives.

Van Dyke, Augustus M. Papers (M 284), Indiana Historical Society.

INDEX

356 □ *Index*